Michael Veitch is well known as an author, actor, comedian and former ABC television and radio presenter. His books include the critically acclaimed accounts of Australian pilots in the Second World War, *Heroes of the Skies*, *Fly*, *Flak*, *44 Days* and *Barney Greatrex*. *Turning Point* is his ninth book. He lives in the Yarra Valley, outside Melbourne.

Praise for *Turning Point*

'Michael Veitch recounts the events of the Battle of Milne Bay, showing how a mix of luck, dreadful conditions, fateful decisions and blind courage stopped the seemingly unstoppable Japanese in August 1942, all told with his trademark attention to detail.'

Herald Sun

'An excellent book that clearly and fairly shows what really happened at Milne Bay in August 1942.'

Baird Maritime

'In many ways a significant event in the history of Australia's participation in World War II, this book brings to life the people and the formidable situations they endured – making it a commendable resource for students of the history of the war in the Pacific, as well as an engrossing read for the general reader.'

ReadPlus

'Veitch's account is one of the best and most readable. He has a great eye for interesting details, and writes credibly about the men who took part.'

Daily Telegraph

'This beautifully written book is heartbreakingly sad at times but also uplifting, and it is impossible not to feel a sense of pride in the determination of the allies.'

Weekly Times

'Told for the first time, this is the epic story of the Milne Bay campaign of 1942 – which saw Japanese land forces suffer their first defeat of the war – and has properly been called the RAAF's forgotten finest hour.'

Sunraysia Life

'Veitch has succeeded in bringing to life the story of a little known but decisive battle, with its mix of tragedy and heroism.'

Australian Defence Magazine

'Author Michael Veitch has combined some of the most detailed and intense insights recorded into a new book on the savage battle that took place at Milne Bay, Papua New Guinea in mid-1942.'

Down Under Aviation News

THE BATTLE FOR MILNE BAY 1942 –
JAPAN'S FIRST LAND DEFEAT IN WORLD WAR II

TURNING POINT

MICHAEL VEITCH

hachette
AUSTRALIA

□ hachette
AUSTRALIA

First published in Australia and New Zealand in 2019
by Hachette Australia
(an imprint of Hachette Australia Pty Limited)
Gadigal Country, Level 17, 207 Kent Street, Sydney NSW 2000
www.hachette.com.au

This edition published 2022

Hachette Australia acknowledges and pays our respects to the past, present and
future Traditional Owners and Custodians of Country throughout Australia
and recognises the continuation of cultural, spiritual and educational practices
of Aboriginal and Torres Strait Islander peoples. Our head office is located on
the lands of the Gadigal people of the Eora Nation.

A catalogue record for this
book is available from the
National Library of Australia

ISBN: 978 0 7336 4867 0 (paperback)

Cover design by Luke Causby, Blue Cork Designs
Cover photographs courtesy of Australian War Memorial (AWM MEA0879, 026630)
Author photograph courtesy Gina Milicia
Typeset in Simoncini Garamond by Bookhouse, Sydney
Printed and bound in Australia by McPherson's Printing Group

MIX
Paper from
responsible sources
FSC
www.fsc.org   FSC® C001695

The paper this book is printed on is certified against the
Forest Stewardship Council® Standards. McPherson's Printing
Group holds FSC® chain of custody certification SA-COC-005379.
FSC® promotes environmentally responsible, socially beneficial
and economically viable management of the world's forests.

'Some of us may forget that of all the Allies, it was the Australian soldiers who first broke the spell of the invincibility of the Japanese Army.'

William Slim

CONTENTS

PART TWO   THE BATTLE

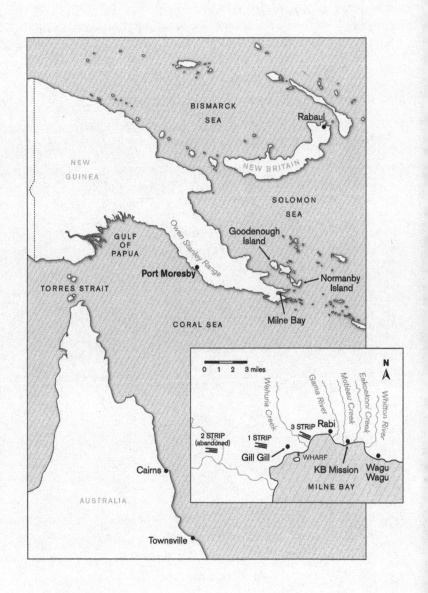

A JUNGLE RUNWAY

On the worst day of the battle – that strange and confusing Saturday when nothing was certain and everything hung in the balance – a pilot stood on the edge of a perforated metal runway, his face expressionless, focusing as best he could on the impenetrable wall of jungle in front of him. His tropical-issue khaki shirt was filthy, and his sallow skin glowed with a permanent sheen of perspiration. He swayed slightly – like a man drunk – from fever and exhaustion, but his hollow eyes remained fixed on the green line to the east. Muffled sounds of battle leached through the tangled, steaming jungle; they were soft and far-off, and even strangely comforting. But he was not fooled. Whatever was happening out there was, he knew, close.

His concentration focused by the sickness, he could distinguish the airy *whoomph* of exploding 3-inch mortars, and the sharp crack of .303 rifles and automatic weapons. Then a deep *boom* from the battery of 25-pounders, like the distant steps of a giant stomping through the foliage. He thought of those artillerymen from the 2/9th Field Regiment he'd seen around the camp before the fighting started: serious-looking AIF blokes who kept to themselves. It sounded now like they'd found their range.

'Jesus,' he muttered.

Over to his left, one of 76 Squadron's Kittyhawks rested at its dispersal, while a couple of fitters were washing off the muck and filth which yet again caked the flaps and undercarriage. At his feet, the metal matting rocked slightly – like the deck of a ship, he thought, sailing on a dark liquid ocean. It oozed up black over his boots. He was used to it now. Didn't even shift his feet.

'What's happening?' he called in the direction of the ground crew, not really expecting an answer, and immediately wished he hadn't. Saying anything brought on a rush of nausea – whether from the malaria or the Atebrin tablets which were supposed to suppress it, he had no idea.

He really should have stayed in the sick bay, but what was the point? Lying there on a filthy stretcher under a dripping tent, feeling useless. It was just as impossible there as anywhere else to avoid the mud, the heat, the insects and the endless, endless rain. So he'd got up, thanked the doc, who just shrugged his shoulders, then made his way over to the operations tent and put his name back on the flight list. Just in time. Because now, for those blokes out there – those poor terrified bastards some-where in that jungle, just a mile or two away – it was on.

He looked up at the sky. Was it morning or evening? He could barely tell. This featureless soup cloaked the entire day in a miserable dusk, and the wet mist hung like lead, never seeming to lift. And behind that, all around, were mountains. 'Clouds filled with rocks,' someone had quipped. Taking off into it was terrifying. Or at least it had been, during the first few weeks. Now he was too tired to notice.

He looked at his watch, out of habit, and swore. It had stopped working days ago.

Five days earlier, the Japanese had finally turned up. Five days of almost continuous flying around this monotonous, dead-end jungle, and he still couldn't get his bearings. In fact – thinking about it – there wasn't actually much flying involved at all. Standing patrols and recce jobs had been the go before the battle started, but now it was all about strafing: strafing the jungle, strafing the mangroves, strafing the landing areas – strafing anywhere the enemy could be lurking under that endless canopy of trees. Sometimes he'd have his thumb on the gun button even before his wheels were fully up, wrenching his aircraft off the runway, then swinging hard around on a wingtip and blasting away at a featureless stretch of grey-green foliage the army boys had fired flares into, denoting the enemy, often just a few hundred yards ahead. As one of the 75 Squadron pilots had put it, 'It's like taking off from the Sydney Showgrounds and shooting up Darlinghurst.' Only you could almost never see what you were shooting at.

But they were out there and getting closer. And those army and militia boys were right in the middle of them. However tough it was for the pilots, it was worse, far worse, for those blokes on the ground.

The stress was incredible. If he messed it up just once – got things arse about or back to front – or missed something in this ocean of green, allowing himself to succumb to a moment's disorientation, he could, in a heartbeat, commit the unthinkable and fire on his own people. The thought went through his mind every time his guns let rip. Or if he banked around too hard, or pulled up too fast, or even too slow, he could stall the plane and go in. At this height, he'd be spread across the jungle floor in an instant. It'd happened just a few days ago to – of all people – the boss, Pete Turnbull, 76 Squadron's CO, a man with a full combat tour in the desert under his belt. Late in the day, he'd come up too slow from a strafe run against a Japanese tank and the air sucked out from under his wings. His big and heavy Kittyhawk had fallen into the jungle like a stone. Or maybe he was just exhausted. At any rate, Pete Turnbull was one hell of a pilot. Now he was gone. Somewhere out there.

Several times a day, the word had gone up. 'It's on!' a voice would yell. He'd haul himself into the cockpit, push the throttle wide open and thunder down the runway, the big prop fanning mud and filth everywhere. Landing was even more of a nightmare: the Kittyhawk thudding onto the deck like an old truck on a rutted road; trying to keep her straight on the sodden and greasy metal surface; working the brakes and rudder to avoid swinging as his tyres hit the puddles and pools; swearing blind. The guns were still smoking and the prop still turning as the armourers scrambled up onto the wings to rip off the covers and replenish the boxes with long, greasy belts of half-inch ammunition. Then, after a cigarette – a few minutes to get over the shakes – he'd be up again. Sometimes they didn't even need to refuel. These trips weren't long enough for that.

Since his arrival he'd gone from novice to veteran, cramming months of combat flying into a couple of weeks, and all of it close by this sodden airstrip the Japanese seemed hell-bent on taking. Streaming out of that jungle and taking. But they weren't going to bloody take it, not if he and his mates in 76 and 75 Squadrons could help it. And the same went for those militia blokes on the ground: just kids, or so they seemed, pale and scared – but determined. Likewise the AIF fellas from the 18th: tough bastards with sand in their boots from the fighting in Libya and Tobruk. But they'd never seen anything like this place.

He could see it in their eyes. They weren't going to let them through either. None of them were.

'Snipers!' someone shouted. 'Watch out for bloody snipers!' The pilot's nausea cleared in a moment. They'd been warned about them: slipping silently ahead of their own positions in bunches of twos and threes, then with climbing irons, slithering up into the fronds of the coconut trees, lying dormant for days, like coiled snakes, living off rainwater and a handful of rice a day, with no expectation whatsoever of coming down alive. Even when wounded, they could still get off a couple of rounds before they bled to death. At least that was the rumour. *Christ, the bastards are barely human.*

'Fuck it,' he said, and spat. Turning with a sudden urgency towards the ground crew, he gestured to a couple of lads in filthy khaki shorts. 'You two, pull her round.' They looked at each other, uncertain. 'Now!' he barked.

Energised by his idea, the pilot now moved with the speed of a cat. Putting his shoulder into the wing root, he indicated another man do the same, and the three of them pushed the big green fighter clear of its dispersal bay. 'Line her up this way,' he said, pointing to the long, straight line of green which ran beside the runway apron, cleared by the machines of the American engineers a few weeks before. Leaping onto the wing, the pilot launched himself into the cockpit.

The young crewmen looked bewildered. 'I didn't hear the scramble, sir,' said one of them.

'Both you blokes get on the tail,' he replied. 'I'm not bloody flying it.'

Positioning themselves on either side of the elevators, the crewmen complied. Then they heard the whirring of the battery and the electrics being engaged.

'Now, when I say move her to the left, move her to the left, okay?'

The two nodded. Then all hell broke loose.

The aircraft's machine guns opened up, lines of roaring flame and tracer shooting ahead of them towards the tops of the coconut trees a few hundred yards away. The foliage disintegrated as if struck by the swings of a gigantic scythe.

'Now left – go left!' he yelled, still seated in his cockpit, his thumb squeezing short bursts on the firing button. The men at the back lifted the tail of the aircraft slightly, and pulled it around on the wheel.

'That's it!' called the pilot. Another burst, another shredded row of coconut crowns.

They got the idea. 'Right a bit!' and back they traversed along the arc of ferocious fire. Spent brass shell casings poured out from under the wings, clattering onto the metal matting. Finally, the guns gave a click and fell silent, and the pilot switched off the aircraft's electrical system and the spinning magnetos went quiet.

Slowly, he pulled himself out of the cockpit and climbed down. 'Better load her up again, boys,' he said. 'No fucking Jap sniper's gonna get me.'

This story was told to me by a 76 Squadron pilot who was there, and who swore it was true. 'That was Milne Bay,' he said.

PART ONE
PRELUDE TO BATTLE

CHAPTER 1
A PECULIAR BATTLE

There was no inevitability to the Japanese defeat at Milne Bay. Today, the clarity of hindsight marks the ten-day battle in the far east of Papua as the zenith of Japan's bloody advance across the south-west Pacific, her high tide of conquest delineated by the piles of blasted olive-green corpses of marines lining the eastern edge of a lonely jungle airstrip. Not a single aircraft had yet taken off from its hastily constructed surface. Even its utilitarian name had yet to evolve from that given it by the engineers who had barely finished carving it into the jungle: 'Number 3'.

Soon after the battle, a small cairn was erected to mark the point at which the Japanese were stopped, from where they would begin their long, slow retreat, ending over 3000 miles away at Hiroshima and Nagasaki, three bloody years later. But no-one could guess this in August 1942, at Milne Bay.

If even a single of the various elements which foiled Japan's audacious plan to force a pincer on nearby Port Moresby had fallen their way – or if they had not succumbed to their own hubris, performed some reconnaissance and planned their attack better – the outcome of the brief but savage campaign could have been different.

Milne Bay was a peculiar battle, fought largely in the dead of night in unspeakable conditions by men exhausted and often sick, with many on both sides new to combat. It was a battle of a thousand crazy skirmishes fought in pitch black, illuminated only by muzzle flashes, flares or the blinding spotlights of the Japanese tanks that pierced the jungle, defying the best efforts of Australian riflemen to shoot them out. It was fought at frighteningly close quarters in blind and savage gropings, where the bayonet was used as frequently as the rifle. The voices of the enemy could be easily heard – laughing, shouting and even taunting – sometimes in perfect English. As the battle went on, the Australians' daily passwords were selected from words beginning with L – Life, Lewis, Lonely, Little – to confound the Japanese attempts to mimic them.

As *The Central Queensland Herald* put it, 'On the ground the fight was against an almost invisible army. Short, sharp bursts of machine-gun fire were the only sounds breaking the long periods of silence, giving the whole battle a macabre quality.'

Although fought within the chronological framework of the long Kokoda campaign, which raged over four months across the great distances of the Owen Stanley Range to the north, Milne Bay was, by contrast, a short, sharp and vicious affair, which see-sawed along a sodden strip of jungle coastline, hemmed in by mountains on one side and the sea on the other. Running through the middle was the miserable stretch of muddy road over which both sides were desperately battling.

It was fought – on one side – by the hardened elite of an army long inured to exactly this type of jungle fighting, whose savagery on the battlefield defied comprehension, and who, in nine months of conquest, had yet to be stopped on land by any Allied force arrayed against them. So confident were the Japanese of victory at Milne Bay that initially they abandoned all pretence of stealth. The spearhead of their navy marines marched into battle shouting, singing, even banging tins to amplify their presence. This was to be another walkover, in which a weak and cowering enemy would wither before them.

Opposing them were men whose experience of fighting was against Germans and Italians in the desert on the far side of the world, and other men who had yet to fight anyone, anywhere.

It was fought in an ocean of stinking tropical mud, under a permanent grey sky which excluded all but the briefest rays of sunshine for the entire battle. And it was fought in the rain. For three weeks prior to the fighting in late August, the heavens had opened in a deluge, extreme even for this notoriously wet region of Papua. Rain fell in relentless downpours that left not a surface dry. Flat land was transformed into a single gigantic bog. Like their fathers had done on the Western Front of the Great War, men waded through thigh-deep mud which sucked their boots from their feet. Canvas tents and beds rotted before their eyes. Roads were virtually impossible to construct, and soon became impassable anyway. Simply walking short distances was a dispiriting and enervating ordeal. The temperature rarely dropped below 30 degrees Celsius, and the humidity, beyond anything experienced by all but a few, sapped the men's energy and made the very air thick to breathe.

And the disease. Because of ignorance, incompetence or both, the men of Milne Force were delivered into battle utterly unprepared for the ravages of the tropics, particularly malaria. Whining clouds of Anopheles mosquitoes rang constantly in their ears, introducing the malaria-causing *Plasmodium falciparum* parasites into their bloodstreams within days. No-one was ready for it. Long-sleeved clothing failed to be issued. Mosquito nets were inadequate or did not arrive. Antimalarial drugs such as quinine and Atebrin were in short supply, and often prescribed in the incorrect dosage. Hundreds were forced to live, fight and die under the dreadful feverish pall of the disease, and many of the survivors would carry the symptoms with them for years.

Even the issue of essential stores such as tents were mucked up in logistical ineptitude that would be comical if not for the consequences. One soldier reported that half his unit were issued only the tents, and the other half only the flies. Both proved inadequate in the nightly downpours, and men were soaked to the skin in their beds, depriving them of invaluable rest.

Despite this, Milne Bay would be, in the end, a noble and unquestioned victory. And an Australian victory at that, but one won also with the incalculable assistance of tireless American combat engineers turned infantrymen, and the material largesse that their great nation could provide. Of this, surely no element was more important than the innovation of prefabricated metal Marston matting, which allowed runways to be laid down virtually anywhere, enabling the deployment of modern and powerful aircraft. Deployed for the first time at Milne Bay, the Marston mat would prove itself in almost every theatre of the Second World War.

Radar, too, played its part, as did the heroic and still under-appreciated deeds of Australia's wartime code breakers and Coastwatchers, who accurately reported from their lonely jungle vigils the progress of Japanese convoys and naval reinforcements, and who monitored the southbound formations of red-circled aircraft, providing timely warning of air attacks.

Milne Bay drew the curtain on the series of disasters that had befallen the Allied forces in Malaya, Rabaul, Timor, Ambon and Singapore, where men were sacrificed in the blind hope that penny packets could succeed where entire battalions had failed. It was the moment that halted the dangerous belief, which was beginning to take hold, that Australians simply could not overcome the Japanese.

Now, finally, the enemy was met in force and in good time by determined men, who decreed solemnly that this enemy would advance no further. They were led, for the most part, by some of Australia's best senior and junior officers: thoughtful, cool-headed men with battle experience, who appreciated the enemy, and who would ask the utmost of their men – who, for their part, were prepared to sacrifice everything, confident that their lives would not be expended cheaply.

It was the moment when the two arms of ground and air power came together in a single, cohesive unit, with interservice rivalries buried. The army and air force, relying utterly on one another, fought as a single weapon of deadly efficiency.

The Japanese marines of the Special Naval Landing Force, selected for their height and strength, many already blooded veterans of China, Malaya, the Philippines and other campaigns, left their ships and landing craft and swaggered along the Milne

Bay track, completely confident of another victory. It was not to be. In this sodden outpost on the far eastern tip of the Territory of Papua, the Australians of two infantry battalions – one experienced, the other raw – forced them back to their ships, leaving hundreds of their number dead or lost in the surrounding jungle, their ambitions to take Port Moresby extinguished.

Milne Bay also represented the first land defeat of Imperial Japan since its humiliation by the west in the 1850s, when it was wrenched open, and began its long descent into militarism, the endgame of which was now playing out in the south-west Pacific.

Of course, no battle in a conflict the scale of the Second World War's Pacific theatre was fought in isolation. Milne Bay was part of a greater struggle, which played out over a vast canvas at places such as Port Moresby, Buna, Rabaul, Kokoda, the Coral Sea, Midway, Guadalcanal and beyond. It was at Milne Bay, however, that the myth of Japanese invincibility was smashed forever. This was no less a shock to the American and Australian forces than to the Japanese themselves.

Yet Milne Bay was not inevitable. Had the Japanese not made the error of landing miles short of their objective; had they not grossly and arrogantly underestimated the forces set against them; had their aerial and tactical reconnaissance located the US and Australian hub at Milne Bay just a little sooner; had the RAAF failed to locate just a few of their targets; had the American assault on Guadalcanal not at the last minute drawn away precious resources earmarked for the Milne Bay assault; had the US engineers not performed a miracle of construction in creating an airstrip in the jungle in three short weeks, then the outcome of the battle, and the fate of Australia itself, could have been vastly different.

If not the turning of the tide, then, Milne Bay was most certainly the turning point.

CHAPTER 2
THE OBSCURE OUTPOST

Milne Bay sits at the extreme eastern point of the vast island of Papua, where the north and south coasts meet at the end of a mountainous, thousand-mile spur. It was named in the 1840s by an obscure British naval officer and surveyor, Owen Stanley, after the equally obscure Sir Alexander Milne, who had never been anywhere near the place and would not have cared less about it if he had. The far more spectacular mountain range which Stanley observed running the length of the island, however, he named after himself.

The bay is a perfect natural test-tube shaped harbour, its mouth roughly seven miles wide, running to its deep-water head twenty or so miles to the west. Here Milne Bay is enclosed on both sides by the steep, thickly wooded slopes of the Owen Stanley Range's far eastern tip, the Stirling Range. Only a short distance back from the water, spurs and razorbacks rise quickly to peaks of up to 5000 feet, leaving only a small, flat ribbon of land hugging the coast both north and south.

In 1942, a somewhat feeble government-built dirt road, in places barely ten-feet wide, ran the length of the northern coast, connecting a series of villages, missions and coconut-processing plants, the largest of which was at the modest settlement of Gili Gili, at the bay's western end. Here, the gigantic Lever Brothers company had established one of the largest coconut plantations in the world, producing the oil from which their internationally famous Lifebuoy soap was made.

Running east, the track hugged the mangrove shoreline, never deviating more than a hundred or so metres from the water as it meandered through smaller plantations and villages such as Goroni, Wagu Wagu and Rabi – the name curiously used by the Japanese for the entire campaign. It petered out at the northern side of the bay's opening, East Cape.

Off the southern tip of the approach known as China Strait lay the tiny but beautiful island of Samarai, the administrative capital of this eastern section of the Territory of Papua, which had been under Australian government control since 1906. Despite its size, Samarai was the largest population centre outside Port Moresby, with approximately 300 people; it also boasted a flying-boat base, which was used by both civil and military aircraft, and which the Japanese would later plan to capture.

Before the war, the entire Milne Bay population was estimated to have been around 800 Europeans and Papuans, who were involved in a variety of vocations, including mission work, plantation growing and processing, and goldmining. Most of the European population were evacuated back to Australia soon after the Japanese seizure of Lae and Salamaua in March 1942, leaving mostly the locals, who were described in a Sydney newspaper article as 'quiet and civilised, and generally speaking good English'.

Ten miles or so from Gili Gili lay the Catholic outpost of Koebule, or KB Mission, a 200-acre property founded half a century earlier by an English missionary, Charles William Abel; it would be one of the flashpoints of the Milne Bay battle. The nuns had been evacuated from this peaceful outpost months earlier, but pastors Father Baldwin and Brother Fraser had doggedly refused to abandon their flock of local Papuans.

Such ecumenical stubbornness was not confined to the lower ranks of the colonial church. In Port Moresby, the Anglican bishop Phillip Strong was likewise resistant to calls to abandon his several Papuan missions, declaring that 'they would have to arrest us and take us away in handcuffs' before he would leave his people. When informed that some missionaries had already been caught by the Japanese and beheaded, Strong remained adamant. 'Whatever they were likely to do,' he stated, 'could not justify a betrayal of trust.'

This caused a headache for ANGAU, the Australian New Guinea Administrative Unit, a military-based organisation hastily thrown together by the commander of the Australian forces in Papua and New Guinea, Major General Basil Morris, to fill the administrative vacuum created when most of the Australian civilian population fled or were evacuated.

Virtually the only flat expanse of Milne Bay, at its far western end, had been exploited by the Lever Brothers, who established vast tree plantations right up to the edges of low-lying boggy areas and waist-deep sago swamps. Around these were sprinkled a collection of colonial-style administration houses and huts and a rudimentary road system. The bay's mangrove shoreline dropped away to deep water in just a few metres, allowing vessels of size to dock extremely close to shore; in some cases the branches of trees brushed up against the ships' hulls.

And it rained. Unlike Port Moresby, which is one of the driest places in Papua New Guinea, with just under 40 inches of rain annually, Milne Bay is deluged by a massive 200 inches every year, and has a relentlessly high humidity at all times. Myriad creeks, rivers and gullies funnel vast amounts of water down from the Stirling Range, turning the lower-lying areas into impassable quagmires.

Hence, depending on who was asked, Milne Bay appeared as both a paradise and a hellhole. Many men of the 7th and 18th Infantry Brigades and others would later recall their first sight of it as their transport ship turned from the China Strait into its wide entrance. Some were entranced by the lush jungle, with the dramatic mountains behind. Others saw it straightaway as a lonely, muddy, mosquito-infested dead end in the middle of nowhere. As one soldier described:

> Even without the war, Milne Bay would have been a hell hole – it was a terrible place. The sun hardly ever shined and it rained all the time. It was stinking hot and bog holes everywhere; it was marshy boggy country. Even without the Japanese it would have been hard to live there . . . a terrible, disease ridden place.

As dubious a location as Milne Bay may have been on the ground, by the middle of 1942 everyone seemed to want it. For the Allied forces, the prospect of a base here would provide vital backup for their airstrips at Port Moresby, offer further protection to the sea lanes to the south, and serve as a place from which to launch air assaults against Japan's new conquests to the north, without pilots having to negotiate the ominous 14,000-foot barrier of the Owen Stanleys.

For the Japanese, Milne Bay's attractions were identical, but in reverse. It was the vital back door to the crucible of Port Moresby, the capture of which would enable their audacious plans for the conquest of the south-west Pacific to succeed. From Moresby's magnificent natural deep-water harbour, adjacent airstrips and facilities, Japan would be able to control the seas to the south, neutralise Australia's northern airfields and isolate Australia out of the war entirely. It would also bolster Japan's newly captured territories in New Guinea and Rabaul, and secure the left flank of the next stage of their campaign: the conquest of Samoa, Nauru, Fiji and New Caledonia, a vast chunk of their proposed East Asian empire.

The race, therefore, was on to see who would be first to establish a military foothold in this lonely corner of south-east Papua. Australia's leaders, sensing that the precious shield of its geographical isolation was on the verge of being shattered by the Japanese descent from the north, knew the stakes to be critical, and were determined to waste no time in making Milne Bay their own.

CHAPTER 3
THE RACE FOR A BASE

Milne Bay was not the Allies' first choice for a base. Sitting in his hot and under-ventilated colonial-style office in Port Moresby in May 1942, Major General Basil Morris felt the awful reverberations as yet another stick of Japanese bombs exploded somewhere near the harbour facilities. Why they were actively trying to destroy something they would presumably need to use themselves, should they ever succeed in their ambition of taking Papua's capital, was beyond him – but then again, Morris had always been more of a logistical and administrative general than a fighting man.

This, he presumed, was why he had the previous year been given the job of running Australia's 8th Military District, covering the mandated territories of Papua and New Guinea. In 1941 these were considered by everyone – himself included – as something of a military backwater, a quiet reward for his organisational and diplomatic efforts in the Middle East. At the dawn of the Pacific War, however, this backwater and its somewhat reluctant commander suddenly found themselves on the front line of the most perilous battle in Australia's history.

In January 1942 he had been forced to abandon the 8th District's original seat of power in Rabaul and relocate to Port Moresby when the Japanese launched a savage and successful assault on the Australian island territory of New Britain. In April and May, the gallant efforts of the RAAF's hastily formed 75 Squadron had seen a virtually untrained gaggle of pilots hold off the Japanese air force for a time, but it was only the intervention of the Battle of the Coral Sea which foiled what would otherwise have been an irresistible amphibious invasion of Moresby, one Morris knew he would be unlikely to survive. Yet the Coral Sea would not be the end of Japan's ambitions towards Moresby. Another attempt, most likely overland, would be made – and soon.

It was with not a little relief, therefore, that Morris greeted the order to proceed to Melbourne to consult with the newly arrived American general, Douglas MacArthur, whose overview of the situation to the north was ominous. 'I can't afford to lose Port Moresby, Morris,' MacArthur told the Australian general.

'We have no intention of losing it, sir,' he replied, with as much confidence as he could muster.

MacArthur explained that although the recent Coral Sea battle had been a success, the loss of the American navy's aircraft carrier *Lexington* had been a disaster, and its replacement, Washington had made clear, would not be arriving anytime soon. Moresby's air defences would need to be bolstered by another air base – somewhere within reasonable flying distance, and from which offensive operations could also be mounted. The only realistic area was to Moresby's south-east, and a detailed aerial reconnaissance was ordered. 'I could see that the location of an Australian airfield in the southeastern corner of Papua was of the paramount importance,' Morris recalled years later.

The Japanese also understood the strategic value of the area. A base here would bring their bombers within an hour's striking distance of Moresby, as well as giving their ground forces a staging post from which to begin an advance on the capital. That would be no easy task, with their men being required to cover a distance of over 200 miles, but they believed it could be achieved by utilising the island's relatively flat southern coast.

In any case, the assault on Moresby from the east would not be undertaken in isolation, but as the second of a two-pronged thrust. The first would arrive from the north, along a steep bush track which Japanese aerial reconnaissance had revealed wound almost due south 60 or so miles – from the coast, over the Owen Stanleys and to the very back door of Port Moresby itself. This track passed close to a small airstrip at a village called Kokoda.

Assaulted thus from the north and the east, Moresby, the Japanese were confident, would soon fall.

•

On 22 May, soon after MacArthur's instructions that an air base be established somewhere in the region, Catalina flying boats returned with the first detailed aerial photo mapping of the area. The first site to be considered lay close to the island's eastern extremity, at the inland village of Abau, 12 miles or so from Mullins Harbour, on the south coast. It was not an ideal location, with MacArthur's engineering officers warning that it would take at least four months to prepare and construct an airfield at this isolated spot. The decision, nevertheless, was taken to proceed – in the strictest secrecy, and with the code-name Boston.

On the journey back to his office in Moresby, Morris was required to spend a day in transit in Townsville. Here he ran into Captain Sydney Elliott-Smith, also on his way back to New Guinea to resume his post as a magistrate and commander of his local detachment of the Volunteer Defence Corps. This impressive young army officer, described by a patrol officer as 'stocky, forceful and very effective in his job', knew New Guinea like few others, and had already been earmarked for high office in Morris's new administrative structure, ANGAU. However, when Morris revealed to him the plans to build airfields in the suggested locations, Elliott-Smith was aghast. For a start, he said, the rainfall there was horrendous – well in excess of 118 inches annually – making the soil around Abau much too boggy for a strip of any kind. Besides, the nearby Mullins Harbour was an utter backwater, barely possessing a road or even a jetty. It would also be difficult to obtain fresh water, gravel and labour.

Far better, Elliott-Smith suggested, to consider the settlements further east, inside Milne Bay, particularly around the gigantic Lever Brothers' coconut plantation, which was on a relatively firm plateau. Being already cultivated, it would be far easier to transform into an airstrip than raw jungle. It also possessed some houses and other structures, a local pool of labour, and at least a rudimentary road system, which could be reinforced by a readily available supply of gravel and crushed coral. The harbour was fine and naturally deep, and already had a few jetties which could be adapted to handle the largest ships.

Morris, a man capable of being swayed by reason, hastily made his way across town, with Elliott-Smith in tow, to the office of the senior HQ Staff Officer of the RAAF's Northern Area, Wing Commander William 'Bull' Garing. Arriving without an appointment, Morris had Elliott-Smith repeat his opinions to the stocky staff officer with three rings on his sleeve.

Both men were convinced enough to convey the new perspective to MacArthur, who had the good sense to request Garing to organise further aerial reconnaissance of Milne Bay, as well as to begin looking for available ground units which could be rushed to the area to provide security for construction crews. Local Australian administrators already in place in the area were ordered to immediately begin organising local labour crews to start work on wharf and dock facilities.

Upon inspection, Milne Bay seemed to bear out Elliott-Smith's concerns, but a definitive on-ground assessment was needed. Garing, a renowned administrator known for making things happen – his sobriquet 'Bull' was not undeserved – gave the matter his utmost attention, as Major General Morris was to soon discover. Upon Morris's return to his office in Moresby a few days later, he was surprised to find the senior engineering officer in New Guinea, Lieutenant Colonel Leverett G. Yoder, of the US 96th Engineer Battalion, accompanied by a small group of Australian and American engineers, standing ready and waiting to depart via Catalina flying boat to conduct initial inspections at Milne Bay.

Yoder concurred with Elliott-Smith, and the very next day submitted a favourable report about the siting of Milne Bay, adding the existence of a large diesel power plant, and a significant supply of Papuan labourers and white overseers on hand. He warned, however, that it was also a place 'open on all sides to enemy attack'. On receipt of his report, on 11 June, the Boston operation was scrapped and an airstrip was ordered built at the Gili Gili plantation at Milne Bay. Again the operation was given a secretive codename borrowed from an American place name: Fall River.

The next day, 12 June, the men of the 46th US (General Service) Engineering Regiment, who had arrived from Texas only a month or two earlier and were still adjusting to life in Townsville, were addressed by their commanding officer. The men of E Company, he announced, should begin packing immediately, as they would be getting into action somewhat earlier than the rest of the battalion.

Just hours later, they found themselves walking up the gangway of the *Bontekoe*, a freighter of the old colonial Royal Packet Navigation Company or KPM line; it was one of 29 such vessels which had escaped to Australia after the fall of the Dutch East Indies. Manned by Dutch and Javanese crews, the ad hoc flotilla would form a major part of a vital supply line between Australia and the south-west Pacific, motoring tirelessly between the mainland and Milne Bay, and beyond.

Five of KPM's ships would be lost during the fight for Papua. US private Walter Wanielista later recalled his first encounter with the ship:

How E Company was selected to be the chosen one, only the Lord knows – a drawing or a dart board perhaps? Anyway, we left for Port Moresby, but of course at that time no one knew where we were headed, and even if they mentioned New Guinea our geography was not that good.

In the *Bontekoe*'s holds were some of the engineering equipment with which they were expected to build an airfield: two medium D4 Cat bulldozers (both in need of repair), two graders, four small dump trucks, one cargo truck and a power shovel. More, the men were told, would be picked up en route.

Beside them, a similar but considerably older Dutch KPM ship, the *Karsik*, was busy loading the experienced Australian troops of 9th Battery, 2/3rd Light Anti-Aircraft Regiment (LAA). While the ageing ship took no time to be awarded the nickname 'Spit, Fart and Cough', the men were more impressed with the Dutch crew's liberal liquor policy, which did much to assuage their grievances.

The 2/3rd had already seen a great deal of the war in the Middle East, having accounted for over 100 enemy aircraft destroyed, but 162 of their men had either been killed or taken prisoner. Hauled back to Australia to meet the Japanese threat, they had docked in Adelaide only the previous March, with jungle training in Queensland beginning a few weeks later. Now they were heading off again to fight a very different kind of war – but to where, exactly, none had the slightest idea.

After an uneventful few days at sea, the *Bontekoe* and *Karsik* pulled into Port Moresby's harbour, where every man onboard suddenly felt decidedly closer to the war. That afternoon, eighteen

Japanese bombers flew overhead, accompanied by the booms of the heavy anti-aircraft guns which opened up on them from around the harbour. More men and equipment was loaded onto the two ships, with the *Karsik* taking on several 25-pounder heavy field guns and eight Bofors anti-aircraft pieces of the 2/3rd LAA; several were not lowered into the ship's holds but placed straight on the *Karsik*'s upper deck, where the men of C Troop were ordered to secure them for immediate action. Just as well, as the wail of air raid sirens soon rang out once again across the harbour. The dock workers, it was observed, barely broke stride: Japanese air raids on Moresby had become a daily – sometimes several times daily – occurrence.

Also making their way onto the *Karsik* at Moresby were several hundred men of the 14th Brigade's 55th Battalion, whose role, at least on paper, would be to provide manual labour and security for the construction personnel. As militia, the 55th were not permitted to serve in areas outside Australia's jurisdiction. This, however, was the Territory of Papua, under Australian rule since its annexation by Queensland in the 1880s. To the men boarding the *Karsik* that morning, however, as Japanese bombers prowled overhead, the distinction appeared academic.

It had been a bewildering few weeks for the men of the 55th. Since December 1941 they had been deployed mainly in coastal defence roles around Newcastle in New South Wales, but as the situation to the north deteriorated, they were ordered in May to move significantly closer to danger at Port Moresby. Here, their weapons were shovels rather than rifles, and they were kept busy building and manning harbour and airfield defences.

Yet they noticed that they weren't spending much time in actual training. Three companies of the battalion – A, C and a section of E (which had at least had some training on antiquated First World War Vickers machine guns) – were informed in mid-June that they would soon be on the move, though none yet knew their new location.

For three days the ships loaded men and material at Port Moresby, interrupted by frequent Japanese air attacks. Up to twenty pieces of the American engineers' equipment would, for the time being, be left to languish on the dock while another ship was sought to take it forward. In its place, it was noted with alarm, was loaded a good deal of highly flammable aviation fuel and ammunition.

Also preparing to depart was the elegant passenger and cargo vessel *Macdhui*, which had already had an eventful war since being painted grey and pressed into service the previous year. In January she evacuated hundreds from the fallen fortress of Rabaul, and was now regularly running supplies between Townsville and Port Moresby. Lying at anchor in the harbour there on 18 June, the *Macdhui* was hit by four bombs from Betty bombers, which ignited her holds full of drums of aviation fuel. Fire quickly took hold before she rolled over and sank half a mile offshore, taking ten merchant navy sailors with her. Waiting to leave, the gunners, troops and engineers looked on helplessly as smoke from the *Macdhui* billowed across the harbour.

Although unused to handling weaponry, another group also preparing to sail would play a vital part in the coming battle: the radar operators of No. 37 Radio Direction Finder (i.e. radar) Unit. With their training thus far having been entirely theoretical, and delivered in stifling Port Moresby classrooms, they had not even sighted their equipment until, brand-new and still in its crates, it was loaded onto the ship alongside them. At least, at Moresby they been given some rudimentary rifle practice, if only, as one of their number remarked, 'to show us from which end the bullets emerged'.

Finally, just before dawn on 24 June, the four-ship convoy of the *Bontekoe*, *Karsik*, plus two escorting vessels, the corvette *Ballarat* and the destroyer *Warrego*, set sail for Milne Bay. Only now was their destination revealed to the engineers, gunners and infantry on board, but as the operation was referred to only by its codename, Fall River, no-one was any the wiser. As Sergeant Wilbert Block of the US 46th Engineer Battalion recalled:

> We headed southwest. Everyone was ordered to stay below deck. No one was allowed topside. We sailed all that day and night. The skipper had ordered several 'Abandon Ship' drills, but there were not enough lifeboats. We had to wear our life jackets at all times. All this made us wonder what we were getting into. We were never told where we were going.

As recorded in their official history, the 2/3rd Light Anti-Aircraft Regiment's gunners onboard the *Karsik* remembered the trip as somewhat surreal:

> The Dutch skipper weighed about twenty stone and drank Bols gin in a huge glass. There was a Dutch engineer, an Australian radio officer, and a deck crew who from the bosun down were Malay.

Twenty-four hours after leaving Moresby, at first light, the convoy approached the narrow passage which guarded Milne Bay's southern entrance, China Strait, passing close by the local administrative centre of Samarai, or what was left of it. Now, it was largely abandoned, with much of its little town reduced to piles of blackened beams and rusting corrugated iron. The previous January, after a Japanese air raid, it was decided to execute a scorched-earth policy on Samarai to deny it to the Japanese, who, it was correctly suspected, wanted its port, harbour and seaplane facilities for themselves. For the sailors on the ships of the convoy heading into the bay, however, it was a depressing sight.

It was in fact the forlorn sight of Samarai that filled the crew of the *Karsik* with sufficient foreboding for them to stage a near mutiny when they signalled to the rest of the convoy their reluctance to enter the bay. 'Nobody knew what was in there,' recorded the diary of a leading seaman travelling with them. It was not until her escorting vessel, HMAS *Warrego*, trained her guns on the recalcitrant merchantman and threatened to sink her that she grudgingly complied.

Sailing due west for the next five hours, the convoy finally arrived at Gili Gili, at Milne Bay's western end. Barely a week earlier, a handful of Australian and Papuan labourers, under the guidance of Captain Mackendrick (Mac) Rich of ANGAU, had begun construction of a rudimentary wharf and pontoon.

Rich himself proved an invaluable asset to the Australian forces at Milne Bay and beyond. Born to missionary parents on Samarai in 1903, he was at an early age fully fluent in several local dialects, and at twenty began a career in Papua's civil administration. By the mid-1930s he was district officer at Kokoda, at which time he also became Papua's first fully licensed radio operator. When the war came, his talents were recognised quickly by ANGAU, which in early 1942 placed him in charge of the Eastern District of Papua, as well as conferring on him the army rank of captain. In his memoirs, Rich recalled the visit from a flustered major in Port Moresby charged with overseeing his hasty transformation from civilian to officer in the Australian Army:

> He brought some military kit, swags, water bottles, blankets and clothing but no badges of rank and we were forced to cast our own 'pips' from lead, which hung more like sinkers from our epaulets and likely to smite one on the jaw if one turned suddenly.

Sergeant Block of the US 46th Engineers recalled his first sight of Gili Gili from the top deck of the *Bontekoe*:

> We stopped in the bottom of a horseshoe type bay, not more than a quarter mile from shore. The skipper did not drop anchor – just stopped. Shortly, native canoes came out to us and a couple of lifeboats were being lowered by the ship's crew.

The *Karsik*, with its nervous crew, was the first vessel to pull up to the small wharf, which, though newly completed, could only accommodate one vessel at a time. As the risk of their discovery by Japanese reconnaissance aircraft was high, waiting patiently for one's turn to come in and dock would simply not do. Block continued:

> The platoon commander and some of us went ashore to look for deep water as close to the shore as possible. The natives knew the shoreline and took us to such a place. This area had no beaches – where the trees stopped, the water began and went straight down for 30 feet. The Skipper moved his boat right up to the trees, tied onto them and pulled himself in.

Even at the wharf, stores were unable to be loaded directly into trucks and vehicles, making the entire unloading procedure long and exhausting. Out in the bay, the *Warrego* made constant anti-submarine sweeps; overhead, Beauforts from 100 Squadron, based at Moresby, also patrolled, an early indication of the deep cooperation between Australian ground and air forces that would exemplify the campaign. All ears were alert to the sound of Japanese aircraft, but to the relief – and not a little surprise – of everyone, the unloading proceeded unobserved by the enemy.

Three days were needed to complete the initial unloading, a task that would have been unachievable without the labour of 250 local villagers. Negotiating the recruitment of labourers was a delicate business requiring tact, diplomacy and an appreciation of Papuan village life. With neither the war nor the Allied cause being their own, it was appreciated early that the local people needed to be won over rather than coerced into offering their support. The brutality of the Japanese towards many Papuans played into the Allies' hands, but their goodwill and cooperation were nonetheless not taken for granted. Loyalties and alliances among Papuans coalesced around individual relationships rather than larger causes, and ANGAU officers such as Mac Rich made securing such loyalties a priority.

Papuan villages were small but tight-knit communities governed by complex social and family structures and hierarchies. In a village of 100 individuals, it was estimated that no more than twenty would be able-bodied males, upon whom the remainder of the community – old people, women and children – relied. Removing too many males for labouring duties would thus deprive the village of those capable of hunting, and canoe and house building, as well as the ceremonial obligations that were essential to village life.

Impressed upon all Australian personnel was the need to respect the villagers, with threats of severe punishment for those who did not, as the Standing Orders for 61 Battalion outlined:

> It is imperative that troops do not commit acts which may, in the slightest degree, alienate the natives and at the same time embarrass the ANGAU officers in carrying out their duties.

Village gardens and plantations were to be respected, all labour was to be paid for, and under no circumstances were Papuan women to be molested, or even approached. Directives concerning the Australian troops' penchant for nude bathing were also issued:

> It is only by retaining the respect of the natives of this country that we hope for the cooperation in the task we have before us. The white population of New Guinea have built up this

respect for the white man and it is for us to see that by no action our prestige is lowered. For a white man to expose his naked body before a native means that we all as a race lose face in the eyes of a native and it is therefore essential if troops bathe in the nude that a sentry MUST be posted to prevent natives approaching. Where available, trunks must be worn.

In large part, the diplomacy paid off, as ANGAU officer Lieutenant Jim Ross recalled:

When [the local people were] called upon to work, the response was gratifying. This in no small way was a result of the confidence they had in the leadership given by the administration [ANGAU] personnel whom they had come to know.

Traditional attitudes towards the Papuan people were nevertheless deep-set, as one air force anecdote regarding 76 Squadron's CO, Peter Turnbull, attests. Fresh from his assimilation lecture in Townsville, upon arrival in Port Moresby, the veteran squadron leader grabbed the nearest local boy he could find to attend to his domestic needs. 'Eh! Boy, these big boots, clean 'em, quicktime – yes?' he said, attempting to speak the local pidgin. 'Certainly, sir,' replied the boy in perfect English. 'Do you prefer that I use Kiwi or Nugget?'

Over a thousand village men and women from the greater Milne Bay area were, at various stages, employed by the army's engineers, each man earning no more than ten shillings a month, with the first task being the construction of a wharf at Gili Gili. In this, their exertions astounded even their white observers. Lieutenant Hugh Griffin of the 55th Battalion was one of those first to arrive, and remembered the ingenuity of the local engineers and labourers, both male and female:

> There were no ropes or picks available, but a few shovels and we managed to acquire sufficient poles for the job. The poles were guyed with native vines used as ropes and rocked into the sea bed forming a framework similar to a pig sty. This frame was then filled with coral and sand by a chain of about eighty women carrying baskets on their heads from a nearby sandy area . . . even the children joined in bringing lumps of coral in their canoes to add as filling.

Large yellow-handled 'hoop iron' knives were used to slash tough kunai grass and small trees to prepare roads and landing areas, and Papuan carpenters constructed and transported the wharf's foundations and decking. In only four days the first wharf was complete, made ready for use just twelve hours before the arrival of the convoy.

At first light on 26 June, it was with great relief that the crews of the *Karsik* and *Bontekoe*, their holds empty, pulled away from the little wharf at Gili Gili and headed east again, towards the open sea. It was only now, however, after their arrival at this strange dead end at the bottom of the world, that the American engineers and Australian infantrymen and gunners could grapple with the scale of the task that lay before them.

CHAPTER 4

THE BUILD-UP

Major Athelstane Garfield Margetts of the 2/3rd Light Anti-Aircraft Regiment, newly appointed as the temporary commander of the so-called Fall River Garrison, in no way relished the job he had been given, and was not in the least certain that it was even achievable. Once again he read over his secret orders, titled 'Fall River Operational Instructions No. 17, June 15, 1942', which stated blandly:

The role of the garrison will be:

(a) to construct the aerodrome

(b) A.A. defence of aerodrome

(c) ground defence of the area against paratroops or small raiding parties by land or sea

(d) provision of such guards as may be required for the protection of equipment supplies, etc

> (e) in the event of an overwhelming force being brought to
> bear against the garrison, it will inflict maximum loss on
> the enemy before withdrawal . . .

The 'garrison' with which he was expected to achieve all this and more comprised a mixed bunch of US and Australian units – or parts thereof – including his own light anti-aircraft men, the under-resourced US 46th Engineer Battalion, six platoons of the Australian 55th militia, a single platoon of the US 101st Coast Artillery Battalion armed with eight half-inch guns, a couple of companies from the 14th Infantry Brigade, a signals company from Western Australia, a US Hospital detachment, an HQ company, plus several others, none of which boasted any jungle fighting experience, nor any time spent in the tropics. With this he was expected to oversee the creation, from scratch, of an airstrip capable of supporting the most modern fighter and bomber aircraft in the world, which would later form the basis of a military citadel, carved out of a 426-acre coconut plantation in the middle of a malaria-ridden jungle, with the enemy at any moment expected to land in force and try to take it. And all this was to be achieved under a cloak of the strictest secrecy in just 25 days.

The problems he faced seemed insurmountable, beginning with the most basic, the complete lack of any decent maps of the area beyond a couple of colonial naval charts of dubious vintage. The men of the garrison would therefore have to make them themselves.

Margetts immediately divided the entire Milne Bay area into sections, each of which was assigned to an infantry officer of the 55th Battalion, who would use his army-issue compass and a prismatic rangefinder taken from a Bren machine gun to survey and map his section. Elementary in the extreme, it supplied just enough information to be collated and overlaid onto the existing naval chart, thus forming a series of maps that were eventually used in the battle itself.

Meanwhile, the Americans wasted no time beginning construction of the airstrip that was designated, quite logically, No. 1 Strip. The widest and flattest part of the coast was situated around Gili Gili, occupied mainly by the Lever Brothers' coconut plantation, at that time one of the largest in the world. After a day or two of surveying, a 55-acre swathe, 300 feet by 8000 feet in size, was selected for its flatness and dryness. The latter was relative, however, with one end of what was to be the runway currently under a swamp, which would have to be drained.

The engineers of the 43rd began removing several thousand trees, blasting and bulldozing stumps and bush, using machines but with a considerable amount of work being done by hand. The technique of removing so many trees was testament to the industrial knowhow of the Americans. Entire rows of tree trunks were holed with a power drill, then small charges of gelignite were inserted in each and wired to a long cable. Then, at a command, an electric plunger was pushed, and the entire row would burst at their trunks, the upper fronds seeming almost to rise up and hang in the air for a moment before crashing to the ground.

The few bulldozers, graders, power shovels and dump trucks worked ceaselessly to clear the stumps and level the ground so that the steel matting could be laid. Even so, the engineers doubted the task could be completed in time. Sergeant Wilbert Block remembered:

> The building of an airstrip in the middle of the jungles and swamps with mountains all around us, looked almost impossible with the equipment we had ... when we first arrived, the ground seemed to be reasonably firm, but with the movement of all this equipment and constant rain, everything turned to mud.

In the memories of all who served at Milne Bay, the mud remained the salient feature, as it pervaded every aspect of life in the garrison. The three weeks prior to the arrival of the construction parties had seen tropical downpours lash the bay's coast and the Stirling Range in a deluge heavy even by its standards. Many veterans, when later reflecting on their time at Milne Bay, do not remember the rain letting up for a moment. Men could literally shower outside. Flight Lieutenant Clive 'Bardie' Wawn of 76 Squadron witnessed a foot-deep tin outside his sodden tent fill from empty to overflowing overnight.

Streams from the 4000-foot-high mountains were transformed into mighty torrents, damaging – in some cases washing away – what few roads existed in the first place. Trucks and vehicles simply slid off the tracks as they became deeply rutted and impassable. Soon, only the most powerful of the American four-wheel drives could navigate the roads in any useful way; most of the Australian vehicles were two-wheel drives, which quickly became bogged. Many more roads would have to be built before the bulk of the 7th Brigade arrived.

Margetts ordered every man who could hold a shovel to go out and dig. To seal the surface of new roads, the trunks of the thousands of coconut trees were laid down, using the corduroy technique, which gave traction for a while. As heavy equipment began to churn up the surface, however, these eventually became unstable again.

Much of this work was carried out by Papuan labourers, recruited by the local ANGAU officers. The Australian and US servicemen were constantly astonished by their ability to work for long hours without complaint, and were surprised by their fluency in English; many in this part of New Guinea had been educated at mission schools. ANGAU officers were instructed to be attentive to the health of the labourers, as many local people had no immunity to diseases such as measles. Any Australian who presented with such an illness had to be quickly isolated; if necessary, they were removed.

The Australians and Americans were ravaged by similarly unfamiliar diseases, primarily malaria. A pre-war survey had found a highly malignant strain to be hyperendemic to this part of New Guinea, present in over 90 per cent of villages in the area. Within days, the first cases among the Allied service personnel started to present. According to one diary, by 11 July five men had been hospitalised with the disease; that doubled the next day. As more troops arrived over the coming weeks, the situation was exacerbated by poor medical advice and a lack of precautions for the tropical climate – so that by the time of the battle, some fighting units were reporting up to three-quarters of their men sick with various stages of the disease.

Dysentery was also common, and tropical parasites abounded. Initially at least, education as to their dangers was sorely lacking, and men began to present with such ailments as ear infections resulting from bathing in local creeks and streams. Bare skin coming into contact with earth could easily result in hookworm, and scratches from the abundant 'wait-a-while' sago palms and many other local bushes and shrubs could quickly become tropical ulcers, which were almost impossible to heal. Medical units would be put to the severest test just keeping the men fit. Private Allan Dolly of the 9th Battalion dubbed the Milne Bay fighting area 'the last place God made and didn't finish'.

Day by day, however, more men and equipment arrived, and more roads were established, or at least begun. Laying down crushed rock and coral was found to be a relatively effective way of securing the boggy road surfaces, and was in abundance along the long shoreline. Still, the road signs reading 'Maximum Speed Limit 20 mph' were looked on with wry humour.

In the days that followed the initial deployment, more ships arrived, including the British vessel *Chochow*, which pulled up at the Gili Gili wharf on 5 July, loaded with some of the tons of American steel Marston matting which would form the surfaces of the runways. Developed just the previous year by the Waterways Experiment Station, a research facility built by the US Army Corps of Engineers in Vicksburg, Mississippi, 'perforated steel planking' (or PSP) became known by the name of the small town in which it was first tested: Marston, North Carolina.

Strong, quick to construct and able to be manufactured in enormous quantities, the Marston mat enabled the establishment of forward airfields which could receive the heaviest aircraft in the most difficult of terrains. Rolled out in quarter-inch steel sheets with circular perforations to save weight, each piece was 10 feet long and 15 inches wide, and weighed about 70 pounds. A series of alternating tabs and grooves on each side secured one piece to another, like a giant jigsaw, and almost no further preparation was needed before the surface could accept aircraft.

Millions of sheets of Marston matting were produced throughout the war, and were used in almost every theatre: from Asia to Europe, the African desert, and even Alaska. Its first use, however, was at No. 1 Strip at Milne Bay, and it was an instant success.

The Australian soldiers at the improvised dock at Gili Gili, employed for now as wharf hands, could not fathom what these pallets of strange-looking steel plates could possibly be for as they came out of the holds of the ships, but they were soon to find out. And they would be very grateful for them indeed.

CHAPTER 5
WHERE ARE THE JAPANESE?

A little over two weeks elapsed at Milne Bay between the arrival of the US Engineers and their Australian guards on 25 June and the arrival of the garrison's first proper reinforcements – in the form of the 7th Infantry Brigade – on 11 July, and they were perilous weeks in the extreme. Should the Japanese have chosen this moment to make their landing – as was widely expected – and secure Milne Bay for themselves, they would have met little opposition. When Major Margetts left Port Moresby for Gili Gili, he was bluntly told that, in the case of an attack by the Japanese, no help would be forthcoming.

This reality was also laid out to the men themselves. On a special parade on 7 July, the garrison was informed that, in the event of a Japanese assault, everyone – including gunners, radar operators and guards – were to assume themselves as infantry, inflict as much damage on the enemy as they could, and then head into the jungle and make for Port Moresby. Those unfamiliar with a rifle were told to learn how to handle one, and fast.

A direction like this from a distant HQ was all very well, but Margetts knew the entire area was essentially unmapped and unknown. This, at least, was a problem he could try to remedy. Soon after the mapping parties had commenced their rudimentary survey of the immediate environs, others were sent further afield to get the lay of the land: what it would be like to fight in, and – particularly – how to get out of it in a hurry.

In early July, two patrols from the 9th Light Anti-Aircraft Battalion were sent out, the first to reconnoitre an escape route to Mullins Harbour, about 25 miles away to the south-west. Led by Lieutenant Gerry Chambers, for three days the men pushed through jungle and up ridges to Mullins Harbour, with steadily increasing dread at what would be the consequences if the entire garrison had to join them along this tortuous route, particularly if fleeing the enemy. 'There certainly wasn't much feeling of victory in the air,' he confessed in the unit's official history.

Meanwhile, a second patrol was sent to explore the coastal track hugging the length of Milne Bay's northern shore, the likely site of any Japanese landing. What was its condition? Where were the likely landing spots? How easy would it be to defend? All questions desperately requiring an answer. At dawn on 8 July, a three-man patrol – two coincidentally named 'Paton', Lieutenant Bruce Paton and Private Jim Paton, and Sergeant Scottie Quinn – were taken by boat 45 miles east, towards the mouth of the bay, to the Anglican mission at Dogura (sometimes referred to as 'Dobodura'), from which point they would make their way back by land, heading west along the coastal track.

At Dogura, Lieutenant Paton and his men were presented with a curiously bucolic setting, distinctly at odds with the violence looming above them. Here, among the mission's tidy lawns, orderly little church and playing fields, the staff seemed oblivious to the idea that their idyll was about to become a war zone. Father John Bodger, the minister in charge, greeted the men warmly and offered them a meal and bed for the night. Paton explained their mission, and Father Bodger offered to have a trusted local guide accompany them.

When Paton asked when the mission would be evacuated, he was met with incredulity. The missionaries had no intention of going anywhere, said Father Bodger. Paton's entreaties – he even pointed out that people such as Bodger, as well as nurses and teachers, had already been murdered by the Japanese at places like Gona – fell on deaf ears. 'We too have our duty to perform, Lieutenant,' was the simple response.

At dawn the next day, after by far the most comfortable night the men had spent since their arrival at Milne Bay, Paton's small party began their three-day journey back to Gili Gili. To see them off, some 50 of the mission's schoolchildren lined up in order of height along the path, the girls on one side, the boys on the other, all impeccably dressed. As the soldiers passed between them, a perfect three-part harmony of 'Auld Lang Syne' rang out, resonating through the jungle. It was a moment of surreal beauty, but tinged with immense sadness; according to Paton, it was 'a wonderful experience never to be forgotten'.

Proceeding west, Paton first addressed his primary task of noting possible landing areas that might be used by the enemy. These, he realised with dismay, were just about everywhere. Milne Bay's naturally deep water and steeply falling shoreline were a boon to any ship seeking to pull up and disgorge its passengers and cargo. An invading Japanese landing party would be spoiled for choice among the many sheltered little coves Paton observed. The track itself, he also noted, would provide one of the most difficult battlegrounds imaginable, for both the attackers and the defenders. As he later wrote:

> With the help of the trusted guide, it took three days to cover the distance from Dogura back to Milne Bay over some of the most tortuous country imaginable. Deep ravines alternating with high razorback ridges were the norm as the track, which was suitable for foot traffic only, wound its way through thick jungle for the entire distance.

His conclusion, however, was that, as difficult as this country was, the Japanese could indeed get through to Gili Gili.

The patrol spent two nights in villages high on the ridges, where they were looked after and fed with stews of sweet potato – all strictly paid for. The next morning, when they returned to the garrison, they found it had expanded dramatically in their brief absence. Even as they walked to the HQ staff tent to make their report, a long line of soldiers were disembarking from another large ship. The 7th Infantry Brigade, under Brigadier John Field, had arrived.

•

There are several reasons why John Field was the perfect choice to lead the men of the Milne Bay garrison at this early stage. He was, in the first instance, a thoughtful and intelligent commander who had already proved himself in battle, being Mentioned in Dispatches in 1941. Given command of the 2/12th Battalion – infantry volunteers from Tasmania and north Queensland – he had travelled with them across the Western Desert, fighting the Italians, Germans and Vichy French, bolstering the defences of Tobruk, then serving in Palestine and Syria.

He had a particular knack as a defensive strategist who would not be flustered into making a decision until he had considered all options and angles. And then he would approach his task with resolution and determination. Promoted to acting brigadier upon his return to Australia in May 1941, he was put in charge of the 7th Infantry Brigade, which was to be incorporated into a new, larger force for a purpose so specific that it was to be given a title to match: Milne Force.

However, perhaps Field's most distinguishing qualification was that he was a fully qualified, as well as highly respected, engineer. Born in Castlemaine, Victoria, in 1899, the young John Field was apprenticed to an engineering firm by the age of fifteen, rising in a few years to become the senior draftsman, specialising in centrifugal pumps and pumping plants. By age 26, he was lecturing on the subject at the University of Tasmania, while also climbing up the ranks of the Citizen Military Forces, in which he was made a major shortly before the outbreak of war in 1939.

It was with no little urgency that Field had been brought back from the Middle East. With northern Australia perceived to be under threat of invasion, his capabilities in engineering and defensive construction landed him the job of training the 7th Brigade to meet a Japanese invasion where it was most expected: at Rollingstone, 31 miles north of Townsville. Here, much to the outrage of some of the local sugar cane farmers, who wailed for compensation for the damage wrought on their land, he trained his men to dig in and build. So much work was needed, however, that Field spent little time instructing his infantrymen on how to actually fight.

In the event, no invasion by the Japanese was forthcoming at Rollingstone, nor anywhere else on the Australian mainland, but the threat further to the north was real enough. As Field recorded in his diary:

> We'd just begun the training programme when we were ordered to Milne Bay. Liaison Officer Struss came to see me with the cryptic statement, 'The show is on!' There had been no prior information passed to me on the possibility of a move. Such is the fog of war.

Behind the scenes, things had been moving quickly. As the initial establishment of Milne Bay got underway, General MacArthur decided to reinforce it, though initially with only a single battalion. The commander-in-chief of the Australian forces, General Thomas Blamey, was incensed. Enough 'penny packets' of Australian soldiers, he pointed out, had already been sent into the islands to be swallowed up and annihilated by the Japanese juggernaut. This time, he insisted, 'a self-contained fighting force' must be sent. His argument won the day, and Field's 7th Brigade – comprising three militia battalions, now digging in around Townsville – was chosen.

Field was not to be overwhelmed by the many problems confronting him upon his arrival at Milne Bay on 11 July 1942. Indeed, his very first morning at the garrison had been an eventful one. As soon as the *Tasman*, another venerable Dutch KPM freighter, pulled up to the wharf carrying the forward elements of Field's 7th Brigade, an agitated naval officer, Sub-Lieutenant Ivan Champion, raced up the gangway to alert his new CO of Japanese aerial activity which had been observed overhead all morning.

A childhood friend of Mac Rich, Champion was likewise a former patrol officer and long-time resident of Papua. He had already notched up one close encounter with the Japanese when, the previous April, he had swung his requisitioned Papuan government motor vessel, HMAS *Laurabada*, into a beach at Jacquinot Bay in New Britain. Here, under the noses of the Japanese, he spirited away 156 desperate Australian military and civilian personnel fleeing the Japanese after the fall of Rabaul. The old ship – whose armament consisted of a solitary machine-gun – groaned with the weight, but Champion delivered everyone safely to Port Moresby.

Along with everyone else at the garrison, Champion simply could not believe the Japanese had not already discovered their presence, not to mention the half-completed No. 1 Strip, which was now expanding into the jungle a mile or so away. Japanese aircraft had been coming and going sporadically over the fort-night since their arrival, but the expected attack had failed to materialise. While the men of the garrison were relieved, it was somewhat unnerving. Soon the dismal rumour began to spread that the Japanese were actually waiting for the strip to be completed before launching their invasion, at which point they would simply walk in and take it. The notion did nothing to lift the pall hanging over the garrison.

Nevertheless, the strongest measures to conceal their existence continued to be observed. Radio silence was strictly enforced, with messages received but not broadcast, radar sets were forbidden to be switched on, and no gun was permitted to open fire on any curious Japanese aircraft that might be lurking overhead.

These last couple of days, however, it appeared the ruse was up. In the previous 24 hours, the garrison went onto full alert as a formation of six approaching enemy aircraft was reported by Coastwatchers at their lonely positions along Papua's northern coast. This was later corrected to one aircraft – and then, bizarrely, increased to ten. In the end, a single Catalina flying boat was observed cruising overhead in a southerly direction.

Just hours later, the sirens sounded again as another aircraft was reported, and this one did make an appearance. A gunner from the 2/3rd Light Anti-Aircraft Regiment observed that:

> a twin-engined single-tailed bomber flew over at about 1500 feet. It was not until it changed course that the big red roundel of Japan was clearly seen. According to instructions, no guns were fired. The aircraft left the area in a northeasterly direction without incident.

None of this did anything to assuage the frayed nerves of the men at Milne Bay. When a Japanese aircraft was spotted, all work and activity would cease and, like an animal attempting to conceal itself by blending into the background, the entire garrison would freeze, their eyes and ears straining upwards. Only the movement of the barrels of the anti-aircraft guns as they tracked across the skies, their aim fixed on the enemy, would break the tableau.

The fact that they seemed to have fooled the Japanese thus far amazed the men on the ground at Gili Gili, but all knew that their luck could not last forever.

Onboard the *Tasman*, an agitated Sub-Lieutenant Champion found Brigadier Field, saluted and hurriedly explained the situation, adding that his arrival, as well as the first of the several thousand men of his 7th Brigade, was extremely welcome. With a Japanese presence in the area, it was deemed necessary that the small armada hurry the unloading of the men and their equipment, while the nervous ships' captains looked on.

As Champion escorted Field along the rough track leading away from the wharf for his first look at the garrison, the brigadier saw immediately that there was a great deal of work to be done.

CHAPTER 6
FIELD TAKES CHARGE

As Dudley McCarthy's official history, published by the Australian War Memorial, states, 'It must have seemed to Field on his arrival at Milne Bay that the possibility of a battle might be the least of his worries.' His first inspection was of the vital airstrip, which, to his satisfaction, was in an advanced stage, almost ready for the laying down of the Marston matting thanks to the efforts of the American engineers. The docking and unloading system at the wharf at Gili Gili was still rudimentary, however, and painfully slow.

Milne Bay's vertiginous coral shelf shorelines allowed ships of up to 5000 tons to berth within 40 feet of the bank, and cargo was loaded on a series of floating pontoons, which had been constructed with Papuan labour. It was not possible, however, to load directly into the trucks and vehicles themselves, so hours of labour-intensive reloading were required.

But it was the road system leading away from the wharf that presented Field with his greatest headache. Major Margetts had informed him that, despite his best efforts, there was still not more than 20 miles of roads with anything like a formed surface, and vast sections were just 10 feet wide, making two-way traffic impossible.

An inspection carried out over the next few days revealed at least seventeen small wooden bridges in the main area, all of which would have to be either strengthened or replaced to allow them to accept even moderately heavy military traffic. Although they were infantrymen, Field's 7th Brigade were ordered to put down their rifles and pick up shovels. Milne Bay's infrastructure would need to be built by hand. One of their earliest tasks was to construct passing places and loops on the roads, to allow vehicles to move by one another without the risk of putting a wheel onto the muddy verges and becoming bogged.

With some relief, Major Margetts handed over command of the Milne Bay garrison to Brigadier Field, enabling Margetts to return to the vital build-up of his own anti-aircraft unit, which was soon to be greatly tested in battle.

•

As if preparing the Milne Bay area for an expected Japanese attack was not a formidable enough task, on 11 July Field received instructions from Townsville to begin reconnoitring for a second airfield in the more protected but considerably more inaccessible area of Waigani, four miles inland, to the east of the half-completed No. 1 Strip. For this task, more American engineers – two companies of the 43rd Engineering Regiment, in fact – would soon be arriving from Townsville. Until then, the work would have to be done by Field's men, who, it was becoming increasingly evident, had arrived woefully ill-prepared for the tropics.

Almost all of the 7th Brigade's men were in summer-weight shorts and shirts rolled to the elbows, leaving their arms and legs exposed to the malarial mosquitoes. The repellent cream with which all had been issued was soon found to be useless, and mosquito nets had not yet been handed out, having been stored in an inaccessible part of the *Tasman*'s holds. Quinine tablets were available, but, bizarrely, the men were ordered to refrain from taking them for seven days after their arrival. Added to this was the arrival of several hundred local workers, providing a ready pool of the malarial disease itself, which would soon spread through the ranks of the uninfected. As it had with Major Margetts' men, the first malarial cases from the 7th Brigade began to present within days.

Assessing his own staff, as well as those of the other units at Milne Bay, Field arrived at the conclusion that the only officer with any experience of active service in the present war was himself; four others on his staff had seen fighting in the 1914–18 war. Outside his HQ, established in the old plantation manager's house at Gili Gili, the three battalions of the 7th Brigade were fully occupied making bridges and roads, or labouring on the wharf and at the airfield – all vital tasks in making the place defensible. As at Townsville, however, this left precious little time for Field to provide his men with the jungle training and familiarisation they needed, so his brigade was, he knew, woefully unprepared.

Before arriving at Milne Bay, they had trained around Brisbane and taken part in some exercises, but even there few had had the chance to use their rifles. As one soldier of the 7th Brigade's 61st Battalion remembered, 'I'd only fired seven shots out of my rifle prior to Milne Bay . . . in those days every round of ammunition had to be accounted for . . . we just didn't have much of it.' A man from the 9th Battalion acknowledged that the training had brought them to a level of physical fitness, but that was about it. Their clothing was unsuitable, and their weapons were surplus from the last war. 'We had never advanced over covering fire of any kind,' he recalled.

It was becoming clear to Field that his brigade alone would not be sufficient to defend Milne Bay in the face of a determined Japanese landing. A second AIF unit – preferably a regular one that had battle experience – was also needed. He wrote in his diary:

> I had in mind the strategic importance of the south-east area
> of New Guinea and the earlier futility of defending localities
> in the south-west Pacific with 'Penny Packets'. So many had
> been knocked off before – surely the importance of Milne
> Bay justified its holding in strength.

General Blamey concurred, and selected the desert veterans of the 18th Infantry Brigade, back from the Middle East since May and currently undergoing jungle training around Kilcoy, in south-east Queensland. At their head was the highly capable, though somewhat rotund, figure of Brigadier George Frederick Wootten, who, despite being of only modest height, tipped the scales at 280 pounds. Yet this in no way indicated a lack of dash or skill on the battlefield. When due for rotation away from the battlefield at Tobruk, Wootten had succeeded in extracting his entire brigade on a moonless night in August 1941 without the Germans having the slightest idea.

As far as Field was concerned, the men of Wootten's 18th Brigade could not get to Milne Bay fast enough, for the Japanese were showing more and more interest in this little corner of Papua. In the first half of July 1942, reconnaissance flights became more frequent, and although the cloak of silence was maintained, it seemed almost inconceivable that the enemy remained yet unaware of their presence. In this, the Australians were aided by the single element that was making their own lives such a misery: the weather.

Although the men at Milne Bay felt vulnerable and exposed, the scale of the garrison and its activities were in fact difficult to determine from the air. When for the brief moments the rain and the mist cleared, the garrison appeared as a mere pinprick in the jungle expanse. And with the Japanese lacking in accurate maps of the area, the build-up of the Allied force eluded them.

Then, on the evening of 21 July, reports came through to Field's HQ of a landing being made on the northern coast of the Owen Stanley Range, at the mission villages of Buna and Gona. This was roughly 186 miles from Milne Bay, but only half that distance from Port Moresby. The invasion convoy of four destroyers, one cruiser and a large transport had in fact been spotted by aerial reconnaissance earlier that day in the waters off the southern coast of New Britain, but was later lost. Hence, completely unmolested, the Japanese arrived close off the beach at Buna, where their destroyers turned their guns to shore and opened fire. At exactly 5 p.m., several thousand green-clad army troops scrambled down the ship's rope nets and into assault barges, employing their favourite tactic of striking in the late afternoon, not long before darkness arrived, preventing air attack. The handful of Australian militia troops stationed at Buna were quickly overwhelmed. The Japanese southward drive to the Papuan capital had begun.

The next day Field received an urgent signal from the Coastwatchers along Papua's northern rim, reporting Japanese warships on the move; this led him to believe an attack on Milne Bay was imminent. Beach defences were manned and evacuation kits prepared. In fact, the Coastwatchers were reporting the movements of the Buna convoy. The attack on Milne Bay – the second part of the Japanese campaign to take Port Moresby – was not yet ready. Field had won a reprieve, but it would not be a long one.

Better news received this day was that the final piece of Marston matting had been slotted into place and the No. 1 Strip was now operational. The RAAF could begin arriving as soon as it wished. Although he had not been there at the start, Field appreciated this feat of engineering, undertaken in one of the most difficult locations imaginable. The fact that it had taken a mere 22 days from start to finish, and was three days ahead of schedule, was a further testament to the skill and dedication of the American engineers.

The runway stretched 5100 feet from east to west, and was 100 feet wide. A rise at the western end was still being flattened out, which would add another 300 feet to the total length. Dispersal areas for two fighter squadrons and a bomber squadron had been made just off the main runway.

As remarkable as this airfield in the jungle was, however, it would not be an easy place for pilots to work out of. As Pilot Officer Bruce 'Buster' Brown of 75 Squadron said later, it was quite simply 'the worst airstrip I have ever operated off . . . or am ever likely to'.

CHAPTER 7
AN UNEXPECTED ARRIVAL

Squadron Leader Peter Turnbull, DFC, was not having a good day. Leading his 76 Squadron pilots on their first ever combat mission was supposed to have been a relatively straightforward affair, intended to give the boys their first look at the jungle. The plan was to make a quick strike on some enemy anti-aircraft positions and then bolt home before the Japanese even knew they were there. But it had almost ended in disaster.

The mission was simple enough: take off with five new pilots from Port Moresby's Twelve Mile Strip, drop a couple of bombs on the enemy positions around Gona, which they had overrun during the last few days, then turn around and race home again, flying over the Owen Stanleys. It was just the sort of live training which Turnbull's pilots – fresh from instruction in Townsville, with no experience of New Guinea whatsoever – needed. The Japanese, Turnbull knew, rarely flew standing patrols, and as long as his Kittyhawks didn't hang around long enough for the Zeros to get airborne, his men should be able to get back unscathed and add their first mission to their logbooks.

Turnbull could see above him the reassuring pale-blue undersides of eight P-39 Airacobras from the US 41st and 80th Fighter Squadrons, providing top cover just in case they ran into any trouble. As he made his way towards the target, it may not have occurred to Turnbull that he was making history, leading the first Australian fighter-bomber sortie against the Japanese in the Pacific War.

Around 100 miles from the target, he had more urgent concerns as the weather began to close in and banks of cloud loomed on all sides. Looking around him to keep his young pilots together, he then searched frantically for his American escort, only to find the skies above him empty, the two formations having become separated. Cursing, Turnbull signalled his men to close in and keep an eye on each other. They would proceed to the target alone.

A few minutes later the coast appeared ahead, and Turnbull muttered thanks to the weather gods for clearing their run to the target. Gaining some height, he spotted the Japanese gun emplacements adjacent to the mission buildings a few thousand feet below. His five pilots were strung out in line, just as he had instructed them. Engaging the mechanism to arm his bomb after its release, he prepared to be the first to put his Kittyhawk into a steep dive to the target.

Suddenly the sky above Turnbull was filled with planes. For a moment he believed his American friends had returned, but his blood ran cold as he saw large red circles under their wings.

Two flights of Zeros – eight aircraft – having taken off from their large base at Rabaul, had arrived directly over Gona just as he and his very inexperienced pilots were preparing to dive-bomb it. The timing of the Japanese could not have been more perfect. Breaking radio silence for the first time, Turnbull yelled at his men to jettison their bombs immediately and get the hell out of there. His several weeks' flying in defence of Port Moresby the previous April had taught him that the Kittyhawk pilot who tried to dogfight the fast and nimble Zero was very soon dead.

Pulling the release, his bombs fell harmlessly into the sea, and his aircraft, now suddenly 250 pounds lighter, gave a leap upwards in apparent relief. Some of Turnbull's men had dived at full throttle and scattered into nearby cloud, but now the sky in front of him was full of Japanese fighters, and a line of tracer fire passed close over his head.

These were not the standard high-altitude Zeros, but the relatively new Type 32 variant, known by the Allies as 'Hamp', with clipped wings and more powerful motors, making them superb at low levels. One crossed Turnbull's sights and he immediately pressed the firing button, but thought better of pressing home the attack. Throwing his stick and rudder simultaneously into one corner, his Kittyhawk plunged downwards and rolled, in a manoeuvre known colloquially as a 'bink', which the lighter Japanese aircraft could not follow.

Emerging from the melee, Turnbull turned south towards Moresby, looking around to see who, if anyone, was accompanying him. On his left and right, amazingly, were Flying Officer Max Bott and Sergeant Brian Carroll; both had followed their boss and also fired off a few shots, hoping to hit something before diving away with utmost haste. Now the three of them were speeding along the northern coast of Papua, knowing their best speeds could be maintained at low altitude.

And speed was now of the essence, as they were being doggedly pursued by an indeterminate number of those Zeros which had jumped them over the target. For almost 100 miles the chase ensued, throttles fully open, the Australian pilots putting their faith in their emergency boost, which gave them maximum speed but guzzled fuel at an alarming rate.

Gradually the Japanese aircraft seemed to fall further behind, waning to specks in Turnbull's mirror, before finally breaking off the pursuit. His Kittyhawk's liquid-cooled Allison engine was being belted, its temperature nudging the red. Even worse, the needle on his fuel gauge was dropping rapidly. None of them would make it back to Moresby.

There was only one airstrip in the vicinity, and Turnbull had never landed on it – and nor had anyone else. In fact, he was not exactly sure if it was even finished – but his squadron was slated to be moving there in a few days' time, so he decided to find out. Quickly consulting the map strapped to his knee, Turnbull clicked the dial of his compass around and set course for Milne Bay. What the garrison commander, not to mention the notoriously lively anti-aircraft gunners by the side of the strip, would make of his unexpected arrival was anyone's guess.

Just after half past four on the afternoon of 22 July, the defenders of the Milne Bay garrison turned their heads skywards towards the alarming sound of approaching aircraft. These were not the relatively distant sounds of the odd enemy reconnaissance plane, but low-level, loud and deliberate. All believed that this, surely, was it – the Japanese had given up their feigned ignorance of the garrison and were finally coming to strike.

Gun positions were manned, and slit trenches filled. Then the surprised call went up: 'They're ours!' Moments later, the first aircraft tyres touched down on the Marston matting of Milne Bay's No. 1 Strip. The air force had arrived.

•

In two years of combat flying, the 25-year-old Peter St George Bruce Turnbull had already seen a great deal of war. From Armidale in northern New South Wales, the young country lad had shown a fondness for horses, dancing and girls – who, for their part, seemed happy to spend time in his company too, admiring his striking dark features. Turnbull had joined the Light Horse militia a couple of years before the war, but transferred to the RAAF in January 1939.

Graduating as a single-engine pilot, he was sent to Egypt to take part in the desert campaign against the Italians, and then later the Germans, where he made a name for himself as a skilled and aggressive fighter pilot. With 3 Squadron, flying the Kittyhawk's slightly earlier variant, the Tomahawk, and then later the Hurricane, Turnbull carved a swathe through the Italian, German and Vichy French air forces, clocking up over 100 sorties and 200 operational hours' flying time; he also acquired the status of 'ace', with at least nine credited kills, though the RAAF never officially acknowledged the title with any of its pilots. On a single sortie one afternoon in April 1941, he disposed of four German Messerschmitt 110 twin-engine fighters, for which he was awarded the Distinguished Flying Cross.

In Australia's darkest hours in early 1942, when the Japanese onslaught to the north seemed unstoppable, three new fighter squadrons – 75, 76 and 77 – were formed with the panicked stroke of a governmental pen after a shipload of brand-new American P-40 Kittyhawk fighters, still in their crates, arrived unexpectedly into Botany Bay; they had been destined for the Dutch East Indies. Turnbull, who had already done more than enough to warrant him being allowed to sit out the remainder of the war in training, was instead asked to help instruct the young pilots who would man these new squadrons, and then lead them into battle against a hardened and apparently invincible enemy. He jumped at the chance.

In March 1942 he found himself at Port Moresby's Twelve Mile Strip, a miserable, dusty patch of bush with neither facilities nor comforts, at least as bad as the worst desert airstrip he had encountered in Libya and beyond. It was also under constant attack by the Japanese from their closest base, an hour's flying time away at Lae. Turnbull was one of the few pilots in this new squadron with battle experience, and the younger pilots held him in awe. As far as was possible, Turnbull would do his best to keep them alive, and teach them how to hit back at the enemy.

In this he was enormously assisted by his old 3 Squadron desert CO, now 75's new commander, Squadron Leader John Jackson, a remarkable pilot and true leader of men, who, with Turnbull, helped forge the new charges into something like a cohesive fighting unit. In 75 Squadron's six-week air defence of Port Moresby, the noses of the rapacious Japanese were bloodied for the first time in the war as this small band of Australian pilots fell upon the Zeros and Betty bombers like a pack of wild dogs – scrappy, fearless and determined. Between 21 March and 1 May 1942, 75 Squadron's pilots accounted for over 30 Japanese aircraft destroyed and many more damaged, for a loss of twelve of their own. While this did not represent a significant blow against the Japanese in military terms, it was, as the squadron's official history states, a 'moral victory of incalculable value', throwing into awry Japan's timing for its invasion of New Guinea, and forcing its leaders to realise that their days of unchallenged conquest were over.

Such was the experience 75 Squadron was quickly gaining at Port Moresby that the new CO of the still-forming 76 Squadron, Squadron Leader Bernard 'Barney' Cresswell, was sent there on detachment to gain some combat hours for himself. A pilot of enormous flying – but no combat – experience, Cresswell and another Kittyhawk pilot were jumped by a detachment of Zeros during his first ever combat sortie over Lae on 17 April. Cresswell was unused to the split-second nature of air combat, and a moment's hesitation cost him his life. His burning aircraft was observed to slam into the side of a mountain.

Turnbull, meanwhile, had added another three enemy aircraft to his tally, taking it to twelve, making him one of the RAAF's highest-scoring pilots, and the ideal officer to step into Cresswell's shoes as the men of 76 Squadron prepared for their turn in the limelight. Although torn to be leaving his comrades at Port Moresby, he suspected that he would soon be back there.

In May Turnbull was officially made 76 Squadron's new commanding officer, and at Aitkenvale Weir airfield, near Townsville, he did his best to prepare another group of raw pilots for the heat of battle. At least he had been given more time than had 75 Squadron; he was even joined by a group of experienced pilots just returned from England. One was a true celebrity, Squadron Leader Keith 'Bluey' Truscott, who first made a name for himself on the sporting field with the Melbourne Football Club, and then became a Spitfire ace with 452 Squadron in England, destroying 16 German aircraft and earning himself the DFC and bar.

Truscott's arrival home in May, however, had been bittersweet. He was exhausted, unfit and overweight, and suffering the emotional troughs of what would, in a much later age, be termed 'post traumatic stress disorder'. The first most of the world knew of his return to Australia was his sudden appearance on the turf of the Richmond Oval in Melbourne, having quietly organised to play a game with his old club against their archrivals, the Richmond Tigers. When the crowd realised that it was indeed Truscott out there, back in his old jumper (retrieved from mothballs), they went wild with delight. The returning footballer, and now war hero, acknowledged the adoration of the fans on both sides and played the most atrocious game of his career. At one stage, the opposition slowed down play to give him a chance to kick a goal, but he was hopeless and he knew it, and every muscle in his body ached for days.

The press, starved of homegrown heroes, would not leave him alone. Eventually, he slipped out of the family home and checked himself into the Menzies Hotel under the name 'Squadron Leader Williams' and hid from the world. Then in July, he heard of the death of his great friend and fellow ace Paddy Finucane, who had to ditch his damaged Spitfire in the English Channel. To compound matters, the Air Board attempted to remove the rank awarded to Truscott in England and drop him back to Flight Lieutenant, an insult hurled at many pilots returning from operational flying in Europe at this time. Truscott fought the snub tooth and nail, and with the aid of friends in the press and a sympathetic public, managed to hold onto his two and a half stripes. Posted to the still-forming 76 Squadron, Truscott was now required to adapt to the heavy, solid Kittyhawk after the delicate ballerina of the Spitfire, and did not like it one bit. According to his biographer, Ivan Southall, it did what he asked of it, 'but he couldn't make it dance'.

A brilliant fighter pilot at altitude, Truscott was notoriously inept at low level, particularly when it came to judging the height of the ground. While attempting his first ever landing at No. 2 Operational Training Unit, in Mildura, he came in too slow, stalling just over the runway – at which point his Kittyhawk flipped upside down. With extraordinary skill, Truscott opened up his throttle and pointed the nose downwards, then, still inverted, managed to hold the aircraft off the ground, gain height, right himself and land in his own dust cloud.

Shocked onlookers, as convinced as Truscott himself that he'd been about to die, rushed to his aircraft as it came to a halt. He emerged from the cockpit and fell off the wing onto the ground, 'grey to the soles of his feet', swearing he would never fly again. Only weeks later, however, he was with the rest of 76 Squadron at Aitkenvale Weir airfield, preparing to depart for Milne Bay.

•

On the morning of their departure, Truscott did his best to look past the great long nose of the Kittyhawk as it picked up speed along the runway, the 1500 horses of the Allison engine pulling him forward. He hated the lack of forward visibility of the big aeroplane when on the ground, and swore as the heat shimmer seemed to swallow up the far end of the long dirt runway. Nor was his mood improved by his lack of sleep and general feeling of unwellness. Two other pilots were taking off with him, just a few seconds behind, to his left and right.

Suddenly, the straight ribbon of the dun-coloured runway began to curve to the right. He applied the brake, but this conspired with the aeroplane's torque to take it careening crazily to the side. Onlookers who had gathered to see 76 Squadron off on its first deployment overseas gasped, frozen to the spot.

The two pilots behind him instantly throttled back, but Truscott's reflexes, lightning-fast in the skies over France and England, were now slow and heavy. With a thud, the aircraft left the runway 'like a wildly thrown knife' and headed out of control for a line of trees, beyond which, to the horror of his audience, was the aerodrome's petrol dump.

For two hundred yards the aircraft continued, then came an awful wrench of metal as the Kittyhawk's undercarriage was ripped away by a ditch. An American machine-gun crew scrambled out of their pit just before the wheelless aircraft slid over the top of it and into stacked piles of fuel drums, which 'every living man expected to explode into a flaming pyre'. By some miracle, no fire eventuated, and a shaken but notably un-incinerated Truscott was dragged from the wreck, 'almost incoherent'.

There were no reprimands, no charges and no enquiry. Before he had time to consider how he had escaped almost certain death with nothing but a small cut above one eye, Truscott was given another aircraft, told to blank out what had just happened, and sent on his way. His second take-off that day was uneventful, and half an hour after the crash he was heading for Milne Bay.

Later, he reflected to his friend and fellow fighter ace who had flown and fought with him in England, Flight Lieutenant Bardie Wawn, on how, yet again, he had cheated his mortality. 'It makes you think,' he said. 'I must have another job to do some time or other, somewhere or other.' That 'somewhere' was in the steaming tropics of Papua, and soon Truscott would find that flying against the Japanese would be vastly different from anything he had experienced in Europe.

Preceding their aircrew on the journey north, the bulk of 76 Squadron's staff and ground crew had sailed from Townsville on 14 July. Turnbull had flown up with some of his pilots to Moresby a few days later, but would not linger there, as in a few days' time they were scheduled to relocate to their new base at 'Fall River'. Virtually he alone knew this to be the codename for Milne Bay.

Not much had changed at Twelve Mile Strip since he had last been there in April, although the food was marginally better, and there was the welcome sight of more aircraft, particularly those of the US Army Air Forces, which were now beginning to arrive in numbers. The weather was considerably worse, though, with heavier rain and poorer visibility.

•

Less than a week later, as he flew away from Gona after the abortive attack, Turnbull searched anxiously for the new airstrip at Gili Gili. It was clearly marked on the map strapped to his thigh, but much harder to locate in reality. The primeval green expanse below seemed utterly devoid of human influence, and the weather was not helping. Great banks of cumulus cloud towered all around him, rain thudded against his Perspex canopy, and only occasionally would the mist below clear long enough for him to discern a recognisable feature.

He checked his mirror and craned his head right and left. Good. Bott and Carroll were right behind and beside him, just as he'd instructed them. Where the other three pilots he'd led out from Moresby that morning were he had no idea. Then, below, the misty expanse suddenly parted, drawing back like a curtain to reveal a long, straight shoreline stretching due west. It had to be the north coast of Milne Bay. Waggling his wings, he turned to follow it, with Bott and Carroll still close behind.

Even when he knew what he was looking for, Turnbull struggled to pinpoint Milne Bay's No. 1 Strip until he was virtually on top of it. No wonder the Japanese had yet to molest it – how could they possibly find it? He thought for a moment of what the men on the ground would be making of his unscheduled arrival. Back at Twelve Mile, he knew they could be 'twitchy' at the best of times, and their aircraft recognition was not always accurate.

With flaps down, he descended below the tree line and onto the curious pattern of metal matting. The tremendous thudding of his tyres on the surface was unlike anything he had ever heard, and the aircraft vibrated all over. A great spume of mud and slush, fanned by the prop, flew up and covered his windshield. Then, even more alarmingly, he felt the aircraft begin to slide. Working his brakes gingerly to avoid going nose over, he wrestled the Kittyhawk down the wet and greasy runway, virtually blind, looking out his side window to maintain his bearings. He was aware also of the other two aircraft following close behind. He taxied as far as he could, his fuel tank all but empty. Some of his landings in the desert had been rough, and even those at Twelve Mile were hazardous, but never had he put his Kittyhawk down like this.

From everywhere, people emerged. A jeep came up with two ground crew, who immediately recognised their CO. All watched anxiously as Bott and Carroll made their landings: a spray of mud covered each aircraft as they touched down, but otherwise the two young pilots had made a good fist of their debut. With everyone down in one piece, all could afford to relax a little. 'It's a rough sort of a place, sir,' said one of the crew to his boss. 'Nothing here but tents. Just like Twelve Mile, but wet. The rain hasn't stopped since we've been here.'

After explaining his early arrival to an adjutant, Turnbull inspected his Kittyhawk. He could hardly believe the state of it. The entire underside was filthy, caked with thick mud, particularly on the flaps and undercarriage. The crew washed it off as best they could before refuelling. The metal matting of the runway was unquestionably strong, but the water was in places inches deep, and the mud from the recently cleared ground rose straight up through it, sloshing against their boots.

The three pilots would spend the night at Gili Gili, and then head to Moresby to gather the remainder of 76 Squadron. In a few more days they would be joined by their comrades from the now veteran 75 Squadron. Turnbull could at least warn them that Milne Bay would not be a place to write home about.

CHAPTER 8

THE KITTYHAWKS ARRIVE

On the morning of 4 August, Fall River HQ received a report from RAAF North Eastern Area Command, tapped out in code from deep within their reinforced concrete bunker, 500 miles away in Green Street, Townsville, known cryptically by the air force only as 'Building 81'. Such was the secrecy of the place that an entire house had been built directly over the top of it, disguising it from the air and blending it in with its peaceful suburban surrounds. The message began:

> It would appear that the Japanese are either (a) completely ignoring the presence of our forces at Fall River or (b) they are unaware of their presence. It is felt here that they are paying no attention to you for a purpose, namely, until they are sufficiently consolidated in the Buna area.

In a similarly quiescent tone, the message advised the garrison of suspected Japanese intentions to occupy the Trobriand and Woodlark islands, at least 155 miles to the north, and noted the opinion of HQ Townsville: that the pincer would at some stage close on Port Moresby, at which time 'a heavy load' would be thrown onto the aircraft stationed at Milne Bay.

A few hours later, events would render North Eastern Area Command's report somewhat redundant.

As July turned into August, the garrison at Milne Bay was growing daily, but was still woefully underdefended, with only Brigadier Field's untried and untested 7th Brigade of militiamen in place. Brigadier Wootten and his 18th Brigade, who in fact only received his orders to depart for Milne Bay on 1 August, would not begin to arrive for another week. The RAAF, however, was establishing itself in such numbers that the new No. 1 Strip was becoming overcrowded.

Three days after Peter Turnbull's unscheduled christening of the strip on 22 July, the first eight of his 76 Squadron Kittyhawks arrived, to be joined later that day by aircraft from their more battle-hardened sister unit, 75 Squadron. For many of their ranks who had defended Moresby the previous April and May, this was their second deployment to New Guinea, and the excitement of being sent overseas to fight had long worn off. Not for them the quiet departure from Australia made by the greenhorns of 76 Squadron.

The men of 75, having some idea of what awaited them, and with many suspecting they may not come back, flew from their base at Lowood, west of Brisbane, for a scheduled overnight stop in Townsville, where they threw a party the town would not forget. After a riotous celebration, in which many RAAF personnel, both officers and men, were banned from Townsville's eating and drinking establishments – including the RAAF

Officers' Club itself – they climbed into their cockpits and headed north to Milne Bay, via Cooktown and Horn Island.

Arriving overhead at Milne Bay on the morning of 25 July, 76 Squadron's pilots each took his turn touching down on the metal strip. Truscott, a notoriously rotten lander, began what would become his Milne Bay habit of bouncing three or four times before settling his Kittyhawk on the runway. 'Sounds like Bluey's coming in again,' his fellow airmen would quip at hearing his familiar clanks.

Taxiing down the long, slippery runway that first morning, he looked to the left and right at a scene of chaos. Unaware of the conditions, many pilots had taxied off the matting and straight into the mud. From his cockpit, Truscott saw teams of desperate ground crew, covered in sweat and filth, attempting to wrestle the stranded aircraft back onto the runway.

Emerging from his cockpit, Truscott felt the humidity hit him like a wave. He shook his head as he took in his strange new surrounds, thinking the place to be 'a gloomy, steamy smudge of deep-green hills and glassy water, of orderly coconut rows slashed through with the marks of man. The sweating jungle crowded in upon it and mist sat on the densely scrubbed mountains and the very air sweated.' The first man to greet him was his CO, Peter Turnbull, who appeared, half-naked and filthy, at his wing root. 'What sort of a joke is this, Pete?' he asked, deeply perturbed.

'It's no joke, Bluey,' replied Turnbull with as much jocularity as he could muster. 'You'll need your sense of humour here.'

A few hours later 75 Squadron arrived. Milne Bay was for them too a new and startling experience. Twelve Mile Strip had a dirt runway, partially macadamised, which gripped their tyres well enough, but here the pilots slipped all over the place, and a great plume of slush was thrown up everywhere – it was as if they were landing in a swamp. The clattering noise rose above even the sound of the engine, and the edges of the Marston matting ripped chunks from their rubber tyres. Emerging from their cockpits, the pilots found that the matting was hazardous even for those on foot, their hard-soled flying boots slipping about on the greasy surface.

One witness to the arrival of the Kittyhawks was Warrant Officer Geoff Baskett. 'There was a terrific crash as each of the planes landed on the steel matting,' he recalled. 'None of the pilots had landed on this type of surface before, and one of the pilots told me later that he thought his propeller had fallen off, judging by the noise of the landing.'

With both squadrons now on the deck, No. 1 Strip suddenly looked dangerously crammed. 'If the Japs drop by in the next few hours,' remarked Truscott as the last of 75 Squadron's aircraft touched down, 'these squadrons will be murdered in the mud.' Over the next few days, the issue would be compounded by the arrival of four Lockheed Hudsons from 6 Squadron, which were to perform vital reconnaissance missions.

It was a situation, however, that had been well anticipated. Hence, a few miles to the east, the construction of Milne Bay's second airstrip, designated No. 3, was well underway. Along with consideration of the sheer numbers of aircraft the Milne Bay base needed to accommodate, it was deemed essential to give the pilots alternative landing and taking-off arrangements, so they could cope with various flying conditions. No. 2 Strip, originally pegged out in the swampy area behind Gili Gili, had recently been abandoned due to the difficulty of its terrain and access, but the new No. 3 Strip, running north–south and almost directly down to the water for ease of approach, would form the garrison's most easterly defence. In just a few weeks' time, though still unfinished, it would provide the stage for the terrible climax of the battle for Milne Bay.

Until No. 3 Strip was operational, No. 1 would serve as the mainstay of Milne Bay's aerial arsenal. Working around the clock, engineers and ground staff constructed dispersal areas from the abundance of coconut logs, to provide some protection from shrapnel blasts and bullets, and to prevent a chain reaction if one aircraft blew up.

The newly arrived pilots of the two squadrons had little time to reflect on the strip's shortcomings. Hardly had their propellers stopped turning than they were refuelled and ordered to start flying standing patrols. The garrison's inexplicable invisibility to the Japanese, it was assumed, would not last.

Later that afternoon, four of 75 Squadron's pilots, already in the air providing top cover at 30,000 feet, reflected on how much the conditions had changed since their first stint at Moresby. Back then, the April sky had been relatively clear; now it was a soup of mists, rain and cumulus clouds. Suddenly they heard a crackle over their unreliable radio sets – that much at least had not changed since Moresby – directing them to intercept an approaching enemy aircraft.

Racing through the mist behind their CO, Les Jackson, the pilots swallowed hard as they broke into a patch of clear sky, then sighed as they saw that the 'enemy' was in fact an RAAF

Catalina flying boat. Flicking their aircraft around, they headed back to make their second landing at No. 1 Strip that day.

Ten days later, on 4 August, with the Japanese still having apparently failed to notice the existence of the Milne Bay garrison, something approaching a sense of complacency began to settle on the men. Then, just after midday, as some members of 76 Squadron who had worked to put the morning's standing patrol of eight Kittyhawks into the air were resting inside their tent, an unfamiliar engine note was detected, quite different from the familiar throb of a Kittyhawk's liquid-cooled motor. It was the unmistakable 'chop' of a radial engine approaching from the north.

Leading Aircraftsman John Short initially thought little of it. 'Some silly bugger is playing around,' he remarked to one of his mates. Above the tree canopy, a pale low-wing monoplane appeared. 'What are Wirraways doing here?' someone wondered. Then, as the aircraft banked around, large red circles could be seen on the wings. 'Wirraways be fucked – they're Zeros!' yelled a voice.

Suddenly the air was split by cannon and machine-gun fire. Finally, the Japanese had discovered the garrison at Milne Bay.

•

Three days earlier, on 1 August, the Japanese had only just begun to reconnoitre the bay's mouth, paying particular attention to the partially abandoned Eastern District capital of Samarai Island. Here they planned to land and restore the RAAF's seaplane facilities, which they would use as an advance operations base against Port Moresby. All the while they were oblivious to the extent of the Allied foothold that had been established at the other end of the bay.

On 3 August, a twin-engine G4M Betty bomber circled Samarai completely unmolested, looking for suitable landing sites, when one of her crew noticed two green fighter aircraft flying low over to the west. Remarkably, the aircraft seemed to be losing height, as if about to land in the jungle. The Betty crew returned to their base at Rabaul and reported their sightings.

The next day, a formation of slow fixed-undercarriage C5Ms – the light bomber/reconnaissance aircraft nicknamed 'Babs' by the Allies – was sent out, escorted by four Zeros, with orders to investigate the western end of the bay. What the Japanese airmen saw that day astounded them: there on the shoreline was a fully functioning wharf, apparently servicing a long runway carved into the jungle, with aircraft clearly visible on its unusual-looking surface. The lead Zero signalled his wingman to follow him down for a strafing attack. Pilot Officer Harry Kerr of 76 Squadron wrote simply in his diary that day: 'War started with a strafe by four Zeros.'

Coming in with complete surprise from the direction of the hills, at a height which barely cleared the tops of the coconut palms, the Japanese pilots were met with the astonishing view of a complete military base, with tents, some locally built huts, an airstrip and, more alarmingly, over 30 aircraft nestling under the trees. How could all this have been missed?

Lining up along the runway, they pressed their firing buttons, unleashing machine-gun fire and cannon shells, which tore along the matting of No. 1 Strip. In the sights of the lead Zero was a P-40, apparently being pushed along the runway by several men, who seemed oblivious to the enemy aircraft closing in behind them. Cannon fire ignited the fighter's petrol tanks, and in seconds Milne Bay's first casualty, 75 Squadron's Kittyhawk A29-98, was an inferno. After a few minutes nothing was left of her but the wingtips and a partially melted engine block. The fitters pushing the Kittyhawk into one of the newly built dispersal areas had leaped aside, and by some miracle all escaped injury.

Desperate to get some photos of this secret jungle base while there was still time, the pilot of the Babs reconnaissance aircraft pulled his cumbersome machine up to 13,000 feet and switched on his cameras, escorted by the remaining two Zeros.

But, as the Japanese airmen were about to discover, they did not have the skies to themselves. High above, at 23,000 feet, 76 Squadron was in the air and on patrol, and they now swooped down to meet the enemy. In the long dive, however, their cohesion broke up somewhat, and initially only a few of the pilots managed to engage. Plummeting down towards the slow Babs, Flying Officer Max Bott prepared to unleash his firepower, but the highly manoeuvrable Zeros executed a remarkable pull-up turn to make a climbing pass at him, firing as they did. In aerial warfare, the closing speeds of aircraft often allowed but one chance to hit an enemy, before, in mere seconds, he was miles away in an empty sky.

Behind Bott was Flying Officer Peter Ash, formerly a company director from Newcastle, who suddenly had the now unescorted Babs all to himself. As it reared up in his windscreen, he pressed his firing button and the Japanese aircraft immediately began belching thick black smoke. Then, like a braking truck, it seemed almost to stop in midair, nearly causing Ash to ram it, but he pulled away just in time. Flipping over on its back, the Babs plummeted downwards, crashing with its two crew members into the hills seven miles from the airstrip.

One of the pilots of the escorting Zeros, realising what had happened, broke off his attack on Bott and turned on Ash, who now had a Zero attacking him from behind. Its 7.7-millimetre bullets made their mark on Ash's aircraft, but he escaped before significant damage could be done. Ash's wingman, Sergeant Robert Gray, then fired on Ash's attacker, but once again the nimble Zero executed its deadly manoeuvre of flipping up and around to latch on to Gray's tail. Gray did the only sensible thing, binking away, sending the heavy Kittyhawk downwards and letting gravity and the big Allison engine pull him to safety.

The fight continued, with the pilots from 76 Squadron who had missed the initial fray climbing back up to the combat zone. Sergeants Neville Lundy and John Dempster worked as a team to outwit a Zero which had attached itself to their tails, while Pilot Officer Frank Grosvenor came under attack, with cannon shells tearing into his fuselage as he executed a long-range attack on another Japanese fighter. The patrol's most experienced pilot, Bardie Wawn, was engaged by two Zeros but managed to evade them both.

The action lasted only minutes, but it was a superb debut for 76 Squadron's virtually novice pilots, who were up against the highly experienced Japanese airmen of the Tainan Kokutai, a crack unit which included some of Japan's top aces of the war, such as Saburo Sakai and Hiroyoshi Nishizawa. In fact, so aggressive were the men of 76 that the Japanese believed they had encountered more than a dozen aircraft, claiming four as destroyed. But it was the Japanese who came off worse: the Babs had been lost, and all 76 Squadron's Kittyhawks landed safely.

CHAPTER 9

PROBLEMS WITH THE CAMP

Back at the airstrip, Peter Turnbull and the entire garrison were ecstatic. As one corporal remembered, 'There was great jubilation amongst the pilots and ground crew, a three gallon keg appeared from nowhere and wild celebrations were the order of the day.'

Even more heartening was the fact that the gunners on the ground had also performed well, with the Japanese pilots subjected to a surprising barrage of fire of many types and calibres. Unlike Port Moresby's Twelve Mile and Seven Mile Strips, which had taken months to be properly protected with anti-aircraft firepower, Milne Bay was reinforced from the get-go. By early August, the wharf and airstrip bristled with guns. A and C troops of the 2/6th Heavy Anti-Aircraft Battery both had four large 3.7-inch guns in place, capable of firing up to twenty rounds a minute and throwing a shell more than five and a half miles into the sky, while the 2/9th Light Anti-Aircraft Battery had a similar number of quick-firing 40-millimetre Bofors guns for lower-altitude attacks, many manned by crews who had honed their skills in the Middle East. This was augmented by more Bofors and other calibre weapons being used by the US units stationed throughout the garrison.

On the day of this first attack, even the guns of the corvette HMAS *Swan* went into action against the Zeros, while on the airstrip itself, Corporal Don Cowper, a 76 Squadron fitter who had seen action in Malaya, eschewed the safety of a slit trench, picked up a .303 rifle and, cursing loudly, blasted away at the Japanese aircraft. The damage he inflicted is uncertain, but his positive effect on morale was unquestioned.

In addition, the 9th Battery of the 2/5th Australian Field Regiment began to arrive, with their eight large 25-pound field guns, each manned by a crew of six, many of whom had experienced the fighting in North Africa.

Throughout August, the garrison continued expanding. In the first week or so, new arrivals brought the numbers of Allied personnel at Milne Bay to 265 officers and 5947 other ranks. On the eve of the battle, which began in earnest on 25 August, those numbers swelled to close to 10,000 men, comprising 7500 soldiers, 660 RAAF airmen and 1340 American engineers and gunners. On 7 August, another battalion of US engineers arrived, and immediately began work on the second Milne Bay airstrip.

Life at the garrison continued to be extremely difficult. To the despair of the men of 75 Squadron who had already experienced dreadful conditions at Port Moresby, the military authorities had apparently learned nothing about the care of their men in the intervening months. The food was just as diabolical, with almost nothing fresh: tinned butter that was rancid, tinned bacon which was almost entirely fat, army biscuits so hard they had to be soaked in tea before eating, the monotonous bully beef and tinned pilchards, the latter reportedly quite inedible, and the mysterious and sickly tinned substance known simply as 'tropical spread', whose origins were never properly identified.

The camp continued to teem with diseases. As well as malaria, lice, sandflies, hookworm and ringworm were also rife, as was dysentery caused by the poor diet and sanitation – another lesson the RAAF seemed not to have learned from Port Moresby. Bill Deane-Butcher, 75 Squadron's doctor, was unimpressed by the place from the moment of his arrival on 30 July:

> It was evident that preparations for our arrival had been minimal and we were back to the basics of survival. Where's the loo? Where can we shower? Where do we eat? I had other questions too. Where do I treat the sick? Where are the long-sleeved shirts, long trousers, repellents and mosquito nets? Well there were the nets – a pile of them lay in the mud! . . . waste from the kitchen tent fouled the area. Men formed a line at the primitive pit latrines.

Deane-Butcher was particularly appalled by the criminally negligent advice the men had been given regarding their anti-malarial medicine. Holding off taking anti-malarial tablets until a week after arriving meant many were quickly infected, and preventative measures were useless. Ten to fifteen grains of quinine was the prescribed dosage, but, to Deane-Butcher's frustration, this was not enforced.

Flight Lieutenant Norman Newman, 76 Squadron's doctor, had been instrumental in selecting the initial location for some of the RAAF camps: he chose a spot close to the beach, where the sea breezes dispersed the mosquitoes to some extent. This position, however, was thought to be too exposed to the enemy, and he was forced to relocate the camps under the cover of the plantation's coconut palms. This may have protected them from the Japanese but not from the black clouds of mosquitoes that swarmed in the thick vegetation. Malaria cases soared.

As Private Desmond Balkin recalled: 'The mosquitos were just thick and swarms of them . . . everywhere you went you'd get bitten.' Still, the issuing of long-sleeved shirts was sporadic and haphazard, although men were forbidden to walk barefoot.

Pilot Officer Bruce 'Buster' Brown added in an interview years later: 'My best description of Milne Bay would be that if you were going to give the world an enema, you'd push it in at Milne Bay. It was bloody terrible . . .'

Deliveries of wildly inappropriate stores were received, while equipment that was sorely needed was nowhere to be seen. One large crate was found to contain hundreds of pith helmets, shorts and short-sleeved shirts, while mosquito nets were in short supply. Brigadier Field tried to report the situation to various visiting dignitaries, but came to suspect his entreaties were being ignored.

Field also suspected that the privileged command structure awarded to Milne Force – it reported directly to General Blamey, bypassing Major General Morris's 8th Military District HQ in Port Moresby – would not last. Indeed, a resentful Morris visited Milne Bay himself and told Field bluntly that he believed Milne Force should be brought under his command.

On 12 August Morris's wish came true, though not quite as he had envisaged. Bowing to pressure to streamline his forces, Blamey at the stroke of a pen brought Morris's 8th Military

District under the command of the newly formed New Guinea Force, and appointed his own chief of staff, Lieutenant General Sydney Rowell, as its General Officer Commanding. Morris, meanwhile, was relegated to the significantly lesser position of running ANGAU.

One visiting senior staff officer, the quartermaster general, Major General James Cannan, particularly caught the ire of Field by sneeringly describing the men of Milne Bay as 'uncouth'. Field bit his tongue, ignored the tedious political intrigues in play and instead concentrated on the build-up. He knew his focus had to remain on developing ways to fight the formidable Japanese when and where they chose to appear.

Not for nothing had Field been chosen as Milne Force's leader in its construction stage. Apart from his engineering prowess, he had also won first prize in an army essay-writing competition in the 1930s with a paper entitled 'The New Warfare', which explored the influence of technological advances on modern military tactics. As a naturally forward thinker, simply waiting at Milne Bay for the expected Japanese assault was never part of Field's strategy. Instead, he sent his men out to meet them, or at least familiarise themselves with the areas over which they might soon be fighting.

Men were sent out on long patrols, often lasting many days, during which they would have to be wholly self-sufficient while they explored the many bush tracks in their battalion's allocated area. No bush track, he impressed upon his officers and men alike, was to be assumed to be impassable to the Japanese, no matter how rough or primitive it appeared.

For men untried in battle and preparing themselves to fight in an alien environment, these crash-courses in jungle assimilation boosted their confidence and bolstered their morale. As Lieutenant Eric Schlyder of the 25th Battalion reported after returning with his men after one week-long patrol in the bush, 'The members of the patrol showed great determination and fortitude. For the first 4 days and nights it rained heavily and the troops were only having one meal per day; but no member complained of the hardships under which he travelled.'

Field's time as commander of the garrison was drawing to a close. In a few days his men would receive a significant boost with the arrival of the seasoned men of Brigadier George Wootten's 18th Infantry Brigade. At that point, command of Milne Force would devolve to a man who would come to personify the Australian struggle in this place: a man of few words but with nerves of steel, who would deliver victory and win the undying respect of his men, but who would then be shunned by the senior army command and bypassed by history, and quickly fade into obscurity. This was the inscrutable, enigmatic figure of Major General Cyril Albert Clowes, DSO, MC. To the troops, he would always be known, with eternal respect, as 'Silent Cyril'.

CHAPTER 10
THE PILOTS SETTLE IN

On 8 August, the now very operational and very crowded No. 1 Strip, which had originally been expected to serve only one squadron, was given the name by which it would be known for the remainder of its existence: Gurney Field.

Originally from New South Wales, Raymond Charles Gurney joined the nascent RAAF as a pilot in the 1920s, before accepting a job with Guinea Airways, where he became one of New Guinea's aviation pioneers, famed for his ability to fly into the smallest of airstrips with the biggest of planes, such as the Ford Trimotor and Junkers transports used in Papua at the time. When war came, his knowledge of New Guinea's terrain made him ideal to command the newly formed 33 Squadron, based in Townsville, and ex-Qantas Short Empire flying boats were hurriedly pressed into service. It was, however, a mission with the Americans that would be Gurney's last.

In May 1942, while seconded to fly with the Americans on a mission from Port Moresby to Rabaul, co-piloting a B-26

Marauder, Gurney's aircraft became separated from the formation, and arrived over the target well after the rest of the squadron had bombed and left. Despite facing the full force of the Japanese air defences around this vital base alone, Gurney and his pilot proceeded with their attack.

One of the Marauder's engines was knocked out, and the aircraft headed south to friendly territory, losing height all the way to the Trobriand Islands, where his pilot made the fatal error of attempting a wheels-down landing on what he believed to be flat ground, but which was in fact a swamp. Most of the crew of five survived, but the two pilots were killed as the aircraft flipped onto its back.

Gurney was buried with honours in Port Moresby, and his name was given to the vital airstrip at Milne Bay, near to where he had lost his life. It remained a fitting tribute to the man throughout the war and beyond.

On 7 August, Gurney's spirit and skill could well have assisted some of the pilots of 76 Squadron, who took off from Gurney Field in pursuit of a formation of enemy aircraft reportedly sighted over Samarai Island. No contact was made with the enemy but, somewhat embarrassingly, the five pilots – not all of whom were inexperienced – overstayed their time in the air and ran out of fuel. Brigadier Field, in an act of foresightedness, had arranged for fuel to be delivered to an emergency strip on Goodenough Island – 57 miles to the north, in the D'Entrecasteaux group – for just such a purpose.

The locally built airstrip was 5 miles inland, rough and somewhat rock-strewn, but all the pilots managed to land unhurt. A six-day rescue mission was then mounted, with a Tiger Moth dropping supplies while local Papuans were employed to cut the kunai grass and tidy the runway so the Kittyhawks could refuel and take off.

The rescue was attempted on 12 August. One aircraft tipped on the rough surface and crashed, writing itself off but leaving the pilot unharmed. The others decided to cool their heels a little longer until the runway was improved. The damaged aircraft was not wasted, however. In a remarkable effort, it was stripped of all useful parts – including the complete Allison engine, which was tied to poles and carried through mangroves and onto a beach, to a waiting motor boat, *Bronzewing*, for transportation back to Gili Gili. With the availability of spare parts being just one of many headaches for the squadron fitters, the effort was greatly appreciated. Upon their return a few days later, the pilots of 75 Squadron were given a stern lecture by their CO, Les Jackson, on the importance of watching one's fuel gauge.

It was decided that the two squadrons should each occupy a side of the airstrip, with 75 lining up on the left side of the matting, and 76 on the right. Initially, however, it was more than simply a strip of runway which separated the two groups of young men, and the atmosphere was somewhat chilly. Inevitably, friction was generated between those pilots with experience in Europe and those who had fought during the 44-day defence of Port Moresby, each regarding their own battle experience as more important. Some of the men who had flown in England also seemed to be affecting English accents and mannerisms, which galled the others, who responded sharply when given unsolicited advice on aerial combat.

For their part, the newly arrived pilots from overseas, many of whom had flown the glamorous Spitfire, were irked at having to go back and train for a few hours on an old Wirraway before being allowed to fly the Kittyhawk, an aircraft for which many, initially at least, had little regard. Flight Lieutenant Nat Gould, who had flown with the RAF in England and then in Russia, described the P-40, with its heavier controls, as akin to flying 'a great big steamroller', compared to the 'delicate ballerina' that was the Spitfire. Later, he would come to appreciate the Kittyhawk's robustness over the jungle.

Then, there were the young men – particularly in 76 Squadron – who could boast no combat experience whatsoever, and who felt somewhat like apprentices. According to 75's redoubtable medical officer, Bill Deane-Butcher, this even extended to the songs the pilots of the respective theatres had picked up, those from Europe having quite a different feel from the Moresby veterans. To counter this, Deane-Butcher led singsongs in the mutual mess tents, where the men of each group had to learn the others' ballads.

A novel means – conceived in jest, most likely – was hit upon to differentiate between the men of the two largely identical units: facial hair. Shaving being problematic in the conditions at Milne Bay, a virtue was made out of necessity. The pilots of 75 Squadron, it was decreed, would grow beards but no moustaches, while those of 76 would do the opposite, nurturing the moustache *sans* beard.

More significant than all such juvenile rivalries, however, would be the terrible blowtorch of combat itself, the desperate need for mutual cooperation, and the shared experience of living, fighting and dying in this difficult corner of the world, every aspect of which lay far beyond the experience of every man present.

The climate, too, was a shock for all, but particularly for those with no experience of the tropics. The constant humidity – upwards of 80 per cent – and temperatures which rarely dropped below 30 degrees Celsius sapped energy and challenged morale. The camp for 75 Squadron personnel, such as it was, was situated just a few miles from Gurney Field, but with the dreadful roads, the journey could take hours, the vehicles rocking and bucking hideously on the primitive roads, if not becoming bogged completely. More often than not, men resorted to slogging it on foot.

Many of the problems faced by the RAAF squadrons at Milne Bay stemmed from the seemingly cavalier manner in which they had been sent there, and the lack of a coherent command structure. Normally, a senior RAAF officer would be authorised to develop strategy and tactics, liaise with the army units, or simply look after the men's needs, but, bizarrely, it was only after the battle had begun that the RAAF command thought to appoint such an officer, in William 'Bull' Garing. Almost nothing in the way of direction was given to the men of 75 and 76 Squadrons at Milne Bay. After proceeding there, they were left to work it out for themselves. The commanding officers, Les Jackson and Peter Turnbull, cannot really be blamed, as they were accustomed to fighting battles according to directed tactics, but not to devising them.

At one point the situation became almost farcical when a retired wing commander wrote to the director of RAAF

Operations, offering his services, but was turned down. Later that month, the CO of RAAF Base Garbutt, in Townsville, Wing Commander Frederick Thomas, was sent up, but only as the Air Liaison Officer to the Army, meaning he lacked any overarching authority. In any case, his attachment ceased on 5 August. Thomas later submitted a report stating that 'the units ... were just haphazardly placed in the area with no central coordinating authority. The result was absolute chaos.'

Matters such as accommodation and other essential features of life should 'have really been the job of a small Air Force Command', Thomas continued.

> [These] were being carried out by individuals with conflicting authority ... units of the RSU [Recovery and Salvage Unit] detachment had come from Moresby in a shocking condition ... it would appear from the way they arrived that they had been sent out more for a tropical holiday than ops against the enemy ...

In the circumstances, overall command inevitably devolved to the army and Brigadier Field, but he had no authority to delve into air force matters and would have felt decidedly uncomfortable about doing so. It is to a large extent due to the quality of Field's – and his successor's – leadership that an unprecedented level of cooperation was forged between the army and the air force, which ultimately proved an essential factor in the victory.

First, however, as the army had done on their arrival a few weeks earlier, the men of the RAAF had to come to terms with the elements. As with everyone at Milne Bay, the worst enemy was usually the stinking, ankle-deep mud. For the airmen, it was far more than just an inconvenience, threatening their ability to fly and therefore to fight.

The Marston mat runway was immensely strong (indeed, pieces of it are still propping up fences in Papua New Guinea today), but its perforated design meant the mud underneath would ooze up, covering the runway in liquid patches often inches deep. One ground crewman likened the sight of landing aircraft to 'watching high-powered speed boats on a lake'. More dangerous still was the damage inflicted on the Kittyhawks themselves. If not washed off quickly, the mud which covered the aircraft on landing would harden on the wingtips, affecting its aerodynamics and manoeuvrability, and slowing its forward speed considerably. Being a heavy aircraft, the Kittyhawk required a high landing speed as well as a good deal of flap, but these were prone to severe damage from the mud thrown up by the wheels. One fitter recalled spending more time repairing bent flaps than fixing bullet holes inflicted by the enemy.

To lessen the danger, some pilots would pull their flaps up fully as soon as their wheels hit the runway, making for a faster but riskier landing on the wet and slippery runway. Aircraft could skid wildly for hundreds of yards. Mud smeared Perspex and wheels, bound up brake drums, and found its way into the Kittyhawk's six half-inch machine guns, causing stoppages and pitting vital parts with rust. Alarmingly, great patches of the runway were observed to be sinking into the mud as the runway's use increased, prompting the American engineers to improvise a solution: a grader fitted with a rubber strip would scrape the mud off to the sides on a daily, or even twice daily, basis. Later, gravel was graded over the matting in an attempt to settle the slush, but this created the new problem of stones being flung up by the tyres, rattling like shrapnel against the underside.

Even taxiing the aircraft was a nightmare. The Kittyhawk's great long nose obscured the forward view of the ground at the best of times, but here, a false turn on the Marston mat could see a wheel slip over the edge and become bogged. Woe betide any pilot who did so, as a serious rocket from the commanding officer for wasting the already exhausted ground crew's time was inevitable.

A unique solution to this problem was employed where possible, as photographs of 75 and 76 Squadrons at Milne Bay will attest. To assist with taxiing, two crewmen would climb up and sit at the aircraft's wingtips, from where deft hand signals could guide the pilot along the narrow lanes to the dispersal areas. At the same time, the men's bodyweight helped prevent the dreadful bouncing which occurred as the Kittyhawks travelled along the usually uneven surface.

In July and August, while the elements that would make up the ground battle were still manoeuvring into position, the air war was well underway. From the moment of their arrival, the 75 and 76 Squadron Kittyhawk pilots, as well as the Hudson crews detached from 6 Squadron, began long patrols of the area, ever watchful for the Japanese naval force that was expected to invade at any time. Flying Officer Arthur Tucker, who, a few months earlier, had been a novice during the fight for Port Moresby, was now one of the veterans of 75 Squadron. His logbook records that he began the long trip north from Lowood on 20 July, making his way in stages through Rockhampton,

Townsville, Cooktown, then Horn Island and across the sea to Port Moresby – '400 miles of drink!' wrote Tucker.

On 26 July, along with many fellow pilots, Tucker touched down at 'Fall River'. As soon as was practicable, the pilots began standing patrols. Tucker's logbook: 'August 1 – shipping recco – 2.24 hours – 480 miles.' After the surprise attack by the Japanese on 4 July, more patrols were mounted, with Tucker recording flights of around two hours on each of the next three days. Never had he contended with such atrocious flying weather, details of which he also recorded: 'August 6 – standing patrol – 24,000 feet – 2.35 hours. Complete overcast. Rain to sea level. Landed with 13 gallons.'

In an interview recorded several decades after the war, Tucker remarked that, initially at least, there was not nearly as much aerial contact as he had expected. 'However,' he said, 'I don't think we could emphasise enough how difficult the flying was, even when the Japanese weren't bothering us.'

Here is his description of Milne Bay:

> . . . a strange place, a little like an open-ended shoe box with mountains on one side rising 3000 feet straight out of the water like a wall. In all the weeks I was there, I think [I] only ever saw the tops of those mountains on a handful of occasions. The clouds rose like a sheet to 6000 feet from horizon to horizon.

Out into the Pacific, the cloud ceiling would rise to 2000 or 3000 feet, but the meteorological conditions inside the bay brought that down to 700 or 800 feet. As the pilots patrolled at more than 20,000 feet, they would look down at the top of the thick layer of cloud and feel decidedly uneasy.

The aerial battle, when it came, would, they knew, take place beneath that cloud, as the Japanese attempted to attack the airfield and its installations. This would put the Kittyhawk pilots at a grave disadvantage. The only real edge they had over the far more manoeuvrable Zeros was their ability to dive and escape after attacking from above. With low cloud cover, such a tactic was virtually impossible. Any pilot who tried it down there would end up in the sea.

Now that the Japanese had discovered and attacked Gurney Field, the Allied cloak of concealment was made redundant. Radio traffic was thus permitted, making the lives of the pilots considerably easier – although, as Port Moresby had shown, radios in the tropics proved consistently unreliable.

Since the strafing on 4 August, however, the Japanese had remained oddly conspicuous by their absence, and the aerial attacks that everyone had expected to now commence on a daily basis failed to materialise. Where, asked every man at Milne Bay, were they? Although they could not know it at the time, more than 600 miles to the east, luck had intervened.

CHAPTER 11
SILENT CYRIL

In the official history of the Australian Army's war with Japan in New Guinea, published in 1959, author Dudley McCarthy makes a point of footnoting almost every individual serviceman (and one or two women) discussed in his vast and exciting narrative. Whether their part in the great struggle was large or small – be they general or private – each player is given their own minute biography in the form of a footnote at the bottom of the page.

Lieutenant Colonel Alexander Meldrum, for example, the commanding officer of the 7th Infantry Brigade's 61st Battalion, which was to play a pivotal role in the Milne Bay battle, is introduced on page 160. At the bottom of the page, a footnote details Meldrum's service number (QX55238), his date and place of birth (1892, Lanarkshire, Scotland), the unit in which he served during the First World War (2nd Light Horse Regiment), his home town (Balmoral, Queensland) and the various commands of his long career. Curiously, the soldier's civilian career is also included. In Meldrum's case, this was 'Conveyancer-at-Law and Valuer'.

One can only think that the author pursued this to emphasise the fact that the forces which defeated the Axis powers of the Second World War were essentially civilian armies, summoned in a moment of terrible crisis, and which then melted back to their former peaceful occupations. To the modern reader, it adds a small dab of colour to the picture of a person's life.

A page or so later, we learn of a Private W.C. Whitton (QX36055), a bank clerk of Yeerongpilly, Queensland, who was killed in action on 27 August, the first night of the battle. Then there is Warrant Officer 2nd Class D.R. Ridley (QX49636), 29 years old, a builder's labourer from Brisbane.

The footnote for arguably the most important figure in the story of Milne Bay, however, is almost unique. Listed beside the name Cyril Albert Clowes, Major General commanding Milne Force and overall leader of all Allied forces for the battle, is much of the familiar information – birth date and place, and so on – but his career is listed simply as 'professional soldier'. Indeed, it is hard to imagine this quietly brilliant warrior having embarked on any life other than that which he pursued for nearly forty years, spanning two world wars, and which climaxed spectacularly in August and September 1942 at Milne Bay. The author describes Clowes as 'learned, cautious and taciturn'.

•

The doors had barely opened at the Royal Military College, at Duntroon in Australia's brand-new capital, Canberra, in 1911, when nineteen-year-old Cyril Clowes and his younger brother, Norman, strode in to be counted among the college's first intake of cadets, along with two other men Cyril would encounter years later in New Guinea, George Wootten and Sydney Rowell.

As children, the Clowes boys had been inseparable, and caused much amusement as the 'trotting brothers' who would run as a pair rather than walk to their school, Toowoomba Grammar, simply as a way of keeping fit. The military was already instilled in their blood. Their father, Albert, had arrived from England and practised as a dentist in Warwick, Queensland, but his passion was the military, and at the time of the First World War he was a major in the local militia, in charge of the Warwick Light Horse.

The boys' four-year course was cut short by the coming of the war, and Norman and Cyril both found themselves as young lieutenants landing at Gallipoli on the very first 'ANZAC Day', 25 April 1915. As a forward observation officer with the 1st Field Artillery Brigade, Cyril was directing gunfire onto Turkish positions; he was wounded by a returning shell, rendering him partially deaf for the rest of his life. Norman was also wounded at Gallipoli. Both recovered and went on to serve on the Western Front, where their careers progressed uncannily in step. They served for long periods under fire at some of the war's bloodiest battles, such as the carnage of Pozières, which claimed the lives of over 2000 Australian soldiers for little discernible gain. By war's end, both brothers had each picked up a Distinguished Service Order and Military Cross, and had risen to the rank of major. Their reputations were of competence, combined with an utter disregard for their own safety.

After the war, Norman transferred to the British Army, where he rose to the rank of major general, seeing action in the Western

Desert and becoming a member of General Harold Alexander's staff, and aide de camp to King George VI. Cyril, meanwhile, returned to his former college of Duntroon as an instructor, before seeing further action in the doomed Greek campaign of 1941, where he proved himself a superb artilleryman.

Because of his calmness, organisational skills and ability to quickly assess complex situations, General Blamey sent Cyril Clowes in to command a New Zealand battalion which was in danger of collapsing in the face of a German advance, which would have threatened the entire Anzac left flank and compromised its southern withdrawal. Clowes calmly explained the situation to the men, informing them that they must maintain their position, 'even in the face of extinction', and remained with them to share their fate if required. The men held, and a rout was avoided.

Clowes was brought back to Australia in January 1942 to face another crisis as the Japanese swept towards his homeland. Rated highly by the commander-in-chief of the Australian military forces, General Blamey, Clowes was considered just the sort of officer to put some steel into the leadership at home. Initially given command of the army's 1st Division, protecting the Sydney–Newcastle area, Clowes was deemed by Blamey as the right man to take command of the newly formed Milne Force and repel the expected Japanese invasion in that area.

Despite this record, no biography of Cyril Clowes' life has ever been written. His face has never appeared on a stamp. Even among the historically literate, his name is largely unknown. His reward for delivering the beleaguered Australian forces their first ever victory against the Japanese at a desperate period of the war, when such a feat was barely considered possible, is to have been erased completely from the consciousness of those he so valiantly served, the Australian people.

To be fair, this process was underway even as the battle of Milne Bay raged about him, and the brightness of his star in the eyes of Blamey and MacArthur began to fade. After the victory, he was not considered for any larger or even commensurate appointment; despite being made a Commander of the British Empire, he was given charge of the relatively obscure Victorian Lines of Communication Area for the remainder of the Second World War. This insult he accepted in good grace, and with his characteristic silence.

Clowes' immediate colleagues, however, provided a more sanguine assessment. According to his chief staff officer, Colonel Fred Chilton, Clowes was 'a fine commander and a steady man . . . a cautious man'.

Indeed, caution and unflappability – the very qualities which had elevated him to command Milne Force in the first instance – seem to have been his undoing. As a commander, Clowes never rushed, nor did he allow himself to be rushed into a decision. But when that decision had been made, he was unwavering in its execution – even when, as at Milne Bay, the fruits of the decision were not immediately evident. In the First World War, Clowes had seen the results of poorly planned and badly executed operations, with soldiers uncertain as to their objectives and responsibilities mowed down in their thousands in foreign fields. He was determined never to be that shade of commander, and never to spend the lives of his men so cheaply.

His long-time friend, fellow soldier and ultimate superior officer, Sir Sydney Rowell, said of him:

> Cyril Clowes . . . was the most experienced and skilled gunner
> in the Australian Army. He had earned a reputation in World
> War One for being oblivious to personal danger, and he
> demonstrated his courage again in World War Two. But his
> fame rests not on his technical attainments but his command
> in a crisis.

Above all, Clowes was renowned for being a man of few words, or at least a man of few unnecessary words; he regarded the imparting of superfluous information as having the potential to lead to obfuscation. In a very public war in which publicity, for the first time, played a major part, this may have worked against him, as Fred Chilton added:

> The only thing I think he can be criticised for is his lack of
> public relations – for not sending back phoney reports about
> what a wonderful job he was doing and how many Japs they'd
> killed and all this sort of thing. His reports were confined to
> purely military operations and he didn't give the boys back
> in Melbourne what they wanted. At that stage most of them
> didn't have a clue about fighting battles anyway.

Even to the men who knew and loved him, Clowes was not demonstrably communicative. At Milne Bay, he remained immaculate in his uniform, but did not force his men to be so. With the pipe that never seemed to leave his mouth, he studied the terrain of the bay, assessed his resources and made his decisions accordingly, ensuring that every man under his command knew his role exactly.

In fact, Clowes very nearly failed to take up his command of Milne Force. Receiving his orders in early August, he arrived at Port Moresby with a small number of staff officers, including one of Australia's greatest doctor-soldiers, Lieutenant Colonel George Maitland, recently appointed as assistant director of medical services for Milne Force, who had served alongside Clowes with distinction in the Middle East. Nothing he had seen in the desert, however, would prepare him for Papua.

Also in the entourage was Clowes' chief staff officer, Colonel Fred Chilton, who had already had a most exciting war in command of the 2/2nd Battalion in Africa and Greece. There, cut off in a gorge behind the German lines, he narrowly escaped capture by island-hopping across the Aegean to Turkey, hiding in barns and under the nets of friendly fishermen. Later in life, he would become one of the fathers of Australian intelligence, founding the Defence Signals Directorate.

Touching down in Port Moresby on 13 August, the staff wasted no time in transferring to another aircraft for the short flight to Milne Bay. As usual, the weather was appalling, and became progressively worse the closer they got to their destination. Their young American flying crew looked uncertain from the beginning of the journey, but when the clouds set in soon after leaving Moresby, one of them ventured down from the cockpit. 'Say,' he enquired of the senior Australian officers, 'any of you guys got a map?'

This, according to Chilton, when he recounted the story years later, reduced the small party to stunned silence. A 'very general' map of Papua and New Guinea was pulled out of someone's briefcase and passed to the American, who seemed most grateful. A few minutes later, however, he returned.

'Say,' he began again, 'you don't happen to know if there are any mountains around these parts?'

This shook away any vestige of politeness. 'Yes!' exclaimed the uniformed chorus. 'It's *all* bloody mountains here, up to 12,000 feet!'

Suddenly pale, the airman quickly made his way back to the cockpit, at which point the aircraft 'shot up almost vertically' through a hole in the clouds.

Eventually they came down to the sea near Buna, having flown in entirely the wrong direction. Here, Clowes 'spoke to them very firmly', advising the pilot to stay low to the water and follow the coast around until they located the entrance to the bay. With its fuel tanks nearly dry, the aircraft arrived at Gurney Field, the passengers now very late and very relieved.

Clowes wrote of the incident a few days later:

> Yes we did get here safely in the end, largely by guess and by God though. Pouring rain, the landing strip covered with water, a ceiling of a hundred feet, a complete lack of knowledge of the country and no maps in possession of the pilot, all helped to add an interest to the trip . . . Majors-General may be two-a-penny but before taking to the air with these people in the future, I recommend prior enquiry to ensure a reasonable degree of safety.

Chilton was far from impressed by what he saw at Milne Bay, and somewhat irked that their arrival seemed to take Brigadier Field's staff by surprise. 'When we first got there, we had nowhere to go,' he said. 'We spent the first several days at Field's headquarters.' Clowes did not like the idea of making himself and his staff a target by occupying one of the few obviously European-built houses in the area, and so ordered the construction of inconspicuous Papuan huts, specially fitted out and established his new HQ further west at Hagita.

The first task of Clowes and his staff was to conduct a complete inspection of the camp, guided by Field, whose time as garrison commander was coming to an end. At this stage, despite being months away from the wet season, the rain beggared belief. Lieutenant Colonel Maitland was particularly alarmed. No facilities were initially available for his medical HQ, and he was forced to borrow an office to bring some order to the struggling medical units. Malaria, he saw immediately, was rife, with 92 men already under treatment. In fact, it was on the very day of his arrival that Milne Bay experienced its first casualty, which came not from an enemy action but from malaria, claiming the life of a young private named Neill from the 61st Battalion. The grave in which he was buried was a bare 18-inches deep, such was the paucity of the soil covering the limestone shelf.

The men's personal and anti-malarial hygiene, observed Maitland, was appalling. Latrines were waterlogged, overflowing and badly sited, and even slit trenches were invariably filled with water, providing yet more breeding grounds for mosquitoes.

Transport, too, was an enormous problem, with almost all of the Australian two-wheel drive vehicles spending more time being pulled from bogs than driving. Not even the Bren gun carriers, which moved on continuous tracks rather than wheels, could easily negotiate the muddy roads. This made unloading stores from the now regular stream of ships pulling up to Gili Gili's makeshift wharf slow, difficult and extremely labour-intensive.

What was being delivered continued to baffle the garrison's officers and men alike. Someone at Townsville had thought fit to include on the inventory several cricket sets – complete with gloves and pads – for the troops' entertainment, as if anything even faintly resembling a pitch could be found, not to mention the time to play. At one stage, discipline was tested when several ships arrived with large stocks of beer in their holds, having presumably taken the place of what was most required: bombs and ammunition. After several raucous incidents during which hundreds of empty beer bottles could be seen floating around the calm waters of the Gili Gili dock, a directive was issued to all officers: failure to severely discipline men for such behaviour would be seen as dereliction of duty. The consumption of beer was thereafter outlawed.

•

The Japanese were aghast at what they had stumbled upon at Milne Bay in early August. Their timetable for the conquest of South-East Asia was short, and no Allied base was still supposed to be operating. It was bad enough that Port Moresby remained unconquered, and now there appeared to be another enemy strongpoint. To make matters worse, the Milne Bay garrison had apparently been built right under their noses. Its existence represented an unacceptable threat to any future capture of Moresby by sea, as well as to the overland assault that was already underway from the north. The Japanese command determined, however, to make a virtue out of necessity. Rather than being a target, Milne Bay would become a prize.

The existing plans to capture tiny Samarai Island and use it as a staging point for an assault on Port Moresby were ditched, and a larger operation to storm and capture the airfield in the jungle prepared. It could then be used by Japanese aircraft.

An air assault against the Australians would begin imminently.

CHAPTER 12
JAPANESE PLANS

In the early morning of 8 August, the Japanese 25th Air Flotilla's airfield at Rabaul throbbed to the sound of eighteen Zero fighters warming up for their flight almost due south to attack the Australian and American base at Milne Bay. The armed reconnaissance trip made on 4 August had given the Japanese pilots the lay of the land, and now the process of capturing this readymade base would begin.

The 25th Air Flotilla incorporated some highly impressive units, regarded as among the best in the Imperial Japanese Navy's air wing. Foremost among them was the legendary Tainan Kokutai, which included some of Japan's most glamorous aces, men such as Saburo Sakai, Enji Kakimoto and Hiroyoshi Nishizawa. Between them, these pilots were credited with a swathe of Allied victories. They were anxious to get into the air this morning to begin the attack on this brazen enemy, who had somehow built an airstrip in the backyard of Japan's newly conquered Pacific territory. After air strikes, the navy and army would launch its assault, land along that long dismal shore and overrun the Allied defences. Today was just the beginning.

Saburo Sakai looked around at his fellow airmen, all the while keeping an eye on his instrument panel, waiting for his oil temperature gauge to rise sufficiently before he and his comrades would line up, open to full throttle and take to the air. Sakai was still awed by the wonderful Zero and what a delight it was to fly: its speed, its turning qualities and its amazing ability to climb, bolting to the higher altitudes like a feather on an updraught.

Warming up on the other side of the airstrip were 32 Betty bombers. Sakai and his fellow Zero pilots would escort them to Rabi (as they referred to the Milne Bay area, believing this village to be the site of the Allied garrison), let them do their work, then go in low to strafe the airfield as a prelude to invasion. It promised to be another glorious day.

Suddenly, he spotted one of the ground crew running towards his aircraft and waving frantically, signalling to Sakai and the others to cut their engines. Astonished, they complied and rolled back their canopies as their props came to a halt. Silence descended upon the airfield.

'The patrol is cancelled,' shouted a breathless ground crew member. 'Please head to the briefing room immediately.' In their flying kit, which suddenly felt dreadfully hot and awkward on the ground, the bewildered pilots trundled in.

In the crew room, none could guess what lay behind the turn of events. After a few minutes, their CO, Lieutenant Commander Tadashi Nakajima, walked in wearing the gravest look any of them could remember seeing. The young pilots stood rigidly to attention.

'At 0525 hours this morning,' Nakajima began, 'a powerful enemy invasion force under heavy cover attacked Lunga Roads, Guadalcanal Island. The situation is extremely serious. Our naval forces operating in the Rabaul area have been ordered to engage the enemy immediately, in full strength, and to drive back the American invasion forces at any cost. Our fighter units are to escort the land-based medium-attack bombers, which will attack the enemy ships.'

The pall of silence in the room remained. Guadalcanal? No-one had heard of the place.

Nakajima's next words induced more alarm: 'We will take off at once for Guadalcanal to attack the enemy forces both at sea and on the beach.'

The battle for Guadalcanal, in the Solomon Islands, one of the epic campaigns of the Second World War, had begun.

For once, the Australians at Milne Bay had cause to be grateful for the amazing flying characteristics of the Mitsubishi Zero. A lesser aircraft could not have even been considered to cover the extraordinary distance from Rabaul to Guadalcanal, then attack the American marines disembarking on the north coast of the small island – and then fly back again.

The Americans' aim at Guadalcanal oddly mirrored that of the Japanese at Milne Bay: to capture an enemy airfield and turn it to their own use. Although the Guadalcanal strip was still incomplete, the American senior command said that, should the Japanese be allowed to make it operational, it would provide them with a base from which to threaten more of the Solomons, as well as Fiji and eventually places as far afield as New Caledonia.

Maps were rolled out over tables in the operations room and protractors used to determine that the Zeros would need to fly a round trip of more than 1100 miles to Guadalcanal, which was towards the south of the Solomons chain, and back. And this barely took into account time spent over the combat area, and the possibility of extra fuel consumption in case of stormy weather.

Nakajima informed his pilots that they were about to undertake the longest fighter operation in aviation history. Absolute discipline must be adhered to in order to conserve fuel. Sakai had shown that it could be done by making the mixture as lean as possible and flying high, and they were to do the same. In the worst instance, those running low might be able to refuel at Buka Island, north of Bougainville Island, 180 miles out from the base.

For the next hour, the men, barely believing what was being asked of them, sweated over maps, studied routes, and checked and double-checked their calculations. Drop tanks were filled and attached to the bellies of their aircraft. On the other side of the airstrip, the Betty bombers' tanks were also topped up for a much longer trip – not south to Milne Bay, but southeast to Guadalcanal.

Everyone now looked skyward, expecting the Allies to launch a pre-emptive strike on the Rabaul base in support of their attack on Guadalcanal. No-one wanted to be caught on the airstrip. The bomber crews were also hurriedly briefed. There was not even time to reload with armour-piercing bombs or torpedoes to attack the American ships; they would proceed with the fragmentation bombs they had already stowed, despite these being of doubtful effect on shipping.

At 8.30 a.m., the Bettys and their escorts roared away from Rabaul, while the men at Milne Bay, unaware of the fate they had narrowly avoided, were left to ponder yet another day of skies conspicuously devoid of their enemy.

•

For the Japanese, it was all in vain. That first day of the Guadalcanal campaign was a disaster, in which the Australian Coastwatchers played a vital part – and particularly one of the unlikeliest of heroes, Paul Edward Mason.

Originally from Sydney, Mason had travelled to Bougainville in the Solomons at just fifteen to help his brother, a trader. He fell in love with the place then stayed to run a plantation of his own, after the previous owner had been hacked to death by disgruntled employees. Though short, bespectacled and sporting a slight speech impediment, as well as 'prominent teeth', Mason was a born diplomat, showed great respect for the local culture and successfully navigated the complex web of tribal politics. He also knew the place like the back of his hand, and was a genius with a wireless – which made him an ideal recruit to Commander Eric Feldt's Pacific network of Coastwatchers.

From his jungle eyrie on Bougainville's south-eastern tip, Mason had first alerted the Americans to the Japanese landing and airstrip construction back in June, after which he reported on all the comings and goings of the Japanese shipping. Then, on the morning of 7 August, as the massive fleet of 82 US warships began landing eleven infantry battalions on Guadalcanal, Mason looked up and counted the Betty bombers and Zeros heading towards them from Rabaul. He then tapped out a message that would become legendary: 'Twenty-four bombers headed yours.'

These few words were relayed via Townsville to Pearl Harbor, then, a minute later, to the US ships at Guadalcanal. Forty-five vital minutes was thus handed to the Americans, who immediately suspended their landing operations, ordered their ships to weigh anchor and assume anti-aircraft dispositions, then pulled their men off the exposed beach. Furthermore, the Wildcat fighters from the carrier *Saratoga* were scrambled and in position in step formation high above Savo Island, and they pounced upon the Japanese aircraft when they appeared. The American ships then put up a wall of anti-aircraft fire, making the attack a disaster for the Japanese. In the attack on this day, and in another mounted 24 hours later, no less than seventeen G4M Betty bombers of the 4th Air Group were destroyed, with the remainder damaged.

Paul Mason would spend almost the entire war in his beloved Solomons, hunted constantly by the Japanese, but managing always to stay one step ahead. In late 1944 he was invalided out with pneumonia, only to return shortly thereafter, leading a band of local partisans, which by the war's end would claim to have killed upwards of 2000 Japanese. Awarded both the American and the Commonwealth Distinguished Service Cross, Paul Mason survived the war, and for the rest of his life remained an unsung Australian hero.

In truth, the Japanese would have been far better off persisting with their original plan to attack Milne Bay. Now, with the opening of the Guadalcanal campaign, the Japanese forces would be dispersed even further, to yet another front at an even more distant part of the Pacific. The Rabi plan was still a top priority, but would become a wholly naval operation, under the organisation of the newly formed 8th Fleet Headquarters. The Imperial Japanese Army forces originally earmarked for the invasion, including the crack Kawaguchi Detachment, would instead be redirected to Guadalcanal.

Outwardly, the men of the navy were proud to be conducting this vital mission all on their own, and looked forward to regaining some of the prestige lost after the defeats of the Coral Sea and Midway. Privately, however, some regretted that there would now be no help whatsoever from the army.

CHAPTER 13
NIPPON'S MARINES

The men of Japan's Kaigun Tokubetsu Rikusentai, translating roughly as the Special Naval Landing Force (SNLF), have been described as the marines of Imperial Japan, but the comparison is only partly accurate. Like the United States Marine Corps, the SNLF were regarded – at least during the first half of the Pacific War – as an elite amphibious infantry force which specialised in storming and holding beachheads and accomplishing other difficult military objectives. But while the numerous divisions of the US Marines functioned independently from other branches of the armed services, Japan's SNLF was formed under and remained the exclusive tool of the Imperial Japanese Navy. Their very existence, in fact, arose from the longstanding enmity between the Japanese Army and the Japanese Navy – a situation which condemned Japan's war effort to poor levels of cooperation between the services and enormous wastage of resources.

The bad blood went back decades. Following the 1905 Battle of Tsushima, when Japan's new and as yet untested warships shocked the entire world (not least the Japanese themselves) by demolishing the fleet of Imperial Russia, it was decided that seagoing troops were needed to secure ports and other enemy strongpoints. Rather than relying on the fiercely jealous army to lend troops, however, the navy trained some sailors in infantry and battle tactics. By the late 1920s, these coalesced into standing SNLF regiments of between around 750 and 1600 men, each taking its name from the naval districts in which the men had been raised and trained: Kure, Maizuru, Sasebo and Yokosuka.

The term 'special' in Special Naval Landing Force did not denote that these troops were 'special forces' in the modern military sense; rather, it signified the SNLF's unique role, in that once the military objective had been attained, the men would revert to their role as ships' crewmen and return to sea.

Experiencing a baptism of fire in Manchuria in the early 1930s, the SNLF quickly took on the mantle of an elite force, well trained in the use of light artillery and amphibious operations, high in morale, and seeing much action in the Second Sino-Japanese War, then later in Japan's eruption of conquests across South-East Asia in 1941–42.

At the beginning of the Pacific War, sixteen SNLF regiments were in existence, but that increased to 21 over the course of the conflict. In Malaya and the Philippines, SNLF forces acted as the tip of the spearhead in Japan's favoured shock tactic of sudden attacks by sea, with men screaming onto enemy shores, officers waving Samurai swords, cutting down enemies with ruthless and overwhelming force. In 1941, three units of the Yokosuka SNLF were converted into parachute regiments; they would eventually make more combat jumps than regular Japanese Army soldiers, onto islands such as Celebes and Timor.

As the war progressed, and Japan's fortunes quickly soured, SNLF units suffered commensurate casualties, fighting till their ammunition was exhausted, then resorting to hand-to-hand fighting. Almost always they refused to surrender. Overwhelmed by the sheer might of the Allies, their numbers waned rapidly, with entire regiments sometimes ceasing to exist after a single engagement. By late 1943 the SNLF regiments were a spent force, with few members surviving the war.

Notably, various units of the SNLF became directly responsible for many of Imperial Japan's most heinous wartime atrocities, committed across their conquered territories against prisoners and civilians alike. The shocking acts perpetrated by the SNLF at Milne Bay would be among Japan's darkest crimes of the entire war.

•

In mid-1942, the 1200 men of the 5th Kure SNLF, though yet to be blooded in battle, believed themselves to be invincible and were itching to prove it. Having trained for months now, they had heard fabulous stories of the Emperor's forces sweeping the white enemy before them. Like dominos, colonial bastions, having remained inviolable for centuries, were brushed aside like cardboard castles by the skilful and devoted Japanese warrior. Malaya, the Philippines, Rabaul and even the great British base at Singapore had caved in, their contemptible defenders not even having the honour to die in battle, but surrendering shamefully, and in droves. Soon it would be their turn to write themselves into the history books by opening the final phase of the New Guinea campaign, and securing the southern flank of Japan's new Pacific Empire.

Underlying this confidence was a plan so bold and so brilliant that failure was unthinkable.

At the Japanese base at Rabaul, the commanding officer of the SNLF's 5th Kure, Commander Masajiro Hayashi, listened intently as his superiors outlined the plan to capture the Australian and American base at Milne Bay. It would be an amphibious night attack, involving 612 soldiers brought up the bay by the ships of the 18th Cruiser Division and delivered close to the airstrip.

Hayashi's men would disembark quickly, then advance up a narrow coastal track to whatever Australian defences awaited them, overwhelm them and secure the landing strip. Supporting them would be 197 men from the 5th Sasebo SNLF, under Lieutenant Susumu Fujikawa, along with several hundred auxiliary and construction troops and labourers, many of them Koreans who had been as good as press-ganged into service with promises of pay which never eventuated. The force would be supported by a number of Type 95 Ha-Go infantry tanks, which were light and fast and would tear through the enemy's ranks.

So swift would be the victory that an air force construction party and maintenance unit would be landed at the same time, so they could begin immediate preparations for the arrival of Japanese aircraft. Bombs and aircraft fuel would be carried in the holds of the ships so the planes could start operating almost immediately.

Meanwhile, the 5th Sasebo's main force of 353 troops would be landed at Taupota, on the coast to the north of the

Australians, and strike out twelve miles or so overland, linking up with Hayashi's men as they approached from the east. The defenders of Milne Bay would be pincered and overwhelmed, and a viable airstrip ready for use was the prize. Within hours, Japanese aircraft would be roaring off the runway and attacking Port Moresby, which would now lie barely an hour's flying time away; what's more, the Japanese pilots would no longer have to negotiate those dreadful mountains.

The task would not be difficult. The Australian defenders were estimated to number only a handful and, as had been demonstrated in Singapore and other places, were green and contemptible, likely to surrender at the first shots than put up any kind of fight.

Then, with Japanese control of the air and the surrounding sea lanes, the advance on Moresby would begin in the form of an even larger two-pronged offensive: from Milne Bay in the east, while from the north General Tomitaro Horii's South Seas Force advanced along the track from Buna and Kokoda. With Port Moresby secured, Australia itself would be under threat – and, with her northern sea lanes in Japanese hands, would be checkmated out of the conflict.

After this the fight would be taken to the Americans in Guadalcanal, and with the airstrip there secured, the entire eastern flank of Japan's new empire would be secure. The war itself could then be wrapped up in months.

The Rabi plan was bold and brazen, and called for fit and determined men to move with lightning speed through jungle terrain. The men of the 5th Kure believed themselves up to the task, and were brimming with confidence, as indicated by the first paragraph of their official battle plan, which was captured along with a swathe of important documents after the battle:

> At the dead of night quickly complete the landing in the enemy area and strike the white soldiers without remorse. Unitedly smash to pieces the enemy lines and take the aerodrome by storm. For this reason strict control of sound and light is most important and every endeavour must be made to maintain secrecy of the plan.

Commander Masajiro Hayashi was an experienced naval officer who had seen action in the Philippines and Rabaul. As writer and Milne Bay veteran James Henderson discovered while researching his small but excellent volume on Milne Bay, *Onward Boy Soldiers*, the paymaster of the 5th Kure, Captain Chikanori Moji, kept one of the few surviving Japanese diaries during both the preparation period and the campaign itself; Henderson was also able to interview him after the war. Its contents, and Moji's recollections, are revealing. He recounts that the men were in high spirits and anxious to get into the fight in the week before the campaign began. Commander Hayashi, however, harboured serious doubts about the entire venture.

While the men were entranced by the apparent endless tide of victories believed to be Japan's military destiny, Hayashi was acutely aware of the setbacks, compromises and delays that had brought them to this point in August 1942. The lightning pace of the war unleashed the previous December had seen Japan's goals only partially achieved, and now things were slowing down. The timetable for the capture of Port Moresby, originally intended for May, was seriously behind schedule.

Hayashi had in fact been part of the original amphibious invasion force of eleven transports and 5000 soldiers when it steamed, full of confidence, out of Rabaul harbour. Then, after entering the Coral Sea and just a day or two from their goal, they had made a sudden 180-degree turn and steamed back to Rabaul. Just out of sight over the horizon, the US carriers *Yorktown* and *Lexington* – which Japanese intelligence had completely failed to notice – let loose their aircraft on the escorting Japanese carriers, sinking the *Shoho* and damaging the *Shokaku*. The Moresby convoy, dangerously exposed, had headed back to harbour, and the invasion was 'unavoidably deferred'.

Hayashi was also hearing rumours that General Horii's thrust towards Moresby from the north was in trouble. The mountain country of the Owen Stanley Range, he had been told in furtive whispers, was diabolical, and the Australian soldiers, far from the paper warriors they had expected, were proving tough, determined and increasingly adept at jungle fighting. So tortuous was the terrain over which Horii's men were required to march that only such equipment as could be carried on their backs was taken, the remainder being abandoned to rust and rot beside the track.

In any case, pondered Hayashi, what chance had a group of exhausted and underequipped infantry of taking and holding a vital and defended enemy port such as Moresby, after they'd had to fight every inch of the way, and without the support of heavy artillery?

If they failed to take Moresby, Japan's forces in the South Pacific would be strung out along a long and vulnerable line, which the gathering strength of the United States would be eager to sever. From Hayashi's point of view, General Horii's situation suddenly imbued the capture of Moresby with an urgency, even desperation. And desperation was a state in which no commander ever wanted to find himself.

If only the momentum of earlier in the year had not been lost, Hayashi mused. If the task force had continued on after its capture of Rabaul in January – before the might of the United States could begin to mobilise – then Moresby might already be in their hands. Milne Bay's value had been appreciated by Japan months earlier, but instead of moving quickly, the Allies had been allowed to slip in and take it for themselves. Then had come the shock of the news of the American landings on Guadalcanal. As heartened as Hayashi was by the confidence of his men, he knew they would need every bit of it, especially as they were going in without the support of the army.

Something else Hayashi had begun to notice: the skies above his head, formerly throbbing with countless Japanese aircraft, had become decidedly quieter these last few months. Air protection at Rabi was, he sensed, no longer guaranteed. This was not shaping up as the short, dynamic war that had been promised.

Most unsettling, however, was the question of what, exactly, his men would face at Rabi. In the last days of July, Paymaster Moji observed an increasing level of anxiety in Commander Hayashi. 'He was clearly agitated and his brows were constantly wrinkled,' he recalled after the war. Day after day, in the leadup to the departure of the task force, he had been observed taking long walks with the senior navy commanders, and returning in a dark mood.

Eventually, Hayashi disclosed to Moji that no proper reconnaissance – either of the terrain or the enemy's dispositions – had been undertaken, mainly due to the weather, and what few aerial photographs they had were inconclusive. His own requests to accompany such a flight were continually refused. Nor, incredibly, were there any accurate maps of the area, meaning the exact position of the vital Allied airstrip could only be speculated. It was assumed to be at Rabi, but no-one really knew.

The same went for the strength of the Australian defenders. The more Hayashi asked for details, the more he found them to be vague and based on guesswork. His men, he sensed with increasing dread, would be going into battle blind.

CHAPTER 14
STRIKE FROM THE AIR

Despite the limitations imposed on them by the opening of the Solomon Islands campaign, the Japanese still regarded the capture of Milne Bay as an absolute priority, and on 11 August they returned to Rabi with a show of air power that would demonstrate to the Australians just what a formidable opponent they were up against.

The 4th Air Flotilla was now down to just 22 serviceable bombers with which to soften up Milne Bay before the impending invasion. Escorted by Zeros, the raid was to be timed close to midday, when it was hoped that many of the Kittyhawks would be on the ground, transitioning from the morning patrols to the afternoon, and many of the personnel would be preparing for lunch. When they got close to the target, however, the bay's characteristically foul weather closed in, splitting up the formation and obscuring the target. Lost, the bombers turned back, but were unable to contact the Zero escort, which pressed on.

Almost every modern source varies on just how many Zeros made it to Milne Bay on 11 August; estimates range between six and twelve. What is not in dispute is that the daring young Japanese pilots slipped under the clouds and flew straight up the bay from the sea. This proved to be a mistake, as the open sea provided the only clear direction from which the now fully operational No. 37 RAAF Radar Unit could detect an incoming enemy, free of the obscuring mountains to the north and south.

Radar, in fact, was just one of the timely warnings which should have given the Australians the upper hand that day. Even if the higher figure of a dozen Zeros was correct, they were still outnumbered by as many as 22 Australian aircraft alerted to their presence. Sixty miles to the north, on Fergusson Island, a spotter had been installed, who was able to radio back to Gili Gili a warning: 'Bandits coming your way.' Out on the water that morning, in a small skiff, another group of spotters was being brought back to Gili Gili – one of their number needing medical attention. Seeing six aircraft approach at mast height, they jumped to their feet and waved with delight. Only when the planes were almost overhead – and the faces of the pilots clearly visible – did their red circle markings become apparent. The waving quickly stopped. Taking no chances, a group of locals on board jumped into the sea – but the Zeros had bigger targets in mind.

The men on the boat may have been surprised, but the base was not, even having time to ready its anti-aircraft guns and scramble all available Kittyhawks into the air. A short time earlier, the signal of three .303 rifle shots fired in quick succession had rung out across Gurney Field, sending the pilots racing to their aircraft amid a ricocheting chorus of 'It's on!'

All remaining personnel headed for shelter, but the squadron fire crew stationed themselves at the western end of the runway to tend to any aircraft which crashed during take-off. As the runway itself was usually the target, the fire crews at Milne Bay were always in the thick of the action.

With the Japanese outnumbered by more than two to one, it should have been a one-sided contest, but the inexperienced Australian pilots were in for a shock.

Some of the American personnel were also surprised. The men of No. 8 Fighter Control Unit had sat through a couple of false alarms already that morning, and now failed to take this latest alert seriously. Their midday meal seemed more of a priority, and many were lining up with their dixie tins in front of the 'chow tent' when the Zeros thundered overhead, barely seeming to clear the coconut trees. An Australian signaller who was dining with the Americans that morning later recalled the chaos:

> We had a Red Alert from very early in the morning and it remained a Red for a number of hours. However, nothing eventuated and we decided to go and have lunch. No sooner had we sat down when all hell broke loose, cannon shells were bursting all around the area as we were being busily strafed.

The men waiting in line ducked at the roar of aircraft engines, then scattered, making for the nearest slit trenches, but as they had been somewhat lax with their shovels in carrying out this particular chore, these proved hard to find. Possibly this was because as soon as the trenches were dug, they became water-logged breeding pools for mosquitoes. After this attack, shovels and entrenching tools were used with renewed vigour.

With radio silence now lifted, the Kittyhawk pilots circling above the cloud mass were alerted to the attack, and swooped down. What followed was several crazed minutes of one of the lowest-level aerial dogfights ever fought, in which the Australian pilots were completely outflown. With the cloud base beginning at a perilously low 1000 feet, the restricted layer of clear air in which the engagement could be fought handed the Japanese the advantage. At this height, the Australians' tactic of descending and firing from above, then zooming away in a dive, was completely neutralised.

The Japanese swung around on their wingtips and strafed Gurney Field, but they had been given strict orders to avoid causing excessive damage to the runway. As the Kittyhawks had already taken off, though, there were hardly any other targets available. The anti-aircraft guns on the ground opened up furiously, with every available man racing to a gun pit and feeding ammunition to the crew. Some even pointed their rifles aloft and took pot shots, even though the chance of hitting anything was virtually nil. A few pilots on the ground crouched behind a tree and were letting fire with their Webley service revolvers, oblivious to the fact that they were ineffective at little more than 50 yards.

The CO of 76 Squadron, Peter Turnbull, raced to the nearest anti-aircraft gun position and assisted the gunners with aircraft recognition, guiding them away from the Kittyhawks and towards the less-familiar Zeros. Anti-aircraft shells were flying as the aircraft were dogfighting, the gun barrels traversing wildly back and forth to track the low trajectory of enemy fighters as they roared deafeningly close overhead.

Emerging below the cloud base, the Kittyhawks had to immediately pull up to avoid hitting the ground, at which point the Zeros used their superior manoeuvrability to pull up almost vertically and disappear into the cloud. The Australian pilots craned their necks upwards to see where they had gone, before realising that the Japanese fighters, having executed a perfect loop, were now directly behind them with guns blazing. It was a chaotic melee as the Zeros continually disengaged and reappeared on the tail of another Australian.

Flying Officer Michael Butler, a 75 Squadron veteran of the Port Moresby campaign, long remembered the skill of the Japanese pilots:

> After the war we all read that the squadron of Japs flying against us were all highly experienced . . . their judgement was absolutely superb, because as soon as you were getting almost in range they'd commence a stall turn and go up vertically, and they'd leave it so late that you couldn't pull back to fire at them otherwise you'd go into a high-speed stall, and the next thing they're on your tail.

Instead of jumping the Zeros, the Kittyhawk pilots found that they were now the ones outfoxed. The men who had flown Spitfires over many months of combat in Europe suddenly realised that their experience counted for little above the jungle. Flight Lieutenant Bardie Wawn had never witnessed such a confusing and frustrating encounter. Five times he attempted to line up on a red-circled fighter, but five times it evaded his gunsight. Again and again he was forced to break off an attack to come to the aid of another Kittyhawk being pursued by a Zero.

Sadly, he could not protect everyone, particularly his wingman that day, Albert McLeod.

Twenty-four-year-old Flying Officer McLeod was originally from Auckland, but had come to Sydney as a child and worked as a commercial traveller before the war. In May 1941 he walked into an RAAF recruiting office in Burwood to become a pilot. This day over Milne Bay was his first ever engagement. He had been paired with the experienced Wawn, but with no combat experience, and in this claustrophobic sandwich of air between the airstrip and the clouds, he was a sitting duck. In the melee Wawn and McLeod quickly became separated.

On the ground, a crewman, Leading Aircraftsman Alex Farthing, watched as he flashed by overhead. 'He came back over the drome with about five Zeros on his hammer,' Farthing later said. 'He disappeared into the hills – never to be seen again.'

Not until 1967 was the wreckage of Albert McLeod's Kittyhawk A29-93 discovered in dense jungle in the hills above Milne Bay. Part of the fuselage was brought back to Australia and put on display at the birthplace of the RAAF, Point Cook, in Victoria. Surprisingly, however, not one but two sets of wheels were found in McLeod's wreckage, indicating that he may have collided with, or was crashed into by, a Zero. It's therefore possible he took one of his enemy with him to the grave. 'It was the first time I had ever lost a wingman,' said Bardie years later, 'a terrible feeling.'

Flying Officer Mark Sheldon, a former building contractor from Sydney, and at age 28 decidedly ancient by fighter pilot standards, also lost his life on this day. Sheldon had flown Spitfires alongside Keith Truscott as a sergeant pilot with 452 Squadron in

England, then had the rare experience of travelling to Russia, operating Hurricanes with the RAF's 132 Squadron near Leningrad.

Returning to Australia, Sheldon was awarded a commission, and arrived with the squadron on 21 July. On 11 August he was already in the air, flying a standing patrol, when the Japanese arrived. No-one is certain of his fate, only that he crashed into the mountains above the village of Ahioma – witnessed by local villagers gathering pawpaws. Using their machetes, they cut a climbing path through the mountain jungle to reach the wreck and retrieve Sheldon's body, which they buried in a clearing close to their village. A runner was sent along the coastal track to inform the Australians at Gili Gili, and eleven days later a party of four was sent to investigate. One of these was 75 Squadron's doctor, Bill Deane-Butcher, who wrote of the incident in his book, *Fighter Squadron Doctor*:

> Our climb to find the wrecked plane was a source of great entertainment for our hosts. The heat was oppressive, our cumbersome boots kept sliding back and our wrists were exhausted from grappling with vines and branches to haul ourselves up the steep muddy trail. We were no match for our agile companions.

Unable to contemplate the indignity of disturbing Sheldon's grave, which the local population had decorated with a ring of shells and hibiscus blooms, Deane-Butcher instead fashioned a timber cross with Sheldon's name and particulars, and left him in peace. Much later, Sheldon's remains were officially exhumed and reinterred in the Commonwealth War Cemetery at Bomana, near Port Moresby.

Sergeant George Inkster, a quiet young man who had worked in a Sydney theatre before the war, joined the RAAF after being inspired by the stories of the men who flew in the Battle of Britain. With 64 Squadron, he would meet some of those same men, and take part in fighter sweeps in Spitfires over Europe.

In the operations tent at the end of Gurney Field runway, Bill Deane-Butcher heard the distressed radio calls of a pilot being chased by several Zeros as he approached for a very fast landing, his aircraft already on fire. A few seconds later, George Inkster's Kittyhawk came into view above the strip, belching thick black smoke and with several enemy aircraft on its tail, the rattle of machine-gun fire clearly audible above the din of the engines.

Deane-Butcher immediately jumped into the ambulance and, with his orderly, raced down the side of the long runway to where he presumed Inkster's aircraft would land, joined also by the fire tender. Over the ambulance radio, Inkster's voice could be heard becoming more panicked as the fire intensified. Deane-Butcher, who as a young doctor before the war had witnessed the terrible suffering of burns patients, was well aware that the pilots flew in shorts and short sleeves that offered no protection from a cockpit fire.

'Suddenly,' Deane-Butcher later wrote, 'the aircraft changed posture and with nose up, climbed steeply to gain height.' Unable to bear the agony of the burning cockpit, Inkster aborted the landing at the last second and decided to bail out, pulling the stick back to gain sufficient height.

Tragically, he was too late. Just above Deane-Butcher's head, the aircraft stalled in an almost vertical position, and Inkster was seen to leap from the smoking cockpit as the plane keeled over and crashed into the coconut trees. Inkster pulled his parachute cord, and the canopy began to unfurl as he plummeted towards the ground, but to the horror of the handful of onlookers he struck the runway just 20 yards from where Deane-Butcher was standing. Rushing to the crumpled heap, the doctor found that the young pilot was dead.

Flight Lieutenant Bardie Wawn, also in the air, witnessed the incident. 'I was actually diving on the Zero behind George that was attacking him. All of a sudden, his aircraft burst into flames at about 500 feet. His aircraft went into a slow roll and I saw George jump out. But he was too low. His parachute opened just as he hit the ground.'

One of Inkster's ground crew, Aircraftsman Bob Clark, who likewise witnessed the tragic incident, later expounded another theory:

> At the time, RAAF fighter aircraft were scarce and . . . the aircrew had been ordered to save them if possible. When George was hit and his aircraft started to flame, it is surmised that he felt he could land and have the fire put out – thereby saving the craft. Apparently on approach to the Strip, the fire became more intense and he took it up and bailed out. Another 50 feet would have given him a soft landing. But it was not to be.

George Inkster was buried the next day on a hill overlooking Gurney Field. He was remembered by all as a 'very quiet, unassuming sort of bloke' who largely avoided the horseplay typical of the pilots, preferring to spend time talking to the ground crew. On guard duty one night, Bob Clark had an opportunity to look through George's logbook, and was amazed to realise that this quiet young pilot in fact had a full tour of eventful combat flying under his belt.

The fourth casualty on this sobering day for the RAAF was 23-year-old Warrant Officer Frank Shelley, a bank officer from Double Bay, in Sydney, and another who had flown with 452 Squadron in England. Of the circumstances of his demise, however, nothing is known. His aircraft was briefly sighted leaving the combat area, never to be seen again.

The Japanese did not escape the engagement unscathed, with pilots of the combined RAAF squadrons reporting three Zeros probably destroyed, one possibly destroyed, and further hits on several others. The Japanese claimed a highly exaggerated nine Australian aircraft destroyed; such embellishments were typical of Japanese air victory claims in this period of the war.

The next day, the first of the ships carrying the 18th Infantry Brigade pulled up to the jetty at Gili Gili and began to unload. Three days later, on 15 August, the Japanese issued their orders for the invasion of Milne Bay.

CHAPTER 15
FIRST BLOOD AT GOODENOUGH ISLAND

Towards dusk on the particularly wet and gloomy afternoon of 20 August, virtually everyone toiling at No. 1 Strip, recently renamed Gurney Field, stopped what they were doing to look up and watch the big green American Liberator bomber, which had been circling now for the best part of an hour. Lower and lower the aircraft had come, forced down by the ever-decreasing cloud ceiling which now hung above the airstrip at just 400 feet. For the past 90 minutes, the Liberator's pilot, Captain Fred Eaton Jnr from New York, and his Australian co-pilot, Flight Sergeant Marv Bell, had, with their engineer and crew, tried everything they could think of to fix the stricken hydraulic system which had left them with just one functioning wheel out of the three they needed to land safely.

The nosewheel – down but not locked – would, they knew, collapse as soon as it touched the runway, leaving just the port wheel locked and in place, with the starboard wheel not having lowered at all. Even worse, their two wheels now stubbornly refused to retract to allow Eaton to chance a pure belly landing, by far the safest option in the circumstances.

Liberator AL-515 had not been a lucky 'ship' for Captain Eaton. Only a few days before, when bringing a load of ammunition and a Bofors gun up to Milne Bay from their base at Townsville, an electrical fire had erupted at the base of one of the gun turrets, which was only just put out by the quick-thinking crew. He prayed he had just a little more luck in store.

All eyes watched the forlorn bomber as it circled the strip. Frantically, the crew threw out the crates of 2000 pounds worth of Bofors anti-aircraft ammunition they carried, and assumed their crash positions as Eaton came in for a long, low approach in the filthy weather. Everyone at Gurney now lined the runway and held their breath as the fire tenders stood at the ready.

Standing on the runway apron, Corporal Vic Alexander from 76 Squadron was one of the witnesses. 'The single wheel made contact with a plume of blue smoke, bounced and touched again. Then the starboard wing-tip slowly dropped and contacted the metal strip with a long shower of sparks.'

The rain was something of a blessing this day, supressing some of the sparks that could otherwise have turned the aircraft into an inferno. Working the brakes expertly, Eaton managed to keep her straight on the runway till the Liberator's nose wheel collapsed and the starboard props lowered with a horrible sound onto the metal runway.

Then, the great bulk of the plane pivoted in a perfect 180-degree ground loop and came to a stop, facing the way she had landed. Eaton immediately shut off the electrics and a huge cheer went up from inside, and outside, the aircraft. Six valuable airmen then made 'a hasty and undignified exit as they scrambled clear', to fly and fight another day.

RAAF engineers and mechanics fell on the aircraft over the next day, dragging it off the runway then stripping it bare of every useable gun and fitting, particularly the specialised American half-inch exploding ammunition, not being used by Australian aircraft at the time. Sergeant Bert Hill from 76 Squadron remembered, 'The explosive rounds delighted our pilots when we interspersed them in the ammo belts. They later expended them on Japanese stores and barges in their strafing attacks . . . like little kids with new toys on Christmas morning.'

Captain Eaton and his crew were honoured guests of the RAAF for the next few days until a flight could be found to take them back to Townsville. At one stage, Les Jackson, 75 Squadron CO, made a small wager with Captain Eaton: 'I bet that plane of yours gets strafed by the Japs.'

Two days later on 24 August, Les would collect his money when fifteen Zeros appeared over the airstrip in the early morning light, looking for targets. With most of the Kittyhawks either in the air or well protected in the revetments, the Japanese pilots were again frustrated, choosing instead to expend their energies – as well as their ammunition – destroying the already cannibalised Liberator parked on the runway's edge. After three or four passes, the Zeros set it ablaze, igniting what fuel remained in the aircraft's wing tanks, but as it was never to have flown again anyway, their efforts were wasted.

It was on this occasion that one of 76 Squadron's most experienced pilots, Bardie Wawn, came close to falling victim to the

Japanese. At dawn that morning, Wawn was assigned to lead the first patrol, but on this occasion his usually reliable Kittyhawk refused to start. Waving the other five aircraft on, he allowed his mechanic to toil with his engine, eventually producing the cough of blue smoke and sudden roar denoting the Allison engine was back in business and ready to go. Taking off alone, Bardie headed to their designated patrolling area, the far end of the bay, when he noticed two of his Kittyhawks heading back towards him a couple of thousand feet above, obviously checking on the whereabouts of their flight commander.

Bardie was pleased, thinking, 'Good. At least a couple of those blokes have the sense to come back and form up behind me.' Waggling his wings in recognition, he noticed one of the Kittyhawks do the same, and so executed a gentle turn to allow them to get behind him so that he would take over the lead. 'Trouble was,' reflected Bardie years later, 'they weren't Kittyhawks at all, they were Zeros!' Too late Bardie noticed the rising sun emblem and two radial engines flash past, then turn into the ideal attack position he had conveniently permitted them to assume. The Japanese pilots undoubtedly could not believe their luck.

Unbeknown to Bardie, several thousand feet above him, the pilots of his actual patrol were witnessing the scene and, no doubt as bewildered as the Japanese pilots, swooped down. 'Apparently I performed aerobatics in a Kittyhawk that have never been seen before or since,' recounted Bardie.

Ducking into some light cloud, lines of orange tracer arced under and over his aircraft, then: 'One Zero went past my wing tip so closely it nearly hit me, and the other one went past even closer.' Unbelievably, at that moment Bardie's engine began to splutter and fail. Knowing he could not remain in the protective cloud forever, he desperately attended to the failing engine, hoping the Zeros would not find him again. Then, in a flash, he remembered his drop tank: 'In the panic I hadn't switched it over to the main fuel tank.' With the throwing of a lever, the engine roared back into life and Bardie dived away to safety. 'I was a bit lucky,' he would say later, 'they wasted a lot of ammo on me.'

Now, however, on the eve of the battle, the focus would shift for a time away from the airstrip and Milne Bay to Goodenough Island, off the Papuan coast to the north.

•

In the late morning of 25 August, from their commanding but expertly hidden lookouts above the western shore of Goodenough Island, three private soldiers of the Australian Coastwatchers were on alert, having been told via their AWA 3BZ radio sets to expect evidence of Japanese activity some-where in the vicinities of Port Moresby, Milne Bay or possibly Guadalcanal, several hundred miles to the east. As their view was limited to approaches from the west, that was where they focused their army-issue binoculars, sweeping back and forth across the endless blue ocean.

At times over the previous week or so, privates Anthony Morrow and Thomas Royal had had to remind themselves there was a war going on at all, such was the peace and tran-quillity of Goodenough. The local people had been kind and accommodating, supplying them with food and shelter, secure in their belief that the Japanese would not bother to disturb their island paradise, 23 miles across and 17 wide, with the spectacular mountain of Vineuo rising more than 8000 feet in the centre. After all, there was nothing here the Japanese could possibly want: no decent harbour, a handful of small villages and nearly 435 square miles of dense and extremely steep jungle. The Coastwatchers concurred, and could not imagine their idyll being disturbed by the hand of war. On the morning of Tuesday, 25 August 1942, however, the war came to Goodenough Island.

•

At 0500 the previous morning, from their new base 150 miles away at Buna, the seven motorised Daihatsu barges of Commander Tsukioka's 5th Sasebo SNLF had set out on a two-day journey towards their objective, Taupota, on Papua's northern coast, above Milne Bay. From here, they would travel a short distance overland and emerge to surprise the Australian and American forces, linking up with other SNLF forces advancing from the east. Together they would capture Rabi and its base.

After a full day and a morning in these dreadful barges, however, the 352 men under Tsukioka's command were finding the going rough. Packed in full kit into the open, flat-bottomed, 10-foot-wide, 50-foot-long motorised crafts, their second day on the water was beginning to wear them down. Nor was Commander Tsukioka feeling particularly happy about the mission. The whole thing had been a rush job, and a badly planned one at that. He had only received his orders 24 hours before sailing, and although he'd tried to exude confidence while addressing his men, he suspected he was not all that convincing.

To his superiors he had mentioned that although his men had trained in amphibious operations, two days was a very long time for them to spend on the ocean in open barges. The senior officers were unmoved, arguing that the trip would be broken up with a night of camping along the way. Besides, they assured him, the 200-mile route he was to follow to Taupota would hug the coastline, avoiding the worst of the open sea.

This was all very well, thought Tsukioka, as he bowed deferentially to his superior and left, but such a course would make their progress clearly visible to the army of spies the Australians had planted along the coast. Worst of all, there had been no time to order any radio sets from Rabaul, so they would be setting off deaf, with no way to communicate with anyone should anything go wrong.

However, his men were young and fit and aching to take part in the battle for which they had so long prepared. All that was needed for them to be refreshed and eager to continue was a rest and a good meal.

Late in the morning, Tsukioka saw a fine and mountainous island ahead, which his map told him was Goodenough. They were making good progress, and well over the halfway mark to Taupota. Here, he decided, he would feed and rest his men and proceed in a few hours' time. It was a fateful decision which would bear heavily on the outcome of the battle.

High above the water, Morrow and Royal could not believe what they were seeing. For miles, they had been tracking the seven dark dots on the horizon; now the barges were just over 200 yards from the shoreline. The sound of the motors and the voices of the several hundred uniformed men were clearly audible as they motored past, seemingly looking for a place to land. A coded message was immediately tapped out on a wireless set alerting Milne Bay, with the rejoinder: 'Await further instructions.' Those instructions were to observe the Japanese landing point, then to get out of there as quickly as possible.

The men on Goodenough were not the first to sight the small flotilla of barges. As Commander Tsukioka had suspected, their journey had been noted soon after their departure the previous day, and had been reported by observers stationed at Porlock Harbour and Cape Nelson on the Papuan coast. Their first night of camping, at a spot called Fona, had been monitored, with some of the Coastwatchers convinced the Japanese were coming ashore there to stay. The spies made a hasty retreat with their radios and equipment.

With orders to evacuate to nearby Normanby Island as soon as practicable, Morrow and Royal put in a final report to Milne Bay, observing that the Japanese had put ashore on the far south-west tip of the island, at a secluded spot called Galaiwa Bay – and that they appeared to be preparing for lunch.

The Coastwatch team enacted their evacuation plan and made for the place where a small boat had been secreted for the journey to the safety of neighbouring Normanby Island. As they departed, just after 1 p.m. on 25 August, the men looked into the sky above their heads to see ten Kittyhawks descending from 10,000 feet. This, they observed with some pride, was the direct result of their work.

Two flights of five aircraft from 75 Squadron took off from Gurney Field into a typical dismal sky. Flying Officer Geoff Atherton's flight, it was agreed, would attack first, while Flying

Officer John Piper's would stay aloft to provide cover. Initially flying north through a wet blanket of grey, the weather suddenly lifted as they crossed the coast and a bright sunny day emerged, the first they'd seen in weeks. Ahead lay the distinct outline of Goodenough Island, which seemed to rise almost vertically from the sea. Commencing their search in the island's south-west corner, it did not take the pilots long to sight their quarry. Below, on a small ribbon of sand, were seven barges, conveniently lined up along the water's edge. The first shots of the Battle of Milne Bay were about to be fired.

'It was like target practice,' recalled Warrant Officer Bob Crawford. 'We'd just sort of dive down, strafe, go back in a circle and . . . do the same again.'

The Japanese had been caught red-handed. Their barges, fully laden with equipment and ammunition, were torn to shreds by the guns of the Kittyhawks as they swooped. As if on a training exercise, the pilots flew low enough that they could make out the paintwork and serial numbers on the prows of the vessels. Some Japanese were still inside the barges, as John Piper recalled when his flight was called down after Atherton's had exhausted their ammunition. 'We actually saw them skedaddling off the barges and onto the beach.'

Eight Japanese soldiers were mown down, with several more wounded; the remainder sheltered out of sight under the trees. Not a shot was fired in return. Ten thousand shells were expended, setting the barges on fire, leaving them a mess of splintered wood and metal with thick black fumes rising up a thousand feet. More important, the 352 men of Commander Tsukioka's 5th Sasebo SNLF were now stranded on an isolated island, without even a radio to call for assistance. The unit had been dealt out of the battle almost before it had started.

The entry in the logbook of 75 Squadron Pilot John Pettet that day read simply: 'Massacre!'

CHAPTER 16
BATTLE LINES

The task confronting Major General Cyril Clowes, commander of Milne Force, was a daunting one. In one of the most difficult and isolated battle terrains in the world, it fell to him to organise the defence of 30 miles of coastline of a sodden jungle bay for which he possessed no accurate map, and along which at virtually any point an enemy could land in force. He would have no immediate idea of the attacking force's size, its tactical direction, nor when it would arrive. The enemy had complete command of the sea, and he had no way of preventing them from entering the wide entrance to the bay. And once they were inside, he possessed not a single shore gun, nor even a searchlight, with which to challenge them.

Unable to defeat the Japanese at sea, Clowes knew that he would need to beat them on land. For this task, he had at his disposal around 9000 men, of whom approximately 4000 were fighting troops from the two infantry brigades under his command. One of those had never fought the Japanese, while the other – a militia battalion – was completely untested in battle.

Yet the consequences of defeat were unthinkable, not only for himself and the men under his command, but for the Allied cause in the Pacific in general. Failure would lead to a direct threat to the security of his own country.

Such problems would have tested even the most experienced military structure, but Clowes' untested HQ staff had been thrown together at the last minute, and had never worked under the stress of battle. Besides Clowes and his staff chief, Fred Chilton, none had any battle experience whatsoever.

But if the weight of the world was bearing down on the shoulders of Cyril Clowes in the days prior to the battle, none of his closest associates, nor the men, suspected it. Even though he had only taken full command of Milne Force on 22 August, Clowes at all times, in public and in private, exuded an aura of calm and control, and a grasp for detail that had those around him sincerely believing that not even the smallest fact regarding the base and its defence had escaped his attention. In his command headquarters – a purpose-built Papuan hut with a thatched roof and bamboo walls, and which was still being fitted for power and telephone lines – he clenched his pipe between his teeth and pored over lists of displacements with Colonel Chilton and his two senior commanders, Brigadier John Field of the 7th and Brigadier Frank Wootten of the 18th.

The RAAF had finally agreed to appoint a senior overall commander, Wing Commander William 'Bull' Garing, to whom Major General Morris had earlier put the case for the relocation of the original garrison from Mullins Harbour to Milne Bay.

One of the RAAF's most colourful and enduring figures, 'Bull' Garing had arrived just in time. The men of the Kittyhawk and Hudson squadrons, Clowes knew, would play a vital – perhaps *the* vital – part in the battle.

In a decision that would be examined by military analysts and historians for decades, Clowes decided to use his two primary weapons – the 7th and 18th Brigades – in very different ways. Assuming the Japanese landed somewhere close to the Gili Gili base, the inexperienced militiamen of the 7th would be used in a largely defensive role – to hold off the enemy, and gauge their strength – while the veteran infantrymen of the 18th would wait in reserve to launch the counterstrike.

With no idea exactly where the Japanese would land, in early July Field had dispersed some of the 7th Brigade along the 30 miles of Milne Bay's northern shore, giving the job primarily to the 61st Battalion of 'Queensland Cameron Highlanders', whose task was to report any Japanese landing as quickly as possible, and resist it where they could.

The 61st had two of its companies dug in around the incomplete No. 3 Strip and had sent a platoon north to Taupota to counter a possible Japanese landing there. This was an accurate enough guess as the Japanese had indeed intended to land at Taupota, but, as we have seen, they were dispatched by the guns of the Kittyhawks on Goodenough Island. Still more of the 61st was spread further east, with B Company ten miles from Gili Gili at KB Mission, and D Company further along the shoreline at the village of Ahioma, the site of Milne Bay's only other anchorage and the location of a government store.

The 7th's two other battalions, the 9th and the 25th, held the bay's western flank, with the 9th stretching from Ladava Mission to Gaba Gabuna Bay, dead in the centre of Milne Bay's western end, while the 25th stretched further around to cover Gurney Field, and be in position to rush to No. 3 Strip if needed. In fact, many of these men were already camped along the airstrip's defensive line, and barely needed to move anywhere. At the climax of the battle fought at the No. 3 Strip, the men would be fighting almost where they slept. Behind the 25th, more units of the 18th Brigade lay waiting in reserve.

In his headquarters, consulting the disposition map with the CO of the 61st Battalion, Lieutenant Colonel Alexander Meldrum, Clowes noticed some markings on the shoreline 30 miles away at East Cape, right at the bay's entrance. This was far beyond where he had intended any of his forces to be situated.

'Who are these people?' he asked Meldrum, who scrutinised the map beside him.

'Don Company, sir,' he replied. 'Seventeen Platoon.'

'Well, get them out of there,' was Clowes' response.

Several days earlier, D Company at Ahioma had received a report from some villagers of suspicious lights and a possible Japanese spy in the area, and so had sent their 17 Platoon, under the command of Lieutenant Tom O'Keefe, to investigate. Nothing of note had been found, and now they were nearly out of food. Alarmingly, O'Keefe was suffering severely from malaria, and exhibiting bouts of delirium so severe that Sergeant Jack Newcombe had felt it necessary to confiscate his officer's pistol. A few days later, 16 Platoon had been dispatched from Ahioma to relieve them.

Clowes did not like what he saw. Both platoons were now strung so far out that they would most likely be cut off by any Japanese landing to the west. In fact, thought Clowes, all of D Company's position was precarious, so he ordered it back to Gili Gili, where they would be used to reinforce No. 3 Strip.

Time being of the essence, three small civilian boats were found to ferry some of the soldiers back: the *Elevala*, the *Dadosee* and the masted lugger *Bronzewing*, which in a previous life was the property of the actor Errol Flynn, and which had recently retrieved the crashed Kittyhawk from Goodenough Island.

At 3 p.m. on 25 August, Major Harry Wiles, on board the *Elevala*, departed Gili Gili to retrieve the farthest-flung of his men out at East Cape. He found them not in a good way. Their food had run out, and now others besides O'Keefe were ill with malaria. A private had seriously wounded himself, virtually severing his big toe while cutting, of all things, a pumpkin. All were tired and extremely hungry. The *Elevala*, it turned out, could not carry everyone, and some of the fit men were required to walk the 35 miles back to Ahioma, a journey which would take them several difficult days.

After the *Elevala* arrived at Ahioma's little jetty at dusk, men were put to work packing the company's equipment onto the little flotilla of ships for the trip back to Gili Gili, all under the supervision of Major Wiles, who seemed agitated.

After the sun had set, the light of a dim moon managed to struggle down through the scattered clouds. At around 8.30 in the evening, Sergeant Jim McKenzie – one of a party of men organising the stowing of a load of corrugated iron on the *Bronzewing* – had his attention caught by something out to sea. Standing on the deck of the little lugger, he made out a series of shapes, barely illuminated by the moon, apparently moving in a line. 'Sir,' he said, turning to Major Wiles, 'what do you make of those dark shapes out there?'

Wiles looked up; it appeared his worst suspicions were confirmed. 'Just get on with loading the boat, Sergeant,' he replied curtly.

Japan's long-awaited invasion convoy had arrived at Milne Bay.

First taste of war: en route to Milne Bay, some men witnessed the sinking of the MV *Macdhui*, struck by Japanese bombs while at anchor in Port Moresby, 18 June 1942. *Argus Newspaper Collection of Photographs, State Library of Victoria, H98.104/3705*

Part of the Lever Brothers' coconut plantation which would be transformed into the Milne Bay garrison and airstrips. *Courtesy of Bruce Whealey*

Some of 76 Squadron's pilots in their tropical camp. Keith 'Bluey' Truscott is second from left. *Author's collection*

Major General 'Silent Cyril' Clowes, the man who would win the battle of Milne Bay, only to be shunned by MacArthur and Blamey soon after.

Australian War Memorial, 013337

76 Squadron's popular and brilliant leader, Squadron Leader Peter Turnbull. His death during the battle was a bitter blow to the unit.
Author's collection

75 Squadron Kittyhawk pilot, Flying Officer Arthur Tucker posing in his full flying kit. There would be little need for much of it at the low altitudes of Milne Bay. *Courtesy of Peter Tucker*

75 Squadron's redoubtable Medical Officer, Bill Deane-Butcher. The conditions of the camp were beyond anything he could have imagined. *Courtesy of Richard Deane-Butcher*

The runway in the middle of nowhere: No. 1 Strip, Milne Bay. Later renamed 'Gurney Field' in honour of Australian aviation hero, Charles Gurney. *Courtesy of Bruce Whealey*

The Japanese finally discover the Milne Bay garrison. Lucky snap of a low-flying Zero over No. 3 Strip, during the attack on 4 August 1942. *Courtesy of Arthur Tucker*

The weariness of the job showing on their faces. 75 Squadron pilots head to their aircraft once again to strafe the jungle, in September 1942. Left to right: Flying Officer Bruce Watson, Sergeant Cec Norman, Flight Sergeant Roy Riddell, Flight Lieutenant Archie Hall and Flight Lieutenant Nat Gould. *Australian War Memorial, 026658*

A Kittyhawk of 76 Squadron battles the mud of No. 1 Strip. None of the pilots had ever seen anything like it. *Australian War Memorial, OG0061D*

A few days before the battle began, a USAAF Liberator bomber made an emergency belly landing at Gurney Field, providing the Australians their first look at this famous American aircraft. It would later be strafed and destroyed by Zero fighters. *Courtesy of Margaret Whealey*

The Milne Bay mud. Flying Officer Geoff Atherton (middle) looks on as a jeep is bogged in the tropical mire. *Courtesy of Arthur Tucker*

A stranded landing-barge, wrecked stores and cratered beaches mark the site of one of the Japanese landing areas at Milne Bay. Bomb crater courtesy of one of 6 Squadron's Hudson bombers. *Australian War Memorial, 026620*

Soldiers wade through a swampy jungle clearing in a still from this famous footage taken at Milne Bay by Damien Parer. *Argus Newspaper Collection of Photographs, State Library of Victoria, H98.100/2411*

The terrifying leviathans of the fight at KB Mission now just curious pieces of junk. Australian soldiers inspect the two bogged Ha-Go Type 95 Japanese infantry tanks, abandoned along Milne Bay's bloody track. *Argus Newspaper Collection of Photographs, State Library of Victoria, H98.100/2409*

The turning of the tide. The point marking the westernmost advance of Japan's drive towards Port Moresby at No. 3 Strip. Successive waves of Japanese marines failed to take the airfield in a bloody night-time slaughter. *Australian War Memorial, PO2875.043*

PART TWO
THE BATTLE

CHAPTER 17
INVASION

Lieutenant Fujikawa was one of the first to inspect the transport ship *Nankai Maru* when it arrived at Rabaul on 21 August to take several hundred men of the 5th Kure SNLF. He was less than impressed. She was a rust bucket, old and worn out, and her thin, flaking plates offered no assurance that they'd stop a bullet. The second transport ship, the *Kinai Maru*, was comparatively newer, but small. Both vessels had at least proved themselves recently, landing Japanese troops at Buna and Gona in Papua for the trek to Kokoda and, eventually, Port Moresby. But they were very cramped. The trip to Rabi, thought Fujikawa, would be an uncomfortable one.

The next day, 22 August, a final rehearsal of the landing operation was undertaken in full combat conditions inside Rabaul's harbour. The men climbed aboard the barges in complete battle kit, while others worked the ship's davits, lowering them to the water, all in virtual darkness, before they set off to the shore. A light mist moved across the water as they made their landing on a nearby beach under a quiet volcano. Here, just as they had trained countless times before, they pulled the barges up off the shore, quickly grouped together under the orders of their NCOs, and fanned out to take positions over the flat, pebbly beach and foreshore. The entire exercise took just two hours.

Then a sudden squall moved in, blotting out the moon. Standing in the pouring night rain, the men were given a final address by their commanding officer. He congratulated them on performing their tasks quickly and efficiently. In a little more than 24 hours, he told them, they would carry them out again, this time in actual battle conditions.

Twenty days' rations were loaded aboard the transports – which was more than enough time, it was believed, for victory to be achieved. Further supplies would be flown in directly to the airstrip at Rabi as soon as it had been captured. It would all be over in a matter of days.

At midday on 23 August, a small ceremony took place on the top deck of the *Nankai Maru*, in which Commander Hayashi, according to tradition, poured beer for his subordinate officers one by one and gave a greeting, before all joined in a toast to the Emperor and to victory. Standing to attention, the young officers of the SNLF sweated in their uniforms under the burning tropical sun. The token serve of beer – not as cold as it could have been – offered little relief.

Under a low cloud at 0700 the following morning, Monday, 24 August, the convoy, consisting of the light cruisers *Tenryu* – the flagship – and *Tatsua*; destroyers *Urakaze*, *Tanikaze* and *Hamakaze*; transports *Nankai Maru* and *Kinai Maru*, as well as two small and fast minesweepers, pulled out of Rabaul harbour and headed south.

•

At age 31, Flight Lieutenant Henry Robertson, formerly a store manager from the beachside Melbourne suburb of Brighton, was several years older than most of his counterparts in 75 and 76 Squadron. However, the controls of the larger and slower Lockheed Hudson twin-engine bomber demanded skills markedly different from those of the Kittyhawk fighters. Instead of brief but intense dogfights or strafing enemy positions on the ground, Robertson, day after day, in all weathers, would climb into the sky to undertake reconnaissance patrols lasting many hours, drawing on his reserves of intense concentration and stamina, and requiring the steadiest of hands.

Already a veteran of the disastrous campaign in Malaya, where his 8 Squadron Hudsons were virtually wiped out in the Japanese onslaught, Robertson and his crew of two had arrived only recently in Milne Bay with their flight, which had been detached from 6 Squadron, and it seemed that they'd been in the air ever since. One of his crew, Sergeant Frank Carden, said of Robertson:

> He earned the highest possible praise from all at Milne Bay who knew his work – he worked almost to the point of collapse. He was later Mentioned-in-Dispatches but this was a poor reward for his efforts and bravery in those dark days . . .
>
> I admired him and had absolute faith in him as my skipper.

Robertson, in one of only four Hudsons to be split off from 6 Squadron and sent to Milne Bay from their base at Horn

Island in the Torres Strait, became renowned for never refusing nor questioning a request to fly, and never reporting as being unable to do so. He performed his duties almost to the point of exhaustion. He would take off in the most atrocious weather, often with dreadful visibility, and fly out over the ocean and the islands, where he and his crew would, hour upon hour, peer through the gloom and act as the eyes of the Milne Bay garrison.

No more capable a pilot could have been guarding the approaches to Milne Bay early on the vital morning of 25 August, as Robertson lifted off from the slippery runway at Gurney for yet another first-light patrol. Following a prescribed course, Robertson flew north, through the endless grey cloudbank, through rain squalls and avoiding the towering clouds of tropical cumulus, in which the updraughts could tear off an aeroplane's wing as if it were a fly's.

At 8.30, around 150 miles north of Milne Bay, just to the east of little Kitava Island, Robertson noticed the weather begin to break up, and he climbed through a gap to give himself and his crew a better view. With swollen, red-rimmed eyes, under strict intercom silence, the three men scoured the grey, flat ocean below. Suddenly, 'Skipper, look!' broke into Robertson's headphones. Below, some distance off, spread out in double lines, at least seven ships – some of which, he could see immediately, were cruisers – were steaming due south.

Robertson found some cloud into which to vanish, then widened out to begin a long circle of the convoy, using the cloud cover whenever he could. When sure of his position, he radioed in: 'Enemy convoy sighted – two cruisers, three destroyers,

two transports, heading due south, east of Kitava Island.'
Remarkably, he had remained unnoticed by the Japanese.

It was the moment that Cyril Clowes – and the entire
garrison – had been waiting for, or at least had been anticipating with dread. Now, with the invasion imminent, was he
able to assume complete command of all Allied men and assets –
including the Americans – at Milne Bay. This stipulation had
been insisted upon by General MacArthur, who was loath to
allow his US service personnel to be commanded by Australians
until it was absolutely necessary. Now, that time had arrived.

Robertson tracked the convoy as long as he could, then
turned for home as the weather closed in and his fuel ran low.
Landing at Gurney Field an hour or so later, he gave a brief
report and was told to rest a little while, as his flying for the
day was far from over.

At this point, the pilots of 75 and 76 Squadrons were summoned
to their rudimentary briefing tent beside the strip to be told that
the moment for which they had been waiting and preparing
would soon be upon them. Initially, however, the message
wasn't sinking in. A 75 Squadron pilot, Sergeant Roy Riddell,
remembered Intelligence Officer Stuart Collie gravely informing
them that the Japanese fleet had been sighted approaching the
China Strait. 'None of us moved or said anything,' recalled
Sergeant Riddell, 'then there was a pause and Collie said, "The
China Strait is NOT in China. It is between us and Goodenough
Island – just around the bloody corner!" We were a bit more
lively after that.'

An hour later, Coastwatchers on Kitava Island confirmed
Robertson's sighting, and Milne Bay's Kittyhawk squadrons were

ordered to launch an attack. But the weather, which had been particularly bad the last few days, prevented their immediate departure. It was not until 1500 hours that twelve Kittyhawks – an even six from both 75 and 76 – took to the air, with the cloud still so thick that the tops of the coconut trees around the airstrip were obscured in white.

In the meantime, the Japanese fleet had closed to within half an hour's flying time of Gili Gili, just eight miles south of Normanby Island, having turned due west to sail directly through the entrance of the bay. Formating on the single airworthy Hudson bomber – flown, once again, by the tireless Henry Robertson – the Kittyhawks found the Japanese convoy in just half an hour.

For the pilots, however, this was to be an attack like no other, as they had recently all been transformed into makeshift fighter bombers. Under each of their aircrafts' bellies was slung a single 250-pound bomb, which they were to use against the Japanese ships. The only problem was that none of them actually knew how to do it. According to Flight Lieutenant Jeff Wilkinson:

> We were all bombed-up with 250 lb bombs but unfortunately none of us had ever dropped a bomb from a Kittyhawk before. We were told that the only way to do it was to line up the target – go into a steep dive – start pulling out, count to three and pull the lever to let the bomb go.

Not surprisingly, the resulting attack was a haphazard affair. The pilots did their best, but with a cloud base at a mere 1000 feet above the water, the tactic of diving steeply from a decent height was impossible to execute in any case. Making dives that were far too shallow, the pilots yanked at the unfamiliar release handle which had been hastily fitted into their cockpits and hoped for the best.

Flight Lieutenant Nat Gould of 75 Squadron remembered a wall of flak and flame coming up at him from the Japanese ships; it was only by remarkable luck that not a single Kittyhawk was lost. Bombs rained down and straddled the ships, sending up white plumes of water, and a few vessels suffered some damage from near misses, but none severely. Luck, in fact, according to Nat, played a bigger part than any flying prowess. Lining up on a cargo ship with his single bomb in a shallow dive, he yanked the lever and released it, then cursed, seeing that he'd missed the vessel completely. Back at the strip, however, CO Les Jackson heartily congratulated him on a job well done.

'But I didn't hit anything,' said Nat.

'Well, you nearly hit that destroyer,' Les replied, convinced Nat had at least caused some damage with his very near miss.

'Destroyer?' said an incredulous Nat, 'I was aiming for the cargo ship!'

More damage was probably done after the Allied pilots swung around for a series of low strafing attacks; on the *Nankai Maru* alone, this accounted for ten casualties.

Several attacks were repeated on the convoy that afternoon, including a heroic bombing run from Robertson and his crew in their Hudson, but as the sun disappeared, not a single ship had been sunk or turned back. This was to be no repeat of the Coral Sea. As night fell, the convoy steamed on into the bay.

Realising the ships were not to be stopped, Clowes relayed the following message to all Allied units at Milne Bay:

Every indication attack by enemy imminent tonight or early
hrs tomorrow – Troops will stand-to in battle positions until
further notice – Attack may be supported by fire of Warships
and Bombers . . . All localities will be held with the utmost
vigour and determination.

Later that evening, Clowes summoned his brigade commanders
Field and Wootten, RAAF boss Garing, the chief medical officer
and his general staff to his headquarters. Here he laid out the
situation as he understood it. Everyone had their orders, he said,
and reminded them of the importance of their strategic position,
which – for the Allied situation in Papua, the Pacific theatre in
general, and the threat to Australia specifically – must be held.
The Japanese were to be resisted by every man to the best of
his capacity. He wished the assembled men the best of luck.

Filing out of the small room, George Wootten turned to
Clowes' chief of staff, Fred Chilton, and simply said, 'Fuck them!'

The Japanese were on their way – but where would they land?

CHAPTER 18
BLOOD ON THE WATER

After nightfall had seen off the last of the air attacks against the Japanese convoy, the ships regrouped and resumed their course towards Rabi. Many of the untested troops had been shocked by their first taste of gunfire. On the *Nankai Maru*, Paymaster Captain Moji was also shaken, having previously experienced high-altitude bombing attacks, but not the low-level terror of the Kittyhawks raking the ship with gunfire before deafeningly roaring away. There were ten dead sailors laid out on the deck under the bridge, including the ship's chief signaller, who had received a bullet in his abdomen and died instantly.

When calm resumed, welders went to work patching the holes punched into the landing barges by the Kittyhawks' bullets. Extra rations were distributed to the troops – three meals of rice wrapped in bamboo leaves – and tea was brewed for their water bottles.

At 11 p.m. on Tuesday, 25 August, the sea was calm and misty, with a half moon shedding a feeble light on the shore, which was otherwise dark. Suddenly, the great engines of the *Nankai Maru* were stilled, and in the deafening silence the ship drifted in the calm, black water. A signal had been received by the lead cruiser, which carried on its bridge a local who could guide the ship through the bay: a former Gili Gili plantation worker from Buna. This, he indicated, was the landing point.

The shrill blow of a whistle was followed by the sound of boots on the metal deck as men clambered up from the holds below, and the soft clinking of rifles and equipment as they assembled on deck. No-one spoke. The landing master on the bridge ordered the lowering of the first barges, and the men, just as in training, descended the short stairway, filling up the barges in an orderly fashion so as not to upset the trim.

Fifteen minutes later, like black shadows, twelve barges carrying the first of the more than 800 men of the 5th Kure and 5th Sasebo SNLF departed for the dim shore. Neither a beach nor a headland could be made out.

Onboard, Captain Moji watched them vanish into the darkness and held his breath, anticipating the sound of gunfire. But as their motors receded, silence reigned once more. In his head, he repeated the words of the orders given for the Rabi operation: 'At dead of night, quickly complete the landing in the enemy area and strike the white soldier without remorse . . . smash the enemy lines to pieces and take the aerodrome by storm . . .'

After a surprisingly short time, the sound of a barge could again be heard, becoming louder as it returned to the ship through the sea mist. All those watching anxiously on the deck leaned over as the now empty boat pulled up alongside. 'What's happened?' a voice called down to the helmsman.

'Nothing,' he replied. 'No resistance. First landing company ashore okay.'

Almost in disbelief, the second group now assembled on the deck for their departure. Surely, thought Moji, it could not be this easy? As the barges departed again, a shuttle began between land and shore. Barges packed with rows of helmeted marines headed off into the night, while others, empty, returned.

As more and more of the men were landed, still without any sign of resistance, the relief on the ship was palpable, and something approaching a lighter tone took hold. Then, approaching from the east, Moji's ear caught the growing note of a different engine. All on board heard it too, and peered into the darkness, towards the open sea. Suddenly, the air was alive with the yellow flashes of gunfire.

•

Having left Ahioma just after midnight, the little flotilla of *Bronzewing*, *Elevala* and *Dadosee* chugged through the dark with some of the men of 16 and 17 Platoon, D Company, 61st Battalion, which had been withdrawn from the eastern end of the bay. The boats hugged the shore as they made their way west towards Gili Gili and safety. On board *Bronzewing*, which had once been a regular sight on Sydney Harbour, Sergeant Jim McKenzie could not shake the images of those mysterious shapes he had seen at dusk on the water a few hours earlier.

Distributed around the boat were 22 men of the platoon, many sick with malaria. The skipper, a Papuan, had been instructed to steer close to the shore at about 200 yards, making from headland to headland. Following a few hundred yards behind in the *Elevala*, Major Harry Wiles tried to keep sight of both *Bronzewing* and the slower *Dadosee*, cursing the little boat to try and keep up.

As *Bronzewing* crossed Wanaduela Bay, the skipper rose up on his haunches and peered ahead at something in the semi-darkness. 'Look!', he called, pointing. 'Boats!'

Sergeant McKenzie could make them out too. He turned to the skipper. 'Whose boats? Ours?'

'No!' he replied slowly with a solemn shake of the head.

Along the shoreline, McKenzie noticed what he thought to be the twinkling of lights, and felt something pass over his head. 'God almighty!' he shouted. 'Muzzle flashes!'

All hell now broke loose. The little three-boat flotilla had run straight into the Japanese landing party as it disgorged its invasion army. From behind, Major Wiles later noted that *Bronzewing* seemed suddenly 'surrounded by fire'.

Bullets shattered the glass windows and splintered the sides of the boat. Not liking his chances, the skipper jumped over the side. McKenzie took control and steered towards a dark patch of shoreline, knowing that his slow boat stood no chance of outpacing anything on the water.

On the *Elevala*, Wiles found himself 'running directly towards two strings of enemy landing craft, one travelling towards the beach . . . the other moving out'.

Onboard *Bronzewing*, Private George Thurlow picked up his .303 and began returning fire, but doubled up and fell dead as a bullet ripped into his chest. Another soldier made for a Bren gun on the forward deck but was forced to retreat by a line of intense fire.

Now the landing barges began to pursue them; one of the Japanese destroyers was also bearing down on them, the soldiers aboard firing their weapons. McKenzie put his craft's nose to the shore and shouted, 'All overboard for yourselves!' The *Bronzewing* was abandoned. Then came the awful rattle of a machine gun as the Japanese commenced shooting the soldiers in the water. McKenzie remembered:

> I dived deep and swam underwater. Every few times that I
> surfaced, the noise of gun fire and whack of bullets kept me
> low. Reaching the beach I scrambled through undergrowth
> to good cover and then across the road and up a jungle
> path to high ground.

Half the 22 men on the *Bronzewing* were killed in the water or captured and later executed by the Japanese. The survivors managed somehow to scramble ashore through the mangroves, swimming as quietly as they could, as any splashing attracted a stream of fire from the Japanese guns. Eventually they slipped away in ones and twos, regrouped and then, heading inland, made their way back to Ahioma. The way forward, along the Government Track to KB Mission and Gili Gili, was now well and truly blocked by scores of disembarking Japanese soldiers.

Following behind the *Bronzewing*, the *Elevala* and *Dadosee* were lucky enough to evade the Japanese, before likewise pulling in at a quiet part of the shore, where, almost under the noses of the enemy, the men were landed and the boats abandoned.

The *Dadosee* had had its own particular adventure. As she chugged down the bay at dusk with her unreliable one-cylinder engine, a tent fly was hoisted as an extra sail to nudge along their progress. Standing beside Private Kevin Hazell at the helm, Captain Leigh Davidson felt comforted by the presence of a large grey ship – an Australian cargo transport bound for Gili Gili, he assumed – which travelled for a time alongside him.

After passing the ship slowly by, a second vessel then loomed out of the darkness, which Davidson thought odd, as there was only room at the small Gili Gili wharf for one large ship at a time. A voice called out from the lookout at the bow, 'Look out, Kev – big ship ahead.' This time the *Dadosee* passed even closer, directly under the darkened side of the great vessel. Then every man on board felt his blood run cold: Japanese voices could clearly be heard on the deck above them.

Calmly, Davidson directed Hazell to steer away from the ship – though not too abruptly – and make for the darkness as quickly as possible. Corporal Bradford recalled of the incident that they were, in effect, 'leading the enemy navy to the common destination. Our quick-thinking helmsman put us ashore, having come dangerously close to a large, unfriendly and well-laden enemy troop transport.'

•

After the commotion of the skirmish on the water, it was Captain Moji's turn to go ashore, aboard a barge loaded with rations. Standing on a sack of rice at the bow, he saw a small beach emerge from the darkness. The shoreline was teeming with men. Korean labourers, working naked in water up to their waists, had already built a rudimentary jetty from sandbags, and equipment of all sorts was piling up beyond the waterline. As the barge slowed, Moji leaped off, sword in hand, into water up to his knees. Instantly the boat was set upon by an army of labourers, who seemed neither to notice nor care for his elevated rank, hauling off the sacks of rations and adding them to the growing piles on the shore.

Moji inspected the chaotic stacks of equipment, including the bombs and fuel drums for the aerodrome. But only a few soldiers could be seen, the rest having taken off down a narrow track, hoping to storm the airfield which they assumed to be on the other side of the bushes. Already runners had returned, reporting that, so far, the soldiers had found nothing but jungle.

One man who did notice Moji was Platoon Commander Mitsumi, who had landed with the initial wave of the Beach Control Unit, and now appeared to be highly agitated. 'Chief Paymaster,' he said standing before Moji and offering a low bow of apology. 'I am very sorry, but this doesn't seem to be the place we intended to land. We seem to have mistaken the landing point.'

A sense of dread came over Moji. This, he now knew, was the reason for the quiet reception. They had landed at the wrong place.

CHAPTER 19

THE LANDING

Captain Charles Henry Bicks should not have been at KB Mission the night the Japanese invaded. Strictly speaking, he should not have been in the army at all. He was, according to the rules, too old to fight.

In the early stages of the war, the government had been happy to allow the ranks of Australia's militia to continue to be populated by officers of a certain age, many of whom proudly wore ribbons from the First World War on their tunics. Since militia troops could never be sent to fight outside Australian territory anyway, and as the Germans and Italians showed no interest in attacking Australia, their lack of modern leadership was not seen as a problem.

Charles Bicks would be turning 40 in 1942. He'd been born in England and arrived in Australia as an eighteen-year-old in 1920. In Brisbane he raised a family and built up a career as a Commonwealth meat inspector. Despite several attempts to join the AIF when the war came in 1939, he was passed over for younger recruits, and so settled for the militia, where he earned a commission in the 61st Battalion.

The looming spectre of Japan, however, forced a change in policy. In mid-1942 it was decreed that 40 years of age would be the cut-off for militia officers to serve in the field; the brutal conditions of the tropics were considered too strenuous for older bodies. In any case, the militia ranks were now being bolstered by young officers who had combat experience in the Middle East. Still determined to serve, however, some older officers fudged their ages to the authorities, becoming known as 'the thirty-nine liars'.

As a man of integrity, the 40-year-old Bicks decided on a more open approach, appealing directly to the 61st Battalion's notoriously strict commanding officer, Lieutenant Colonel Alexander Meldrum. Desperate to serve in action, Bicks declared himself as fit as any younger officer the CO could name and requested special dispensation to serve in the field.

So impressed was Meldrum by the man's spunk that not only did he accede to his request, he put him in command of a company. The appointment proved a wise one. Bicks showed himself to be a leader fine enough to be awarded the Distinguished Service Order, and it was his B Company which bore the brunt of the Japanese spearhead on the first night of the battle.

In the days before the invasion, Bicks' men had been dug in around the Koebule (or KB) Mission, a series of neat Papuan-style huts in a cleared area intermingled with a mix of rubber and coconut plantations, prettily positioned by the shore. When warning was received that the Japanese fleet was near, Bicks sent smaller patrols further east along the track, one of them a fourteen-man section from 11 Platoon, under the command of another capable infantry officer, 31-year-old Lieutenant Herbert Robinson. Robinson was used to the bush, having once been employed in the Queensland forest area of Imbil as a 'saw doctor', or sharpener.

On the night of 25 August, two miles up the track from KB Mission, at a creek junction called Cameron Springs, Robinson and his men crouched in the rain and the darkness, listening to the distant sounds of the firing and boat engines from the direction of Ahioma as the skirmish with the *Bronzewing* played out. Finally, they all thought to themselves, the long-anticipated battle had arrived.

Robinson had chosen his position well, under a spur of the plunging Stirling Range, where it runs down to meet the Government Track. On the spur itself he had placed a man with a Bren light machine gun; further along the track, Private Walther Whitton stood as a forward sentry. He was certain the Japanese would soon arrive at his position, and was determined, if even for a short time, to control it.

In silence, the men kept their eyes on the track through the jungle and the mangroves, listening to the sounds of the barges, and the distant firing, which soon faded. Many were aware that their D Company comrades were somewhere on the far side of the Japanese landing area, and that they too could be coming this way. The appalling possibility of firing into the dark and hitting one's own was real.

At about 1 a.m., Whitton heard rustling and footsteps as four shadowy figures approached along the track. Instead of immediately withdrawing to report to Robinson, the inexperienced militiaman raised his rifle and issued a verbal challenge: 'Halt! Who goes there?'

The challenge received no answer, but only a short pause followed by a series of gunshots from advancing Japanese scouts. Whitton dropped down dead into the mud. Behind him, the remainder of Robinson's platoon opened fire, killing the four Japanese. Robinson, cursing, dragged Whitton's body into the bush and ordered his men to deploy themselves on both sides of the track for an ambush. The 26-year-old bank clerk from Brisbane became the first Australian to die in the fight for Milne Bay.

Twenty minutes later, more – many more – feet and voices were heard approaching. Even now, their identity caused hesitation, and Robinson, loath to risk firing at his own men, even committed the sin of calling out to them; it seemed to go unheard. As a hundred or so Japanese appeared on the track, they pulled up around the four dead marines at their feet, seemingly unconcerned that the men who had shot them could still be in the area.

Now Robinson did not hesitate, and at his shout of 'Fire!' the Bren gun on the spur opened up on the centre mass of the gathered bodies. Some Japanese fell, but the rest scattered and began their standard outflanking manoeuvre – pushing deep into the forest and working their way around to an enemy position – which had proved so devastating to Commonwealth forces in Malaya. Some took off towards the northern, mountain side of the Government Track, while other marines entered the water.

Holding their rifles above their heads, they waded around to outflank Robinson's men from the south.

The Japanese on the northern side soon came under fire from the man Robinson had put behind the Bren gun, Private Latorre, but eventually overwhelmed him. He was never seen again. Robinson saw the trap being set and withdrew 200 yards back up the track to another defensive position, but in the confusion his small party became fragmented. One group of three men vanished, while Sergeant Don Ridley and Private Frank Fraser became surrounded. Ridley had taken a bullet in his thigh, and Fraser was also slightly wounded.

The two men crawled to each other in a small patch of clearing, with Japanese soldiers around them in the darkness. 'Got any ideas?' asked Ridley. They discussed various ways of getting back to Robinson's position, but each seemed impossible. Finally, Sergeant Ridley made the only suggestion he could think of: 'Lie doggo. It's our only chance'.

Adopting a suitably corpse-like posture, the two men lay on the jungle floor until the firing died down and the Japanese approached. Ridley heard footsteps close by, then nothing. The weight of a boot was placed on his back, then he felt the searing pain of a bayonet entering his thigh. Convinced he was living his last moments, he somehow managed to suppress his agony, keeping his body prone. After some brief but terrifying seconds, the Japanese soldier answered a command, and could be heard heading off into the bush to rejoin his detachment.

Remaining still for as long as he could manage, Ridley slowly looked around, and to his amazement saw Fraser looking back at him. 'Christ, you're alive too!' was all they could say to each other. Neither could understand how they'd survived the ordeal.

After applying a field dressing to Ridley's wounds, the two men moved away from the track and up the slope towards the ranges, where, in a patch of open scrub, they observed a group of about 40 men making their way west. Initially wary, they soon recognised Australian uniforms and joined the group: it was the stragglers of D Company returning from Ahioma. All managed to avoid the Japanese, and made it safely back to Gili Gili.

It was reported afterwards that Fraser's hair turned white virtually overnight. Sergeant Ridley's wife testified years later that her husband was haunted by his near-death experience for the rest of his life.

•

In his new position, 200 yards west of the ambush, Lieutenant Robinson counted his casualties and tried to assess the strength of the Japanese force which had landed. But, as would occur throughout the battle, the ability to accurately determine numbers and situations was swallowed up by night and the jungle. As Robinson would learn, this was to be a battle fought in the shadows, amid short bursts of sudden violence where men on both sides had little idea what was happening around them; of surreal images of figures clutching rifles, briefly illuminated by a flare or a gunflash before they dissolved again into the darkness.

At around 2 a.m., one such surreal image presented itself when Robinson caught the approaching sound of an engine and the grinding of metallic tracks. A piercing light broke the darkness, then, to his horror, a tank rolled into view, making its way steadily towards his position, firing a machine gun into the jungle on both sides of the Government Track. This was the first of the two Type 95 Ha-Go infantry tanks brought in the holds of the *Nankai Maru*, the first Japanese tanks to be landed in the entire New Guinea campaign.

Advancing behind the tank's powerful single headlight, Japanese infantry could be made out, walking four abreast. The tank would move ahead, firing its 7.7-millimetre machine gun to clear the path, then stop or even back up to rejoin the infantrymen. With no answer to this new threat, Robinson could only withdraw towards B Company's main position at KB Mission.

The tank approached to within a hundred yards, then Robinson ordered his men to open up with their automatic weapons. The tank fired back blindly into the dark, then paused. Now Robinson took his chance to pull back. All night this pattern was repeated: every few hundred yards, a stand would be made, and gunfire directed towards the advancing Japanese, who would stop briefly before consolidating again.

Eventually, the Japanese brought up their mortars, and the sound of explosions combined with gunfire. Robinson was thankful of the darkness, which concealed the size of his pitifully small group from the enemy, who were undoubtedly convinced they were facing a much larger force.

•

At KB Mission, the sounds of battle could clearly be heard, and were getting louder by the minute. The sinister rumbling and revving of the Japanese armour also now drifted through the darkness, above the noise of the incessant rain. An hour or so before dawn, however, it seemed the entire world had become one giant conflagration as the mission was lit up by a huge sheet of orange flame, followed by a thunderous explosion in the jungle to the north. If there were any still unaware of the Japanese landing, the warships' barrage left no room for doubt that the battle was now on.

As was to become a pattern during the next ten days, the night would belong to the Japanese, while the daylight was the realm of the Allies. Every evening, the Japanese warships, making full use of their nocturnal immunity from air attack, would enter the bay, treating the waters as their own, and attack the Allied positions. Before dawn, however, they would slip out and disappear, relying on the open ocean's murky gloom to hide them from the defenders' aircraft.

On this first night of the battle, the cruisers laid off Gili Gili, while the destroyers aimed their guns at KB Mission, almost close enough for the muzzle flashes to reach the shore. Fortunately for Milne Force, the Japanese naval gunners' accuracy was consistently poor, their proximity to their targets actually hampering their aim. Unable to lower their trajectory sufficiently to cause great damage, the vast majority of the shells wheeled over both Gili Gili and KB Mission, exploding harmlessly in the scrub and jungle beyond.

At KB Mission the barrage was brief but terrifying, particularly when heard by the wary remnants of Lieutenant Robinson's platoon as they approached, with the Japanese not far behind. Making their way over the little bridge bordering the mission's eastern boundary at Eakoeakoni Creek, the Australians might have felt some relief at being out of the jungle. Exhausted, they filed onto the lawns surrounding the neatly built thatch-roofed huts.

A brief consultation between Robinson and Captain Bicks revealed the situation to the company commander for the first time. Robinson thought the open spaces of the mission to be indefensible, and that a withdrawal to a stronger position was required. This would be to the far bank of the Haumo River, several hundred yards to the west of the mission's boundary.

Like a pursuer that refuses to be shaken off, the rumble of the Japanese tank could be heard approaching along the Government Track to the east. Although exhausted, Lieutenant Robinson and a handful of his men doubled back through cover to observe their advancing enemy, closing to within 150 yards of the Ha-Go tank as it prepared to negotiate the narrow wooden bridge.

Like many men of the 61st Battalion, Robinson had grown up around Queensland's Darling Downs, and was well used to handling hunting rifles; indeed, he was renowned as one of the battalion's better shots. Now, he lifted his .303 rifle and adjusted its sight, just as the Japanese tank driver raised his head and shoulders above the hatch to navigate the narrow bridge. Robinson squeezed the trigger and, amazingly, his shot struck the man in the head, killing him instantly. The tank lurched off the bridge, landing nose-down in the mud below. Robinson's marksmanship would hold up the enemy's advance, but not for long.

In the east, the first brushes of light grey appeared in the sky. At Gurney Field, some miles away, the aircraft engines roared to life. The sound reverberated along the northern section of coastline that morning, bringing hope and comfort to the men of the 61st Battalion. Further east, at the rear of their position near their landing areas, the Japanese heard it too, pausing in their tracks to take in its implication. News from their forward soldiers had been scant, but now the question of whether the invasion timetable had been met – it required the Allied airfield to be stormed and captured before dawn – was answered emphatically in the negative.

It was now time for the Kittyhawks to join the Battle of Milne Bay.

CHAPTER 20
THE KITTYHAWKS STRIKE

Just when the RAAF pilots and airmen at Gurney Field believed that no more rain could possibly be wrung from the sky, it turned on a deluge like nothing seen before. In the two days prior to the battle, they recorded over a foot and a half, and the runway reached the point where it seemed to be suspended over a sea of mud. Men bounced on it as if walking across a trampoline, and the makeshift methods the engineers devised to clear the seeping goo were stretched to their limit.

The tension of the living conditions and the inaction was taking its toll. The Japanese had been expected for weeks, and eventually the pilots' adrenaline had begun to stale. The Zeros had appeared sporadically to strafe and attack, but the men were desperate to get their hands on the enemy, particularly as their living conditions, in Southall's words, were devolving 'to a mere existence of mud and muck and misery'.

Squadron Leader Keith Truscott, who had been unlucky enough to be rostered off flying duties on each of the occasions the enemy had made an appearance, was known to relieve his frustration by simply taking off in his Kittyhawk, unannounced and alone, and flying around – sometimes for hours. Where he flew and what he did was never discovered. Perhaps he did it simply to buy himself some time in the cooler air, away from the mud and the heat, and especially the snakes, spiders and other tropical crawlers, which he particularly loathed.

All this changed, however, the morning the Japanese barges pulled up onto the beach at Goodenough Island, offering themselves as target practice for the Kittyhawk pilots. Finally, the men knew, the battle was coming – and they were ready for it.

In the early hours of 26 August, 75 Squadron's Pilot Officer 'Buster' Brown was awake, serving as duty officer at Gurney Field, listening to the sounds of mortar and machine-gun fire several miles away up the Government Track. At any moment he expected the telephone to ring, but for now he was happy to let the men sleep. Over the next few days, he suspected, there would be very little of it to be had.

The quiet came to an abrupt end around 2 a.m. as a screeching whine passed overhead, followed by a tremendous explosion some way off. The guns of the Japanese cruisers had opened up, probing for the airstrip. Brown grabbed the telephone receiver and managed to contact 75 Squadron's commander, Les Jackson, to ask if he'd heard it.

'Do you think I'm bloody deaf?' was Les's characteristic response.

For Jackson, getting back at the Japanese was a deeply personal matter. The squadron's former and beloved CO, his own older brother, John, had been shot down and killed on virtually the last day of the six-week campaign earlier in the year defending Port Moresby. Now, as his replacement, Les would have a chance at revenge.

Soon all the pilots were awake and consulting with their ground crews, who had been working throughout the night in the most trying of conditions to ready as many machines as possible. Well before they could see the runway, the men were seated in their cockpits, praying for the night to pass.

Truscott, enlivened at the prospect of finally being able to get to work, strode over the mud to as many of the pilots as he could, offering a grin and a wisecrack, and assured them that the Japanese had come here for one purpose and one purpose only – to be defeated – and we lucky few were to be the ones to deliver the defeat. Always a natural leader of men, Truscott's enthusiasm was infectious.

Gradually, the trunks and palm fronds around them began to emerge out of a ghostly grey light. Propellers turned over and spun, and fourteen Kittyhawks lined up to take to the air, the roar of their powerful twelve-cylinder Allison engines instilling confidence in the hearts of the Australian soldiers, and dismay in those of the Japanese.

At 5.30 a.m. on Wednesday, 26 August, the Kittyhawks roared off the runway at Gurney into a gradually lightening sky, to begin their own campaign in the fight for Milne Bay.

•

Eight miles away, Paymaster Captain Chikanori Moji surveyed the scene before him, his spirits sinking. For the Japanese, the dawn had come far too soon. The Beach Master, Platoon

Commander Mitsumi, had been quite correct, and they had landed at least four miles east of their intended point. Despite working tirelessly through the night, the several hundred Korean labourers – augmented by the men of Moji's own pay corps, now performing manual work – had yet to complete the unloading and stacking of the mountain of stores, ammunition and rations needed for the Rabi operation. Everyone was exhausted.

Along the beachline, crates, rice sacks and boxes were piled high, but in the encroaching dawn great swathes of material had simply been dumped into the water from the landing barges, whose impatient drivers had no time to linger at the water's edge before shuttling back to the supply ships. With the cover of darkness to be soon lifted, the ships were anxious to pull away to beat the dawn and escape the prospect of air attack. As a result, hundreds of aviation fuel drums, aircraft drop tanks and countless other supplies were floating in the water, to be gathered as best they could and piled up chaotically on the shingle beach.

Moji shook his head. Everything was dangerously concentrated in this one spot. This was not the way it should be done, but at least they were protected from view by the palm trees.

Scant news had been heard from the troops further up the track, but it was obvious that, wherever they were, neither Rabi nor the Australian airfield had been taken; possibly they had not even been reached.

Moji looked around at this small 150-metre strip of beach, which he would later learn was called Wahahuba. The plan had been to come ashore much further west near the Australian garrison, where the distance to their objectives would be short.

But without proper maps, everyone was blind, and now the Australians were fighting back – much harder than anticipated – and starting to inflict casualties.

The sound of aircraft engines drew Moji's attention, and for a moment hope stirred that they were Japanese planes, whose support would soon be greatly needed. Instead, emerging from a cloud like a flock of great dark birds was a formation of American B-17 bombers, having been called up during the night from their base at Mareeba, in Queensland, now heading east in pursuit of the Japanese convoy. His men could just make out an attack on the destroyer *Urakaze*, which opened up a furious anti-aircraft barrage, sending one of the American aircraft fluttering down into the water. A cheer went up among the men on the beach, stirring them with confidence – and leading one of them to commit an error of diabolical proportions.

As the B-17s turned around and headed back, they passed over the Japanese landing activities. Prompted by the success of the naval gunners, one soldier rushed to a quick-firing anti-aircraft machine gun which was sitting among the stores, awaiting transportation to the airstrip once it was captured. Ignoring his comrades' shouts to desist, the soldier swung the barrel into the air and let out a stream of bright-red tracer fire, which sailed high into the sky above the tree line, instantly pinpointing their position for passing aircraft. As the drone of the B-17s receded, a sharper, harder sound took its place: that of the approaching Kittyhawks, who could not believe their luck.

•

Fourteen Kittyhawks had been sent aloft to attack, with another fourteen remaining behind at Gurney to respond to any threat to the airstrip. Leading their men, Turnbull, Jackson and Truscott initially thought their time would be wasted. The targets were the ships, but in the early-morning gloom they had not located them. In fact, they saw nothing as they headed down the length of the bay, so as they came back again they chose to hug the beach, which itself was difficult to make out. Then, right in front of them, a red stream of tracer shot up from the trees like a beacon. Ducking down even lower, the Kittyhawks inspected the shoreline. There, under the trees, was a line of motorised barges and, on the beach, pile upon pile of supplies.

It was this moment, according to Captain Moji, 'which marked the beginning of the nightmare battle of Rabi'.

From a position under cover a little way up the beach, Moji and the 5th Kure commander, Lieutenant Fujikawa, at first thought not much harm had been done, as a couple of the aircraft made strafing runs close to the beach without hitting a thing. But when the Kittyhawk pilots found their aim, devastation erupted. Like cabs on a rank, the pilots took turns to swoop down, line up and press their firing buttons, then turn around and do it all again. Boxes disintegrated, ammunition exploded and fuel caught fire, creating an inferno. Thick black smoke began to rise up, and the shredded crowns of trees caught fire.

Flying Kittyhawk A29-133, 75 Squadron's Pilot Officer Bruce 'Buster' Brown remembered that first morning's attack clearly:

We began in line-astern formation, each aircraft coming in from over the bay and diving at the beach. With our firing run at a selected target completed, we did a left-hand turn over the bay and left again to bring us back for another attack. When we landed at about 7.20 a.m. we had each fired off 1500 rounds of ammunition. We did not carry bombs: the ammunition loading was one tracer, one ball, one incendiary, one armour-piercing and one explosive, which meant that whatever we hit was either damaged or destroyed.

Brown's aircraft, named 'Polly' after his wife, survived the war and is today on permanent display at the Australian War Memorial in Canberra.

As Truscott came in for another swoop, he noticed, bobbing among the fuel drums in the water, the elongated shapes of drop tanks destined for the bellies of the Zero fighters. This filled him with fury. The arrogance of it, he thought: as if they could simply walk in to Gurney, get handed the keys and start using it. 'Over my dead body,' he yelled into his radio/telephone, and urged his charges to target the water. Soon the sea itself was an inferno. Then came an almighty explosion as the aerial bombs, likewise destined for the airfield, cooked off in the blaze and exploded. Now attention was given to the ten or so Daihatsu landing barges, which, as they had on Goodenough Island, shattered under the bullets and caught fire.

In disbelief, Moji and the Japanese on the ground watched their entire supply of food and ammunition vanish. Then all headed for the jungle as the ground they crouched on was targeted by the Kittyhawks. As was to be the pattern, the pilots could rarely see what was beneath the roof of the palm trees, but they raked their unseen enemy nonetheless. Such was the ferocity of the attack, the explosions could be heard by the ground crews back at Gurney Field, who were enthralled to know their pilots were bringing the attack to the Japanese.

Moji's men scattered as best they could. Many were caught as bullets flew in from above or ricocheted noisily off rocks. Moji himself dashed into the conflagration to rescue tins and briefcases containing unit records, before retreating to the meagre safety of a palm tree stump.

All day the Kittyhawks attacked. When their fuel ran low and their ammunition was spent, they would return to Gurney, skid down onto its slippery surface and yell, 'Quick, refuel and rearm!' to their indefatigable ground crew, who in seconds would be crawling over the aircraft like ants. Then off they would go again, firing futher thousands of rounds into the Japanese positions. Later that day, the attack was joined by a Hudson from 6 Squadron, which dropped a series of bombs onto the beach, creating large craters by the shoreline.

It was a spectacular opening bout in which the RAAF pilots and crews performed brilliantly, and although, on that first day, they were all 'tired enough to die', not a single aircraft was lost.

With light fading, the fighters left and the Japanese emerged to assess the terrible destruction. Scarcely a rice grain or a piece of bread was left unscorched. Even worse, the landing barges were now shot to pieces and useless. The Japanese had hoped to use these to coast-hop around the Australian forces spread out along the bay, repeating the tactic which had worked so well in Malaya.

As bad as things were for the men at the landing area, thought Moji, what would it mean for the exhausted – and hungry – men at the front?

Yet the Japanese at Milne Bay were optimistic. Come nightfall, the ships would return and more supplies would be delivered. Casualties, despite the inferno, had been light. The men were still in good spirits, and those green ones had now experienced their first taste of war. They would regroup and continue the attack by night, when the aircraft were grounded.

Indeed, although Moji did not yet know it, further along the Government Track towards KB Mission, the Japanese were gaining the upper hand.

CHAPTER 21
TO KB MISSION

With their Ha-Go infantry tank nose-down in a muddy ditch, its driver dead, and with the sky now full of marauding Australian and American aircraft, the men of the 5th Kure and 5th Sasebo SNLF were forced to pause at their position on the eastern border of KB Mission to await supplies – and perhaps a clearer idea of where their objective actually was. It was becoming obvious that this supposed airfield was not the promised easy jaunt up from the beach. All night they had been marching along this hideous track, and so far there was no sign of anything except mud, jungle and Australian soldiers lying in wait. And where was this Rabi place anyway? Without proper maps, the Japanese had little idea where anything was, only that they were stuck in daylight on one side of a small bridge, with an unknown number of Australians on the other. For now, they would rest and wait.

The Australians were happy for this lull, particularly at Clowes' headquarters, to the rear at Hagita. Colonel Chilton later recalled:

The Milne Bay Battle was often very confused. There were no maps, no real communications – you just didn't know what was going on. We had this rough sketch . . . and that's all we had to fight the battle on . . . you just didn't know where people were.

This included the Japanese, whose exact numbers were still unknown. The most important question, however, was whether it was their main force attacking, or a feint designed to draw the Allied forces away from the base at Gili Gili. Certainly, thought Clowes, it was curious that they had landed so far from their presumed objective, the airstrip. The Japanese were, after all, spoiled for choice in possible sites from which to launch an attack. Clowes could not discount a landing to his west, forcing him to defend on two fronts, nor one from across the Stirling Range to the north, pinning him with a double prong against the eastern attack – a tactic which, as we have seen, the Japanese had every intention of employing.

Then there was the possibility of a direct assault on the long and thinly defended beach at Gili Gili itself, the most direct route to Gurney Field. Until he was convinced that the enemy had fully shown his hand, Clowes would tread carefully, keeping George Wootten's battle-hardened 18th Brigade intact around his base at the far end of Milne Bay.

He was, however, prepared to use some of Wootten's men to reinforce Bicks' inexperienced militia company at KB Mission. The daylight lull would allow a build-up on both sides, which, later that evening, would erupt into one of the most ferocious engagements of the campaign, centred on the hitherto tranquil grounds of KB Mission.

In the meantime, Captain Bicks was ordered to send out a series of fighting and reconnaissance patrols to determine what kind of strength they were up against. The first of these, an eight-man team from 10 Platoon, departed just after dawn under Lieutenant Roger Sanderson, but it was a confused affair. The militiamen of the 7th Brigade were never properly trained in this type of aggressive fighting, which was why Clowes had earmarked them for defensive roles.

One man who remembered the patrol was Corporal Cyril McCulloch. 'We made our way along the track,' he said, 'half on the left side and the other on the right . . . the jungle was very dense . . . our forward scout was approximately 20 yards ahead of the patrol.'

The 30-year-old Sanderson, from Adelaide, ordered his men to fix bayonets as they approached the jungle around Wagu Wagu Creek. Then there was a burst of fire and their forward scout fell. The men fanned out and entered the green wall of jungle, but found it so thick that no-one could see more than 10 feet in front of him. So close were the Australians to the Japanese that the shouted orders of their officer could clearly be heard.

'I could hear Lt Sanderson firing his Tommy-gun,' remembered McCulloch. 'He was the only one with an automatic weapon.'

In the confused jungle firefight, Lieutenant Sanderson and another soldier were killed before the remainder withdrew, none the wiser to the strength of the enemy.

It was here at Wagu Wagu that the Japanese first employed what would become a feature of their attack on Milne Bay: their use of English to throw doubt among the Australians. As English had been taught widely in Japanese schools, many had a passable facility with the language, but even those with no command whatsoever would try it out in the jungle battlefield, with varying success.

'Give up the fight!' was one of the phrases Corporal McCulloch remembered hearing, in what he thought was very convincing English. Other Australians would recall a myriad of false orders, insults and often disconnected sayings and phrases being thrown about during the campaign, particularly in the early stages, when Japanese morale was still high. 'Take it easy! Don't fire! Pull back, Dig! Aussie man go, Japan man come!' were all heard in an attempt to unnerve the Australian soldier, or lead him astray.

Usually the peculiar context gave the Japanese away, such as when 'Keep to the middle of the road!' or 'Good morning!' was shouted in the afternoon. Only one example was recorded of the tactic being effective when a Japanese soldier managed to 'order' some Australians to pull back with a convincingly pronounced, 'Withdraw!' About 50 men from three separate companies fell for it and began to pull back towards Gili Gili via the beach. They were intercepted near the company command post, where they were greeted by Captain Bicks, clutching a rifle.

'Where are you fellows going?' he demanded.

'Sir, we were told to withdraw,' offered the bewildered men.

'Like hell you were,' said the CO. 'This is where you stay!'

The men formed a defensive position around their company HQ, where they remained, still somewhat bewildered, for the remainder of the engagement.

Another, larger patrol was planned for later that day, involving two fresh companies from the 61st, which were to bolster Captain

Bicks and his men at KB Mission, and another from the as yet unused 25th Battalion, currently awaiting the call to action in their camp around Gurney Field. Brigadier Field's orders to the 61st Battalion's commander, Lieutenant Colonel Meldrum, were succinct: 'Take your A and C Companies and push them in ... we must get the job done today in case reinforcements arrive tonight.'

•

Around this time also, an exhausted Major Wiles turned up, emerging from the jungle with the remnants of his D Company, having run headlong into the Japanese invasion force onboard the *Bronzewing*. They had managed to scramble ashore, but had left several of their number dead in the water. Nothing had been heard from them since the invasion.

Their appearance at KB Mission was doubly relieving, as Wiles was one of the few people who could report on the Japanese force firsthand. Captain Bicks had estimated himself to be facing around 150 Japanese, but Wiles put the estimate closer to 1000. Bicks related this sobering news to battalion commander Meldrum, who told Brigadier Field that facing an enemy of that size was far more than his raw company could cope with. Field's assurances of reinforcements only partly assuaged Meldrum's concerns.

The second patrol that day was another messy affair, not even getting underway until late in the afternoon after several hours awaiting the arrival of the 61st Battalion's A and C Companies. When they still had not shown up by the start time, Bicks decided he could delay no longer and began with the forces he had at his disposal: his own B Company and the 25th Battalion's C Company, under Captain Phillip Steel.

Bicks ordered Steel to advance his men up the beach side of the track, while he would move up the mountain side. At 4.30 in the afternoon, with many of the men well aware that by 6 p.m. it would be virtually dark, they advanced up to their start line along Eakoeakoni Creek, the eastern boundary of KB Mission, where the Japanese tank had come to grief.

Private Eddy George recalled: 'As we moved up . . . to take up our positions, I thought to myself – this is not a movie – we are not acting and it's for real. I'd done a bit of boxing pre-war and I felt much the same as the first fight I had, a bit nervous.'

At 5.45, explosions could be heard tearing up the jungle ahead of the men, the results of shells fired by the 25-pounders of the 2/5th Field Regiment, which was situated further back near No. 3 Strip. At the same time, a swoop by the Kittyhawks came in, employing a tactic that would do so much to cement the battlefield cooperation between the men in the air and those on the ground.

Infantry, advancing towards the enemy in the featureless jungle, would aim a flare pistol in the direction of the Japanese lines and fire it above the tree canopy. Subsequent flares of a different colour would denote the distance – in hundreds of yards – to the target. The pilots would then strafe along that line, being careful not to stray across it, lest their own men be put in danger. Over the course of the next week, this would adapt and evolve into the most perfect system the conditions allowed, and help meld the army and the air force into virtually a single weapon, to which the enemy had no answer.

One private in B Company later recounted:

The airmen ... were flying in gathering dusk, through the rain clouds and skimming along the top of the tall coconut trees and perhaps in danger more from the elements than the enemy. They seemed to have a complete disregard for their own lives.

Time was against them on this late afternoon, however, and the pilots of 75 and 76 Squadrons, rather than risk a tragic error in the fading light, soon broke off the attack. The same went for the artillerymen, who no longer felt confident to range their big guns with sufficient accuracy.

From their positions 800 yards away at Wagu Wagu Creek, the Japanese opened fire on the advancing Australians, targeting particularly those seen to be carrying submachine guns, a weapon the Japanese did not possess. Some men crossing Eakoeakoni Creek encountered a virtually sheer bank, which had to be climbed to get to the eastern side. Here, Private Roy Hildred and the other men of Bicks' B Company were subject to withering Japanese attacks. 'Sticks and leaves and bark falling like confetti,' he remembered. Although the enemy did not have light machine guns, he said, 'their firepower was unbelievable'.

In the fading light, confusion set in, with units becoming separated. Communication had been poor, leaving many of the men of one unit unaware of the presence of others. Lance Corporal Errol Jorgensen of the 25th Battalion recalled: 'I didn't know B Company 61st Battalion were there. Never had a bloody clue. That's why we were so confused.'

Finding their small group of eight men out in the open and under sniper and grenade attack in fading light, Jorgensen led his men back the only way he could think of: by the sea. The men waded out and retreated back to their original positions at KB Mission. An order had apparently been issued for them to retreat 500 yards, but they had not received it.

Across both companies now, men were falling back, dispirited by the confusion, the bad light and the apparent Japanese command of the battlefield. The Japanese, growing in confidence – particularly now that night was coming – followed. Wisely, Captain Bicks had pulled his men back to the far bank of Motieau Creek, on the mission's western edge, where the wider spaces and adjacent swampy areas of the mission could be covered and defended.

Lieutenant Robinson, who had led his men from 11 Platoon over this very ground earlier that day, was forced to fight a rearguard action as groups of three and four Japanese began to infiltrate the boundaries of the mission. As night came on, a series of rolling skirmishes took place, with platoons of Australians denying the enemy a firm foothold.

At 9.30 p.m., the Japanese spirits were boosted when the booming guns of one of their destroyers opened up, having re-entered the bay to resume the fight. Again, however, their shooting was largely ineffective, as they were still unable to sufficiently de-elevate their guns. All their shells were therefore wasted, exploding harmlessly in the trees beyond the mission.

The Japanese spent all night trying to force out the defenders. At one point a marine emerged onto the battle area with a flamethrower, which lit up the night with an orange burst. This, however, simply alerted every Australian soldier in the vicinity to the courageous but possibly foolish man's location. A second burst ignited a tree, but when the flamethrower fired again, Private George Orphant, sheltering in the nearby undergrowth was ready:

[T]hey hit the tree with the flame and it went straight up in the foliage. It was quite close to me because they had crawled up close. I don't know how many threw grenades at him but I had a couple of shots at the area before the other boys let him have it.

A cascade of rifle fire and hand grenades poured down on the lone operator, who soon lay dying, his weapon hissing uselessly by his side. The agonised groans of the enemy soldier brought a revelation to Private Eddy George:

I felt good to hear him groaning and moaning and calling for help, before expiring in front of our position. I said to myself, 'you Nips are no super fighters after all – bullets in the right place hurt you too' – my morale was lifted.

•

By 4 a.m., Bicks realised that his prospects of holding KB Mission for much longer were meagre. His men had not slept for two days, and increasing numbers were withdrawing wounded. A tank attack was also expected at dawn, for which Bicks had no defence. With the Japanese slowly beginning to outflank and infiltrate the Australian positions, Bicks ordered a withdrawal from Motieau Creek to the larger Gama River, a mile to the rear.

The Japanese, equally exhausted, were unable to take advantage of their gains. Besides, with the sun soon up, the relatively open spaces of the mission would be a killing ground for the strafing Kittyhawks, which they knew would soon arrive. Far better for them to remain in the safety of the jungle, they reasoned, and wait it out for another attack that evening. Giving up much of the ground they had won that day, the Japanese withdrew to a defensive line beyond Eakoeakoni Creek. The Australians, curious at the sudden quiet, sent a patrol back into the mission to reconnoitre the enemy, only to discover they had departed.

Captain Bicks and his militiamen had performed better than anyone could have hoped, particularly considering this was their first time in battle. As the men of the 61st withdrew towards Gili Gili, the AIF men they met along the track were shocked into silence at their appearance. Finally, the derogatory epithet of 'choccos' – meaning 'chocolate soldiers', who would quickly melt in the heat of battle – was being put to rest.

Private Eddy George later reflected:

I felt really pleased that on our baptism of fire we had done OK and not been moved. My morale was high, also my confidence in my ability as a soldier. I now realise that the hard training and unit discipline which we had endured as rookies, had paid off.

Three officers and fifteen men from the 61st and 25th Battalions were known to have been killed on this evening of 26 August, with a further sixteen wounded and a number missing. Bicks had not slept for 36 hours, but remained alert and responsive to every aspect of the fight. For his cool-headedness in action, he was later awarded the Military Cross.

•

Not that he could have known it, but Bicks had been assisted by another Japanese tactical mistake made earlier in the evening, when Commander Hayashi, who had planned for a major night assault to dislodge the Australians, split his forces at the last minute, ordering the bulk of his 5th Kure SNLF to leave the Government Track and advance on KB Mission through the jungle.

His reasoning was sound – to avoid the traps and ambushes set up by the tenacious Australians along the track – but the jungle proved impassable for his men, particularly at night. In the thick foliage, they became lost and separated, advancing at a snail's pace, forcing Hayashi to postpone his major attack for another 24 hours. It can only be speculated whether Bicks was capable of holding off the Japanese if they had attacked at full strength, but for now his work was done, and as the dawn came up his company was withdrawn.

The main battle of KB Mission would take place that evening, and the Japanese commander would not repeat his mistake.

•

Two hundred and twenty miles to the west, at Port Moresby, General Officer Commanding New Guinea Force, and Clowes' immediate superior, Lieutenant General Sydney Rowell, was beginning to receive increasingly agitated messages from GHQ in Brisbane. General Douglas MacArthur, apparently accustomed to a continuous stream of communications regarding the

progress of any engagement under his command, was not happy
at the relative silence from Milne Bay. George Vasey, Blamey's
chief of staff, and often the meat in the sandwich between the
American and Australian commands, wrote as candidly as he
dared to his old friend Rowell:

> The lack of information from you on the operations at Milne
> Bay has created a very difficult situation here ... only two
> minutes ago I have been phoned by Sutherland [Major General
> Richard Sutherland, MacArthur's notoriously abrasive chief of
> staff] asking me what report I had, and what offensive action
> had been taken by Cyril. I was compelled to answer that I was
> unaware ... You possibly do not realise that for GHQ this
> is their first battle and they are, therefore, like many others,
> nervous and dwelling on the receipt of frequent messages.

What little information GHQ in faraway Brisbane could glean
from the Milne Bay front, however, did not make them the slightest
bit happy. Why had Clowes allowed the Japanese to gain a foothold
in the first place, instead of using every available soldier to push
them back into the sea? According to Vasey, the impression being
given at GHQ indicated 'a lack of activity on the part of our troops
in the area'. Clowes' perceived lack of action led to demands he
immediately throw everything he had at the Japanese.

'Enemy landing at Milne Bay may be a prelude to landing in
numbers,' thundered Blamey to Rowell. 'The land force must be
attacked with greatest vigour and destroyed as soon as possible.'

Hour by hour during the first 36 hours of the battle, Rowell
read carefully GHQ's increasingly febrile requests, opinions
and armchair readings of the situation – and ignored them.

Putting his faith instead in his subordinate Clowes' ability to read the situation on the ground, he delayed the messages, even sometimes altering their intent before passing them on. He sent Clowes short and encouraging missives, such as this, received late in the evening of 26 August: 'Confident you have situation well in hand and will administer stern punishment.'

Rowell's reply to GHQ was less circumspect: 'I took a lousy view of your signal telling us to be offensive as the convoy might be a prelude to further landings. That is very true but you must move slowly in two feet of mud, however much you desire to run.'

The rift between Rowell and Blamey, already deep, became a chasm that would never be bridged, and led to the bitter disagreements which renowned soldier and author David Horner dubbed Australia's 'crisis of command'.

•

On the ground at Milne Bay, however, Cyril Clowes was watching the unfolding situation with his usual sagacity. Although curious as to why the Japanese had not landed – nor attempted to land – at other areas of Milne Bay, he was not yet prepared to risk the defence of his primary resource, his airfields, by committing the main weapon of his counterstroke, the 18th Brigade, to battle.

Nor was he able to glean what the Japanese ships were up to at night, when they had the run of the bay. The sounds of ships and their motorised barges could be heard across the water, shuttling back and forth from the shore, but whether they were embarking more troops, resupplying or evacuating the wounded could only be guessed at. At first light, Clowes waited to receive the dreaded report that fresh forces had been landed at other parts of the bay, but no such news came in. An attack from the north, or even one overland from Mullins Harbour in the south-west, could not be discounted, and for these reasons Clowes felt compelled to keep his main reserve intact, and able to move where needed.

Besides, it was still extremely difficult to assess what exactly was happening. The appalling state of the one main road – along which the battle was being fought – made it almost impossible to maintain regular runners or efficient communications. Cables, recounted one signals soldier, ran 'like spaghetti everywhere in the jungle', and were constantly being cut by the Japanese or worn down by the elements.

The weather, as usual, shrouded everything in mystery. As the official history recounts:

> The rain shrouded the scene, drumming through the trees
> and over the grey sea, turning the roads into morasses. The
> tropical mists added their gloom to the scene so that the whole
> encounter seemed unreal and unpredictable.

Over the next 24 hours, a South Australian battalion would need to draw upon even greater resources of bravery and resilience, as the battle of KB Mission reached its terrible nocturnal crescendo.

CHAPTER 22
CHANGING ORDERS

If, at 43, Lieutenant Colonel James Gordon Dobbs, commanding officer of the 18th Brigade's 2/10th Infantry Battalion, was somewhat more advanced in years than most of his fellow officers ('elderly' is how one soldier described him), it in no way impaired his fighting spirit.

From Prospect in South Australia, Dobbs had come up the hard way, having enlisted as a private in a machine-gun company during the First World War, and working as an accountant during the inter-war years. After serving in the Middle East with the 2/27th Battalion, he was chosen to command the first AIF battalion raised in South Australia for World War Two, the 2/10th, dubbed – with a touch of élan – 'the Adelaide Rifles'. In this, Dobbs' first battalion command, he was eager to give a good account of himself.

Despite being renowned for his strictness, Dobbs, by all accounts, was well liked by his men. On one occasion in early 1942, before the battalion had relocated to Queensland, he personally rounded up a group of privates who had gone AWOL at Sandy Creek, north of Adelaide; he was henceforth known to his men as 'the Sheriff of Sandy Creek'. However, it was his rigour and attention to detail in bringing his men up to the highest standards of physical fitness for which he would be most appreciated by the battalion, particularly when they were to face the almost unendurably taxing conditions of Papua.

Two days into the Battle of Milne Bay, however, Dobbs' battalion had seen frustratingly little action. Having arrived on 12 August in very cramped conditions aboard a small KPM steamer, the SS *Both*, Clowes situated the 2/10th along the outer edge of Gili Gili's defensive perimeter, roughly four miles north-west of the main base, and a mile or so west of the 61st Battalion, which was dug in around the incomplete No. 3 Strip. The tasks assigned to the 2/10th were to secure the northern flank of the Gili Gili base area, to repel any attacks attempted from the northern coast through the Stirling Range, and to work on the wharf, unloading ships.

A few hours after the Japanese landed on the night of 25 August, the 2/10th was ordered to a new position half a mile to the south, towards Gili Gili, where they set up a perimeter defensive position. Later that day, the 2/10th's C Company, under Captain Campbell, was carved off and sent over to reinforce the 61st at KB Mission, but at 6.30 that evening the remainder of the battalion was ordered further away from the fighting, to the outer western perimeter, near Gurney Field. A deeply frustrated Dobbs later remarked that being mucked about like this 'would not have given the Battalion a fighting chance to do a sound job had it been called upon to deal with an enemy attack at dawn'.

As the sounds of the action being fought by Captain Bicks at KB Mission reverberated around the bay on the night of 26 August, Dobbs decided he'd had enough of waiting in the wings. At 4.30 a.m. he buttonholed one of his signals sergeants and made his way towards the HQ of his immediate superior, Brigadier John Field. The unexpected deputation was challenged by a sentry, but Dobbs was determined to see his boss, despite the lateness of the hour. Wanting to know what all the fuss outside was about, Field himself appeared, and ushered them in.

'Look, sir, I want you to let me take the battalion out and have a crack at the Jap!' implored Dobbs.

Though impressed by the man's enthusiasm, Field declined the request, as the 2/10th was currently plugging the hole left when the 25th Battalion had been moved up to KB Mission. Besides, only the overall commander, Major General Clowes, could authorise such a move.

In the early dawn, a disappointed Dobbs made his way back towards his men in a jolting truck that struggled through the mud. Just before 11 a.m., however, he was urgently summoned back, and this time Field was ready to receive him. Yes, Field said in quite a different tone from earlier that morning, an offensive plan was an excellent idea, and Dobbs' 2/10th was perfectly situated to execute it.

•

Things now moved quickly, with the arrival of a series of muddied pieces of information, which prompted a series of reactive moves that would lay the foundations of this most fluid of battles.

Since their early-morning meeting, reports had been processed from those men now returning through the difficult Stirling Range on foot from their positions along the northern coast of Milne Bay, led by Major Harry Wiles. All were exhausted and some in a bad way – wounded, and riddled with malaria. Having briefed Captain Bicks, Wiles proceeded back to Gili Gili, where he repeated his estimation that there were close to 1000 Japanese, possibly more, preparing to bear down on the base at Gili Gili from the east.

More curiously, however, several large groups of the enemy had been observed travelling to the east, *back towards* their landing point. This remains an enduring mystery of the Milne Bay battle. It may simply have been Japanese runners returning to their supply base for rations, or others seeking shelter deeper in the jungle. However, the suggestion, although erroneous, that the Japanese might be *withdrawing* sent a flurry through the command at Milne Bay. To fall upon an enemy in retreat was the goal of every general, and now it seemed there was an opportunity to inflict a severe blow against the Japanese at Milne Bay – or, at the very least, finally ascertain their true numbers, which remained unknown.

At Brigadier Field's HQ, a hasty plan was drawn up: three companies from Dobbs' battalion – A, C and D – would move to the village of Rabi, then climb into the Stirling Range, head north-east roughly 5 miles to a local track junction, swing south towards the bay, and then stream out of the bush to hit the enemy at KB Mission. At the same time, Captain Geoff Miethke's B Company would move directly to KB to meet the Japanese head-on.

Dobbs was delighted. This was just the sort of fast and fluid fighting he had been itching to let his men have a crack at. Returning to his own HQ, he shuffled the makeup of his four companies, stripping platoons from one to make up numbers in another. He described his force as 'a large scale fighting patrol ... if time and space meant anything, we must move lightly weighted ... after having wandered up hill and down dale through jungle looking for Japs'.

Favouring mobility over firepower, Dobbs ordered his companies to carry little more than light machine guns, hand grenades and rifles. C Company's Captain John Brocksopp was ordered to leave behind all his powerful Bren guns, and others were limited to one per platoon, although extra Thompson submachine guns were found and distributed. Only one emergency ration pack was permitted per man, and even such basics as signal cable and entrenching shovels were discarded. Dobbs did, however, allow the battalion a single 3-inch and a few 2-inch mortars.

It was at this point that Dobbs made one of the most controversial decisions of the battle, one which undoubtedly cost lives, and could have affected the outcome of the entire campaign.

Although the exact status and location of the two Japanese Ha-Go tanks unloaded at Milne Bay were unknown, Dobbs became convinced that they had become bogged or been knocked out, and ordered his companies to discard their primary anti-tank weapon, the Boys anti-tank rifle. (One tank had fallen from the bridge over Eakoeakoni Creek, but it had already been recovered by the Japanese.)

Developed in England in the late 1930s, the Boys rifle had been the primary infantry anti-tank weapon during the early years of the Second World War. Just over five feet long and weighing 35 pounds unloaded, it was heavy and cumbersome, and was notoriously difficult to fire, having a tremendous recoil that could break the shoulder of an untrained user. It fired large 10-inch-long bullets, which, at close range, could penetrate the thin armour of light tanks. For understandable reasons, the weapon was nicknamed 'the elephant gun'.

Private John Duncan of the 61st Battalion remembered of the Boys:

> I only ever fired two shots, you have got to pull the butt in and it's got a great big rubber sponge and you pull it in and fire it and boom, they go off with a big cloud of dust and you go back about two feet, it pushes you along the ground.

Cumbersome as the Boys rifle may have been for a mobile infantry force, it was no more so than the mortars they were taking already, and was the best weapon for stopping a Japanese infantry tank. But, if their commander was correct, the 2/10th would not need them. If they did encounter a tank, they could deal with it using another ordnance Dobbs had conversely allowed his men to carry, the infamous 'sticky bomb', one of the most ridiculous weapons of the entire war.

Even though the British Army wanted nothing to do with the 'No. 74 anti-tank hand grenade', a zealous Winston Churchill rushed this large and over-engineered hand grenade into production, oblivious to the protests of his generals. The grenade's operation was anything but straightforward. Upon removal of a pin, two spring-loaded metal hemispheres were released, exposing a canvas core covered in a sticky coating. The grenade was then hurled against a metal surface – such as a tank – to which it would supposedly adhere, and after a five-second delay the nitroglycerine charge would explode. Such was the theory; in practice, the sticky bomb proved complicated to use and prone to accidental breakage.

The worst aspect of the sticky bomb, however, was that it refused to stick. During its trials on Boscombe Down, even a slight film of mud or dust on a tank's armour plate would cause it to slide off, a fatal flaw which would only be amplified in the tropics, where the humidity also corroded the mechanism, reduced the effectiveness of the glue, and even allowed the growth of mould inside the bomb. Yet, this was the weapon Lieutenant Colonel Dobbs ordered his men to take into battle against the Japanese at KB Mission.

Several officers made their objections known, including the battalion adjutant, Captain Theo Schmedje:

> At first we were to go inland and come down from the hills to attack, then we were to go along the coast. Dobbs was ordered to discard this and discard that – 'we'll go out lightly armed,' he said. I would like to have known precisely what his orders were. I was very critical about going ahead without anti-tank rifles. I said, 'Sir, two or three anti-tank rifles wouldn't hurt – I'll carry one myself if necessary.' But he said, 'No anti-tank rifles!'

At midday on 27 August, the 2/10th left its base area around Gili Gili to proceed the few miles to the tiny village of Rabi, when an incident occurred which could well have been considered an omen of the upcoming battle. Travelling ahead of the main body of the battalion in a Bren gun carrier – a small tracked vehicle resembling an open and turretless tank – adjutant Captain Theo Schmedje was stopped on a bend of the Government Track by a sentry, who informed him that 'somewhere ahead' was an anti-tank mine which had been laid down by Australian sappers a few days earlier.

Schmedje looked at him with incredulity. 'Where exactly is this mine?'

The sentry indicated a general area over his shoulder. 'Ah, I don't know, sir,' he said sheepishly. 'It's . . . somewhere around here, and I've got to warn people.'

Scarcely believing what he was hearing, Schmedje informed him that a lot of men would soon be passing, demanded the man not leave his post, and strongly suggested he find an engin-eering officer to remove it. Not having time to sort it out himself, Schmedje continued on his way, avoiding any areas of the road that appeared to have been recently disturbed.

A short time later, however, another Bren gun carrier was dramatically less fortunate. For reasons that were never explained, no sentry was on hand to warn the 2/10th medical officer, Captain Ronald Lyne, and his staff of eight orderlies as they passed by that same spot. Moments later, a tremendous explosion was heard by the men following several hundred yards behind. The carrier had hit the mine, which ruptured its petrol tank and created a terrible inferno.

The first men to catch up were confronted by a horrific scene. The explosion had killed several orderlies outright, and burning petrol was everywhere, including over the men themselves, inflicting horrific burns. The explosion had been so great that the carrier's eight-cylinder engine had been blown clean out of the vehicle: it was found some way up the track.

All nine men on board the Bren carrier, including Captain Lyne, either died instantly or over the next few days. The loss of life was of course tragic, but the incident would have an even larger impact on the battalion, which would now be going into battle without properly trained medical assistance.

•

As the three 2/10th Battalion companies earmarked for the coming battle – A, C and D – formed up a little to the west of Rabi to begin their ambitious push up into the jungle, a runner managed to catch up with Lieutenant Colonel Dobbs and summon him to a field telephone. On the other end of the line was a flustered Brigadier Field. Dobbs was immediately ordered to abandon his proposed trek through the hills, turn around, head straight to KB Mission and dig in.

Before a disbelieving Dobbs could protest, Field cut him off. 'Circumstances have changed,' he said. Another of this day's chaotic events had unfolded.

As one of the last stragglers to arrive back at the base area from the 61st Battalion's D Company, Captain Leigh Davidson had undergone a gruelling 48 hours. Having leaped off the *Dadosee* under enemy fire in the dark, he had led his men through the tortuous hills, evading the Japanese, despite being desperately ill with malaria. Eventually his sergeant had been forced to intervene: Davidson appeared to be leading the exhausted men high into the Stirling Range. Admitting he had no idea where he was going, Davidson sensibly allowed his sergeant to lead his men back to Gili Gili.

Despite his condition, Davidson was asked to report on what he had observed – and particularly his estimation of the numbers of the enemy. To the astonishment of the 61st Battalion's intelligence officer, Davidson said he believed around 5000 Japanese had already come ashore. Although this was a wild exaggeration, it was immediately communicated to Brigadier Field, and accepted as accurate.

Field now ordered Dobbs to forget about traipsing over the mountains and head straight to KB Mission, where he was to dig in and defend. The question 'Dig in with what?' might well have arisen in Dobbs' mind, as he'd previously ordered his men to discard their shovels in favour of mobility. A later 2/10th Battalion report stated that 'at no time during the initial instruction given to the Battalion, had there been any suggestion that it would, or even may, have to fight a defensive action'.

Having prepared themselves to fight a fast-flowing battle in which speed and surprise were to be of the essence, Dobbs' 2/10th men would instead have to position themselves in front of the enemy and wait for him to attack. There was no plan; everything would have to be improvised, and they would have to fight a battle in a manner none of them had trained for.

From mid-afternoon on Thursday, 27 August, the men of Dobbs' 2/10th Battalion began to arrive at Gama River, where Captain Bicks' 61st Battalion men were now situated, a mile or so west of KB Mission. Bicks was deeply perturbed to learn of Dobbs' intentions to defend the mission itself, as the terrain offered no natural defences and could be observed easily by the Japanese ships making their nightly forays into the bay. The mission's firm ground posed a double concern: on the one hand, it was one of the few places in the area where tanks could operate effectively, and on the other, it was extremely difficult for any defenders to dig into and hold. All this Bicks had found out the hard way the previous night, when he'd been forced to withdraw.

Dobbs listened, thanked Captain Bicks for his advice and proceeded towards KB Mission, doubtful that his men would encounter any tanks in the first place. After the battle, Dobbs stated that he 'would never have scrapped his instructions on the word or opinion of any Captain'.

At the tiny village of Kilarbo, Dobbs had arranged to connect with Captain Geoff Miethke's B Company, who would guide him along the last section of the track and into KB Mission. To Dobbs' protest, Clowes had the previous day ordered that Miethke's company be temporarily placed under 61st Battalion command in order to bolster Bicks' position at Gama River. In the previous 24 hours Miethke had come to know the area a little. But when Dobbs rendezvoused with Miethke, he was less than impressed to find him half-naked and bathing in a river.

As they pressed on to KB, Miethke paused by a deep and relatively dry creek bed, and suggested that it would offer an excellent defensive position, as it provided both protective cover and a clear field of fire onto the mission. Dobbs, already feeling tested, simply snapped: 'My orders are to occupy KB Mission, and I will carry out my orders.'

Late in the afternoon, the men of the 2/10th made their way towards the western edge of KB Mission. Occasionally, necks would crane as another Kittyhawk zoomed overhead, sometimes seeming to barely clear the tops of the trees. Then, as the aircraft banked into position, the now-familiar thudding of machine-gun fire was heard tearing through the enemy lines somewhere up ahead. It was a comforting sound, and one which evoked the eternal gratitude of the men on the ground, who understood they were well supported by the fellows in the air.

At around 5 p.m., however, the men stopped in their tracks as another, ominous sound was heard: a crash, the splitting of trees, and then abrupt silence. All knew immediately what it signified: one of the Kittyhawks had hit the jungle.

CHAPTER 23
THE RAAF'S WORST LOSS

It had been another busy day for the men of 75 and 76 Squadrons at Gurney Field. As usual, at first light they had taken to the air, patrolling the bay to determine what the Japanese had been up to during the night. Swooping low along the shoreline, they looked out for signs of new landings and troop movements. Some pilots peeled off to make a similar inspection of the southern shore – one of Clowes' fears being that a landing would be attempted there – but nothing was discovered.

Heading back to Gurney just before 8 a.m., the pilots discovered that the action was happening right over their airstrip. The sky was suddenly full of planes – they'd run slap-bang into the middle of a Japanese raid.

The Japanese air campaign in support of their forces at Milne Bay, severely hampered by the weather as well as by attacks carried out by US airmen on Rabaul and Buna, nevertheless managed to launch a number of attacks, including one the morning of 27 August. From the start, however, it had not gone well for the Japanese.

A force of eight D3A dive bombers, known to the Allies as 'Val', and seven escorting Zeros had been told to attack Allied positions at 'Rabi', but once again the weather intervened and scattered the force. Only half the bombers arrived over the airfield, and their protective cover of Zeros was nowhere to be seen.

To make matters worse, the Japanese command at Rabaul – who were not in contact with their ground forces – had informed their pilots that the airstrip would by now be safely in Japanese hands. Some reports suggest that the aircraft had knowingly taken off from their bases at Buna and Rabaul with insufficient fuel for a return trip; some witnesses claimed to have seen Japanese aircraft preparing to land, before streams of gunfire prompted them to reconsider. Instead of landing on the Australian airstrip, they would have to attack it.

Not knowing whether Japanese soldiers were in the area, the Vals made several confused circuits, trying to identify targets, a judgement they based largely upon whether or not they were being shot at. Eventually they gave up and proceeded to KB Mission, where they dropped their bombs haphazardly to little effect.

A second group of Japanese bombers then arrived, flying up the bay and running straight into the Kittyhawks as they returned from their morning patrol. With no escort to be seen, the bombers immediately jettisoned their ordnance and flew close together like frightened deer stalked by a lion. One managed to slip into the clouds and escape, while the others relied on the fire of their rear gunners for protection.

It worked for a time, but eventually the Kittyhawks gained the upper hand, using side deflection shooting – which sent one Val straight into the water and the other two out to sea. Of those, one ditched into the bay near East Cape, where its rear gunner was captured – one of few prisoners taken during the campaign.

•

Meanwhile, the Kittyhawks headed back to land, just in time for the Zeros to arrive and carry out a series of largely ineffectual strafing attacks on Gurney Field. Amazingly, none of the Australian aircraft were hit, the only casualty being, once again, Captain Eaton's already wrecked and stripped Liberator, which was – somewhat uselessly – strafed for a second time.

The leader of 76 Squadron, Peter Turnbull, found himself under attack as soon as he landed from the morning's patrol, and raced to a gun pit where he pulled rank and took over the gun itself. Whether he hit anything is unknown, but his chances would have been considerably better than those of Flying Officer John Olivier, who stood up in his slit trench and started blazing away with his .38 service revolver. For his foolishness, Olivier received a bullet through his shoulder, which needed to be patched up by the squadron doctor, leaving 76 Squadron needlessly short of a precious pilot.

Still aloft, Sergeant Roy Riddell, a 75 Squadron veteran of Europe, was twisting his aircraft in an attempt to gain advantage over a Japanese pilot when, close by, he noticed his friend Flight Sergeant Stewart Munro in trouble. Caught with a Zero on his tale, Munro's Kittyhawk was streaming smoke as he attempted to outrun his enemy by flying north, towards the hills. It was to no avail and Munro crashed, killing the quiet 21-year-old dairy farmer from Grafton instantly.

Witnessing his friend's death put a bitter taste in Roy Riddell's mouth. The two men knew each other from home, as Munro's parents owned a property close to Riddell's in Queensland. 'We'd both flown together in England, even both been hit over there,' he recalled decades later in an interview with the author. 'He was my friend and I felt pretty strongly about it.'

Noting the markings on the Japanese aircraft, Riddell rejoined the fray of whirling aircraft and, a short time later, found himself in a head-on encounter with the very aircraft which had claimed the life of his friend.

At 700 feet over the base, like enraged bulls, the two aircraft locked into a head-on charge. At that moment, Riddell cared little for his own safety. He simply wanted that Japanese pilot dead. A burst from the Japanese aircraft sprayed Riddell's Kittyhawk, but he knew he had the advantage in firepower. He pressed the gun button on his control column and left it there for a burst that lasted many seconds.

As the two aircraft closed towards each other at 600 miles per hour, spectators on the ground were convinced they would collide. Perhaps the Japanese pilot sensed the Australian's resolve, because at the last second he pulled away. Riddell, seizing the advantage, likewise pulled his nose up slightly, his stream of bullets tearing off most of the Zero's starboard wing. Flipping over on its back, the broken aircraft crashed straight into the bay. Roy felt nothing, except the grim sense of a job done.

The formidable barrage of anti-aircraft fire from the ground was also taking its toll on the weakly protected Zeros, which lacked armour plating, self-sealing fuel tanks and bullet-proof windshields. Two more Japanese pilots left the combat area for the protection of the bay, fatally damaged, both of them experienced members of the elite Tainan Kokutai. Petty Officer Enji Kakimoto's aircraft had ruptured oil lines, while his leader, Lieutenant Joji Yamashita, was trailing a white plume of petrol from his main tank. Signalling 'I am done for', Yamashita headed to attack a formation of US B-26 Marauder bombers, which had appeared over Milne Bay just at that moment. He was reported to have landed a few hits on the American aircraft before breaking away and diving headlong into the sea.

Kakimoto, meanwhile, watched his oil pressure drop to dangerous levels, and his engine began to run rough and overheat. Putting as much distance between himself and the hornets' nest of the Allied airstrip as he could, he successfully put his Zero down on the water and began to swim for the nearby shore.

At this point, two of his fellow Zero pilots, apparently more determined to prevent a downed aircraft from falling into the hands of their enemy than with protecting their own hides, came in to make a series of low and slow strafing attacks in order to sink it. It proved no easy task, and in their repeated attempts to scuttle it, they remained oblivious to Roy Riddell and Squadron Leader Les Jackson, who were prowling above them.

'Les and I were up at about 1500 feet, [and] the Japanese were just above the water,' said Roy. Knowing this was the ideal – indeed, the only – method of tackling a Zero with the odds in your favour, the two pilots swooped. 'Les picked one,' added Roy, '[and] I picked the other.'

Caught unawares at the top of their climb, the two Zeros were simultaneously hit from behind. 'They were so busy trying to demolish the plane below they didn't see us. I hit him from about fifty yards, and he got the lot. They both went straight into the water. We were lucky.'

This time, Roy allowed himself to enjoy the victory. 'I'd been shot at myself over the last few days,' he said. 'I remember hitting the button and letting out a great yell of delight.'

Having survived the crash and made it to shore, Kakimoto was then forced to watch the deaths of his two colleagues and was then captured by local villagers, who presented him to the Australians tied to a bamboo pole. Kakimoto was forced to endure the humiliation of captivity for two years, before leading the famous Cowra breakout in August 1944, in which he committed suicide rather than be recaptured.

In all, the Japanese had lost four Zeros and two Val bombers in this single engagement, for the loss of just one Australian, Flight Sergeant Munro. His remains would not be recovered for another year, in the hills 2000 feet above the Hagita Mission. The wreckage of his Kittyhawk, A29-108, was lost, not to be rediscovered until 1988. Curiously, as had occurred with Albert McLeod's Kittyhawk, part of the undercarriage of an aircraft that was not a P-40 was also discovered. One can only speculate that yet another Kittyhawk pilot had managed to take one of his enemy with him.

Two of the Zeros had been brought down by anti-aircraft fire, and the others by the guns of Roy Riddell and Les Jackson.

It had been a disastrous day for the Japanese airmen, with little damage to the enemy to show for it. For the Kittyhawk pilots, however, it was very far from over.

•

Having spent the previous day on the ground, 25-year-old Squadron Leader Peter Turnbull was eager to get back into the fight. Though a quiet man – some in the squadron went so far as to describe him as 'mysterious' – Turnbull was a natural leader, and seemingly devoid of physical fear. In the Middle East with 3 Squadron he had flown over 100 operational sorties, become an ace and earned a Distinguished Flying Cross (DFC), for which the citation mentioned, among other things, his 'magnificent fighting spirit'.

The strain, however, was beginning to tell. Every day, tens of thousands of rounds were being fired by the endless circuit of Kittyhawks, which would land, refuel and rearm, then take off to attack again. Every available man – cooks, guards, orderlies – worked endlessly to reload the aircraft ammunition belts, which the armourers would then pack into the wing boxes and rush back to the aircraft. Bill Deane-Butcher, 75 Squadron's doctor, summed up the atmosphere in his memoir, *Fighter Squadron Doctor*:

> During this intense flying period the living conditions were appalling. Rain was heavy and our unwashed clothes were constantly wet. With no laundry or showers we were dirty and miserable. Pilots kept flying regardless of diarrhoea and shivering attacks. Tents leaked and there was mud underfoot even in the tents.

The diet of bully beef and biscuits was relieved only
when one aircraft demolished a cow! Cooks converged from
nowhere to claim fresh meat from the unfortunate beast.

Despite being marked by HQ with 'Operational Tiredness', and
being overdue for an extended rest from flying, Turnbull led
the early-morning patrol on 27 August, and was lucky to escape
unharmed when surprised by the Japanese Zeros on landing.
When things had calmed down somewhat, he heard reports from
other pilots who had spotted troop movements heading towards
KB Mission, as well as the two enemy tanks. Roy Riddell clearly
remembered taking some shots at them, recalling that their odd
yellow-green camouflage in fact made them highly visible.

In the late afternoon, amid the urgency of the building
Japanese attack, Turnbull decided to mount one last sortie in
the fading light. Only two Kittyhawks took to the air: his own
and that of his wingman, the experienced Flight Lieutenant Ron
Kerville, an excellent pilot who Turnbull knew was skilled enough
to handle a landing on the difficult strip, even in poor light.

Turnbull was cheerful as they prepared to take off, giving
Ron a slap on the back. 'Don't worry, old chap,' he said. 'If your
engine conks out, just swim for it!' As he was being strapped
in, he quipped to his ground staff: 'Well, boys, if I don't come
back, tell my mum my last words were "Stuff the air board!"'

The two Kittyhawks roared down the runway into the early
dusk, creating the usual spray of muck in their wake. Making a
wide arc, Turnbull patrolled down the coast towards KB Mission,
while Kerville provided cover above. As usual, visibility was
poor, and the trees hid almost everything from view, but just

as the light began to fade, Turnbull spotted one of the tanks as it broke cover making its way up to KB Mission. He banked and made a low, strafing pass, opening up on the tank from just 600 feet. His orange tracer lit up the gloomy sky and bounced off the steel surface of the tank, the shells ricocheting crazily.

Then, when he was almost level with the treetops, Turnbull's aircraft made a sudden brief, near-vertical climb, flipped over and vanished into the jungle below. Watching in horror from above, Kerville made a desperate call over the radio/telephone. 'Red Leader's down! Red Leader's down! Christ! Ground fire, I think. They got him!' There was no fire and no explosion; the aircraft simply vanished, swallowed up by the canopy of green.

After the war, Kerville recalled the event:

Turnbull carried the dive very low and his aircraft, during the recovery, turned over, hit the trees and disappeared into the dense undergrowth. I called up on the radio in the hope that perhaps he was not badly hurt – but unfortunately he was killed.

There was conjecture for some time as to the cause of Turnbull's crash. When his aircraft was found a week later, it was seen to have carved a 100-yard gash across the jungle floor, the trees wrenching off the propeller, radiator, windshield and part of one wing. Turnbull's body was strapped upright in the cockpit, but no bullet holes were found, either in him or the aircraft. It seemed that, brilliant pilot though he was, Turnbull, exhausted, had misjudged his height, possibly clipped a tree and pulled up too quickly into a high-speed stall, transforming the aircraft into little more than a mass of falling metal.

Back at Gurney Field, the loss of Turnbull was received with shock, the ground crew and airmen waiting vainly in the dark for any sign of a miracle. A distraught Keith Truscott had to be restrained from taking off to strafe the Japanese in the dark. When he had calmed down, leadership of the squadron passed to him.

A week later, 76 Squadron's medical officer, Norm Newman, buried Peter Turnbull beside the beach. A machine gun from his aircraft, Kittyhawk A29-92, is on permanent display at the Australian War Memorial.

Later, in a letter to Peter Turnbull's mother, Ron Kerville gave an account of her son's death:

It was just about dusk when we took off together to attack a Japanese tank located on the roadway right on the shore of Milne Bay. Peter was in good spirits as we talked over the method of attack and as we flew out to locate the target he told me exactly what to do if my engine failed – 'Hop out old boy and swim for it.'

He was really happy to be flying again after a few days on the ground. He told me to keep top cover – watch his attack and then follow him in. As I did so, I saw his aircraft dive from about 600 feet and from about 500 yards out to sea. His guns opened fire in a long burst – tracer could be seen flying in all directions from the tank and I could not tell whether it was return fire or Peter's own fire. He carried the dive very low and his aircraft during the recovery turned over, hit the trees and disappeared into the dense undergrowth.

I called up on the radio in the hope that perhaps he was not badly hurt – but fortunately he was killed instantly, for which we were all thankful as the target was 400 yards inside enemy territory. The thought of him being in Japanese hands at that stage of the struggle was not a pleasant one. Although he passed on, I assure you Peter's spirit still lives in the squadron of which he was so proud – we will never forget him.

CHAPTER 24

THE FIGHT FOR KB MISSION

At KB Mission, the men of the 2/10th Battalion had fanned out and searched its 200 acres as best they could. Many were intrigued to inspect the bodies of Japanese soldiers killed in the skirmish with Bicks' men the night before. Some were surprised at the standard of their uniforms, which were well made, with padded helmets sporting the Japanese naval anchor signifying them as marines. Many had leather water bottles – some filled with tea – and neatly rolled puttees around their ankles. Some Australians expressed their surprise at the apparent height of their enemies, having expected to encounter shorter, scruffier men.

In the weakening light, Dobbs now took command of even the smallest detail of the defence, spreading his men in a rough perimeter around the few buildings, cleared areas and small rubber and coconut plantations of the mission compound, personally selecting not only all the defensive positions but also, in many cases, the individual soldiers who would occupy them.

When some pointed out that there were no tools with which to dig in, Dobbs pointed at the many sturdy coconut trees and stumps behind which they could take shelter. At one stage, he mused to a private that the coming battle could well become 'another Tobruk', referring to the epic eight-month siege in North Africa the year before, in which he had played a part.

Somewhat more concerned with the here and now, the men attempted to scoop out the ground using their tin helmets, but found it in most places to be an impenetrable mesh of vines and runners. Battalion adjutant Captain Theo Schmedje was moved to voice his concerns. 'I don't think we're in the right position for defence, sir,' he told Dobbs. 'We are in the killing ground.'

'I appreciate that but we have to get into position quickly as I think an attack is developing,' replied Dobbs.

A reluctant Schmedje had no choice but to accept the decision.

Finally relieved, Captain Bicks could at last withdraw his exhausted men of the 61st Battalion back along the track towards the next Australian strong point of No. 3 Strip. As darkness set in, they struggled through mud that was at times thigh-deep, each man having to hold onto the equipment of the man in front to make their way.

Coming in the other direction, the tail end of the 2/10th made their way towards the mission, the sound of squelching footsteps punctuated by the clanking of rifles and equipment. Occasionally a small torch or match would cast a ghostly pall of light on the passing faces. In the gloom, the two columns of warriors exchanged greetings – 'Good onya mate . . . Well done, Dig . . . Give it to the bastards . . .' as one headed back to safety and the other moved up into battle.

The 435 men of Dobbs' four stripped-down companies were arranged defensively in a rough oval shape, intersected by the Government Track, with Dobbs' battalion HQ in the centre. On the beach side of the track, facing the expected direction of the Japanese attack, was Captain Brocksopp's C Company, with Miethke's B Company beside him on the mountain side. Behind them, A Company and D Company held the rear, under Captains Sanderson and Matheson respectively, with instructions to cover any withdrawal, and to counterattack if an opportunity presented itself.

As it had been impossible to dig any defences, men huddled with their machine guns and rifles in twos and threes around the bottom of coconut and rubber trees, or dispersed among the bushes. A line of shallow drainage ditches cut through the mission to the sea, and these too were occupied by men.

Captain Schmedje spent his time reconnoitring various paths of retreat, should the position – as he grimly suspected it would – prove unable to be held.

Two patrols were sent out east along the Government Track with the double task of determining the movements of the Japanese and locating Turnbull's crashed aircraft, but in the failing light nothing was seen. The final order passed around to every man was, first and foremost, not to move, under any circumstances. In the 2/10th Battalion's history, *Purple and Blue*, Lieutenant Colonel Frank Allchin recalled, 'This being the unit's first experience of a night operation in the jungle, orders were firm that there must be no movement after dark, nor during any fighting, unless along a route that was clearly defined . . . any other movement could be presumed to be enemy movement.'

Captain Miethke remembered it somewhat more bluntly: 'Dobbs said that anybody who moved would be shot at, in case it was a Jap.'

A soft, drizzling rain set in as the men huddled in their positions on the ground. Wrote Allchin: 'The men were quiet and doubtless some seized the opportunity to sleep.' Others kept watch. No smoking was allowed. Minimal talking was permitted, but in any case, no-one felt like chatting.

At around 7.30 p.m., in almost pitch dark, the rumble of an engine was detected somewhere towards the east. It grew louder. Then the changing of gears was heard, making it sound like a delivery truck struggling up a hill; then came a slowing-down, as the vehicle appeared to negotiate a creek or narrow bridge. Over 400 pairs of ears strained to listen above the pattering of the rain.

The sound of the engine grew closer, and paused. Then occurred one of the most peculiar incidents of the entire campaign, as KB Mission was bathed in the sound of singing. Every Australian there that night heard it. From the Japanese, the sound of a single voice – purportedly a fine one – chanting from somewhere deep in the jungle. This was then taken up by a group of voices in a different position, but seemingly closer to the Australians, then by yet another, till all were singing in perfect unison. Hundreds of voices from different points of the jungle joined in.

The cycle was repeated three times, its purpose as enigmatic as the sonorous tones themselves. Whether it was a religious rite or battle song, the passing down of orders, or a way to unnerve the enemy remained a mystery; nothing like it was ever witnessed again in the many subsequent battles in which the Australians faced the Japanese. In the rain, the Australian soldiers listened to the peculiar, even beautiful sounds, and gripped their weapons tightly.

Like nocturnal ghouls, the Japanese marines of 5th Kure slid out of the safety of their daytime hideouts and emerged into the night, armed and ready for battle. Forming their usual lines of four abreast behind the two rumbling tanks, they spread out along the eastern boundary of the mission.

A bright light pierced the trees in the distance, then edged closer. Then a moment of rare comedy, as a booming voice, which turned out to be that of Lieutenant Colonel Dobbs himself, rang out: 'Put that bloody light out!' The order was not obeyed. Everyone saw the joke but Dobbs himself. Perhaps, in his dogged refusal to believe in the presence of the Japanese tanks, he could not now fathom the notion that they had suddenly materialised on his battlefield, or perhaps he genuinely thought one of the 61st's Bren gun carriers was rumbling around with its headlights on. The men, however, knew exactly what it was – and, more pertinently, that their Boys anti-tank rifles were currently several miles away.

'Poor old Jimmy Dobbs – he's lost his glasses,' mumbled one soldier to another as they allowed themselves a grim chuckle.

Twenty minutes later a second tank rolled up the Government Track to join the first, their powerful headlights sweeping back and forth across the grounds of the mission. Then, slowly, they both rumbled forward, and the battle for KB Mission began.

•

One of the Bren light machine guns opened up, the bullets ricocheting harmlessly off the tanks' armour plates. Rifle fire came from everywhere, trying to knock out the piercing lights, but to the frustration of the Australians the tanks appeared impervious to their bullets. In fact, as was later discovered, the powerful lamps were cleverly recessed into the body of the vehicle, shielding them from direct fire.

A burst of machine-gun fire from the tanks' two 7.7-millimetre machine guns swept back and forth, spraying red, blue and green tracer. Beside and behind the tanks, the Japanese infantry worked in unison with the lumbering steel monsters. Time and again the pattern was repeated: the tank would advance with its blinding beam, sweeping back and forth and looking for targets and firing, then halt and switch its light off while the infantry caught up. Then the light would come back on and the firing recommence.

In the scrub around the perimeter, Japanese gun positions were set up and an intense firefight ensued. Small-arms and Bren gun fire poured down on them, and great cheers arose from the Australians as several positions were destroyed. For the first hour or so the tanks stayed close to the Government Track, moving and firing with impunity. Then the dark was suddenly illuminated by fire, as tracer bullets set alight the grass roof of one of the huts; despite the rain, it burned fiercely. Suddenly silhouetted, a section of C Company was forced to escape towards the beach, from where they resumed firing.

To confuse the Australians, the Japanese threw fireworks in all directions, and resumed their unnerving calls in English:

'Stand up, Corporal Smith,' and so on. They also fired mortars and grenades, which sometimes exploded high in the coconut trees. Corporal Louis James recalled receiving 'a shower of red "hopper" ants and the biggest spider I'd ever seen that must have been blown out of the coconut trees right near my face'.

Working in tandem, the tanks drove back and forth among the men, attempting to shoot the Australians or run them down. The Australian positions were identified, and subjected to withering machine-gun fire.

Fortunately, the machine gunners inside the tanks had limited vision, as well as a restricted field of fire, particularly at closer targets. Nevertheless, it became clear to the Australians that, without sufficient weapons to counter them, they had little chance of winning the engagement. Corporal James recalled the frustration: 'I can remember people virtually screaming, "Where are those bloody anti-tank rifles – when are they coming?"'

Realising the extent of his error in not including the anti-tank rifles in the battalion's armoury, Dobbs immediately sent word to rush several forward. Time, however, was running out. With increasing desperation, the Australian attacks on the tanks became bolder, with men using the only weapon at hand which could potentially stop them: the sticky bombs. One of B Company's lieutenants had three at his disposal, but each of them failed. Some, he found, were corroded with mould, or had faulty fuses or detonators.

With incredible bravery, the men of B Company launched attack after attack on the Japanese tanks, hurling their useless ordnance from closer and closer range. Each time, the sticky bombs refused to stick, rolling off the sides of the tanks, and even failing to explode. A little before midnight, the Japanese tank commanders realised that the Australians possessed no weapons that could harm them, and their tactics became bolder. They charged larger groups of men with the intention of running them flat; the Australians had no choice but to scatter into the night.

Nor would there be any help this night from the big guns of the 9th Battery of the 2/5th Field Regiment, whose 25-pounders were situated back towards Gili Gili. The reasons for their non-appearance at KB Mission are contested. Two artillery observation officers – Lieutenants Esmond Gilhooley and Athol Baird – along with a small escort, had been sent to KB Mission to liaise with the battery by telephone, but most accounts simply state that, with the hasty set-up at the end of the day, there was no time for them to be deployed.

Military historian Nicholas Anderson argues, however, that Dobbs himself refused to allow the battery to fire its guns, believing they could not be calibrated or ranged in time, given the available light and maps. According to Anderson, 'the battery proved on subsequent occasions that these concerns were unfounded'.

When the attack came, Lieutenants Gilhooley and Baird, along with their escort, became riflemen and fought alongside the 2/10th Battalion infantry, firing from one of the mission's grass huts. Both men were killed early in the engagement when their position came under heavy fire. Signaller Clem Constable remembered seeing Gilhooley firing his pistol and advancing towards the Japanese, and did not see him alive again.

Aided by the tanks, the Japanese began making a series of frontal attacks on the Australian defensive perimeter, but rarely strayed from the line of the Government Track. Some men reported explosions in the jungle to the north, but these turned out to be feints, designed to draw the Australians towards supposed encircling movements. Not once did the Japanese deviate from their directive to crash forward through the Australian defences, being content to hold the small amount of ground on either side of the track, and from there to proceed straight to their goal of the airstrip.

Parts of the defensive perimeter began to crumble, but in other areas the Australian resistance was fierce. Firefights erupted everywhere. Bullets made odd swishing and popping sounds as they passed through the fronds of trees and the long kunai grass. The Bren guns were found to draw instant retaliation from the Japanese when fired, so Miethke had them shift their position constantly, firing in bursts, but not so long as to allow the Japanese to range on them.

In one such position, Private Bob Abraham – of Semaphore, Port Adelaide, and whose occupation was listed as 'Canister maker and farm labourer' – was attacked by a group of ten Japanese and shot multiple times in the legs. Clutching his Bren but unable to move, Abraham would heroically endure the most terrifying of nights.

Occupying the ground inland from the Government Track was B Company's 11 Platoon, under Lieutenant A.R. Scott, who led a series of desperate counterattacks on the tanks with sticky bombs, only to be let down by his equipment as they bounced off like tennis balls. Lieutenant Murray Brown, commanding 14 Platoon, became infuriated by his impotence in the face of the Japanese armour. 'I emptied my pistol into it,' he recalled.

'I might as well have pissed on it! I was just furious because there was nothing you could do!' At one stage, a tank suffered a direct hit from a 3-inch mortar round, but to no visible effect.

Everywhere, Miethke's and Brocksopp's men performed dozens of astonishing feats of spur-of-the-moment valour, charging into the dark-grey shapes moving towards them, firing from the hip and hurling hand grenades. The latter proved one of the most effective weapons, scattering many Japanese forward thrusts.

Private Jim Kotz, a 28-year-old labourer from Adelaide, grabbed a Bren gun, the use of which had already caused three men to be wounded, charged forward under fire towards a Japanese machine-gun position 15 yards in front of him and wiped it out. Then he turned and ran, again under fire, and scattered hand grenades at three other groups of Japanese who had broken the perimeter and were firing on the company command post. Wounded in the chest, he refused to be carried out; he would walk back with the remainder of his company. He was later awarded the Military Medal.

In the dark, hand-to-hand fighting broke out, with the bayonet used extensively. Private Harry McLennan of C Company – a 30-year-old labourer from Broken Hill – leaped from his position to kill at least five and as many as eight Japanese in the semi-darkness.

At one point the Australians watched as, almost for the first time since any of them had been there, the clouds parted and a bright moon cast an unearthly pale glow over the battlefield.

•

By the early hours of Friday, 28 August, the Australian casualties were mounting: there were around 40 dead and another 30 wounded. Those figures could have been much higher had the Japanese been more accurate with their shooting. As it was, many aimed too high – a common error when firing at night – sending bullets whizzing over men's heads and into the trees. On one or two occasions, soldiers reported being struck by falling coconuts from the tree under which they were sheltering.

While the fight was intense for the men of B and C Companies, forward of the mission, the soldiers of A and D Companies, to the rear, had little to do but lie in their positions in darkness and observe the fireworks of battle occurring a few hundred yards ahead. Many were itching to move forward and join their comrades, but their orders were clear: any movement was forbidden.

Battlefield communication began to break down. All orders and instructions were issued by voice and runners, but with a number of officers killed or wounded, many positions had no idea of the overall situation. Runners were targeted and shot down by the Japanese, meaning some messages to advance or withdraw remained undelivered.

With the Japanese beginning to infiltrate the mission defences, the Australians were forced to move back to avoid being surrounded. In the darkness and with the poor communication, some suddenly found themselves in the midst of advancing Japanese.

C Company, on the beach side of the track, was bearing the worst of it. Their commander, Captain John Brocksopp, a 29-year-old Adelaide solicitor – described by one of his fellow officers as 'the coolest man you ever saw, you would have thought he was at a garden party' – ordered a counterattack, which nearly resulted in the death of one of his platoon commanders, Lieutenant Brown. Moving against a group of Japanese sheltering near a grass hut, Brown emerged to throw several grenades in their direction, unaware of the tank idling beside them. The dreaded spotlight came on, illuminating him like a candle, and immediately a burst of machine-gun fire wounded his right foot and took the top of his left ear clean off. By incredible luck, he escaped by dashing back into the darkness.

Brocksopp concluded that there was now no position left for any counterattack to restore, and contact with much of his rapidly fragmenting company was faltering.

Battalion adjutant Theo Schmedje went forward to assess the situation firsthand, only to be confronted by a group of advancing Japanese. Drawing his pistol, he opened fire and yelled with such gusto that the enemy temporarily scattered, giving Schmedje a chance to turn and run hard the other way. 'We're not bright,' was the profoundly understated message he delivered to Dobbs. Both agreed that a withdrawal was imperative, and runners were sent out ordering a pull back to Motieau Creek, 300 yards to the rear, which the still intact A Company was ordered to defend.

Across the track, Miethke's B Company did not receive the order to retire, but with his 2IC, Lieutenant Scott, already killed, and his men down to just five rounds of ammunition each, he knew his company was fracturing. Miethke later described Scott as 'a very tough, courageous officer'. Scott had been hit in the calf, and Miethke was attending to him personally, when a bullet struck the wounded lieutenant in the throat, killing him instantly.

Having successfully fended off four frontal attacks by chanting Japanese soldiers and their tanks, B Company was slowly being split in two. Some platoons struck north towards the hills to beat their way around to the rear from that direction, while others retreated along the beach. With the Japanese now beginning to break through in numbers, distinguishing friend from enemy was almost impossible, and the risk of firing on one's own in the near-darkness was real.

Caught with a section of his men behind the rapidly advancing Japanese, Miethke led them back towards the creek in a series of fighting withdrawals: one group held off the enemy, while another leap-frogged between them. Eventually they reached the line of the creek. Where the remainder of his company was at that time, Miethke had no idea.

Of the many individual encounters with the enemy this night, few were more dramatic than that of Sergeant George Spencer, a 33-year-old agricultural labourer from the tough Mallee country of eastern South Australia. In charge of C Company's 13 Platoon, which was in position on the coastal side of the Government Track, Spencer suspected the Japanese had observed his unit's location, as their advances seemed to split in two and make straight for him. He watched as B Company, to his immediate left, was hit first, then it was their turn. Around him, Spencer's men began to be hit, suffering terrible wounds far worse than those inflicted by conventional bullets, leading him to suspect the Japanese were using dumdum rounds, which were designed to expand on impact and inflict the worst possible injuries.

One of the tanks began to target his platoon directly, firing a withering stream of bullets into his meagre defences. Men were killed and injured beside him. Spencer knew his position was desperate and untenable. How he wished at that moment for one of the Boys rifles, which at this range could punch a hole straight through the tank's thin armour. Instead, all he had was a small supply of the infamous sticky bombs. He had never used one but had been shown the method: pull the pin to remove the cover and expose the adhesive, then release to trigger the five-second delay fuse. Throw.

With the tank preparing to charge down on their position, Spencer knew it was the time to act. Grabbing a bomb, clipping four grenades to his webbing and holding his rifle in one hand, he turned to the remainder of his platoon. 'Hang on,' he ordered, then leaped forward and ran.

Bullets followed his path, hitting the tree trunks as he dodged between them. Then the dark swallowed him up. Spencer later remembered hearing the booming voice of Lieutenant Colonel Dobbs issuing some kind of command, and made towards the sound of the tank. The 30 yards to the enemy seemed like miles, and bullets again whizzed over his head, some smashing into a tree behind which he had paused for shelter. The trunk, he remembered, was sticky, and in a disconnected moment it occurred to him that these were rubber trees.

Now the tank's light was switched on, and it began to try to trap Spencer in its beam, lighting him up like a moth to give the following infantry a target. A macabre dance began, in which the tank fired and then manoeuvred to keep Spencer in its sights, while Spencer confounded it with desperate sideways dashes into the darkness.

Seizing his moment, he emerged onto the track and, barely feet from the vehicle, pulled off the sticky bomb's cover and hurled it. It hit the side of the tank – and rolled off. Undeterred, Spencer sprang even closer and, like a footballer, kicked the bomb along the ground, managing to lodge it directly between the tracks. Now the Japanese infantry, infuriated at his daring, advanced towards him.

Spencer wrenched two grenades from his belt and threw, then dashed back behind a tree. Iron fragments blew in all directions as the grenades exploded and the Japanese, some screaming in pain, fell back. Not a sound, however, emanated from the sticky bomb, which Spencer realised was a dud.

Bolting back to 13 Platoon, the unhurt Spencer found a runner waiting for him, with orders to return to talk to Lieutenant Colonel Dobbs, who assured Spencer he was going to recommend him for the Distinguished Conduct Medal. He then handed Spencer another sticky bomb, promising him that if he attacked again and was successful, he would put him up for the Victoria Cross.

Spencer assured his CO that he would do his best, but Dobbs was renowned for being reluctant to recommend decorations for valour to anyone, so he was sceptical of his chances.

Returning to his position, Spencer found that it had already been abandoned, and that the tanks had pushed on to somewhere behind him. Looking around, all he could see were advancing Japanese. Pulling back to the reserve line of the scrub, he encountered Captain Schmedje, who informed him that A and

D Companies had also scattered, and that a general withdrawal back to the line of Motieau Creek was in progress. By now the Japanese were all around them, and the best Spencer could do was lead a small party of men from various companies north into the foothills to safety, where they awaited the dawn.

For George Spencer, the battle of KB Mission was over. Although he'd shown tremendous gallantry several times, the recommendation for a medal never arrived.

At the line of Motieau Creek, confusion reigned as the fractured Australian units tried to find each other in the dark. As Captain Schmedje later recalled, 'withdrawal at night in the heat of battle, no matter how well trained you are, cannot possibly succeed very well'.

C Company's commander, John Brocksopp, had by now lost contact with so many of his men that he decided to return with his sergeant, Mick Winen, to locate them. As the two men moved carefully around the now Japanese-occupied mission, they came across a group of their dead and began to remove their dog tags. Engrossed in the grim task, Winen felt a sudden nudge from Brocksopp and looked up. Standing just a few feet from them, leaning against a coconut tree, was a lone Japanese soldier, staring at them blank-faced. The two Australians slowly stood, and the three watched each other in silence for a series of eternal seconds, before Winen and Brocksopp backed away into the dark.

From the Motieau Creek line, a new defensive position was agreed upon, a mile or so back along the Government Track to Gama River. But as the shattered 2/10th began pouring west along the track and through the scrub and jungle, they found themselves amid a Japanese advance in the same direction. In the awful confusion, Australian officers and sergeants called orders to groups of enemy soldiers, and men quickened their pace to catch up with others marching ahead of them, only to realise at the last second that they were the enemy.

CHAPTER 25

THE BLOODY TRACK

There was no confusion as to the intentions of the two tanks which now began to rumble their way along the Government Track, west of the now conquered KB Mission. The efforts to stop them, however, were largely chaotic. Improvised ambushes were hastily organised and badly executed. Sergeant Winen's dairy noted that at about 2 a.m. on the morning of 28 August:

> Within minutes the Japs came down the road behind the two tanks but we never got a chance to use the last of our ammo. Some trigger happy bloke gave the game away and again lead started flying. Lt Mackie yelled to us to get moving and keep in front of the Japs.

Another diary recalled simply that 'there were a lot of panicky troops about'.

As they approached the ford overlooking Gama River, a Boys anti-tank rifle, which had finally been delivered by launch from Gili Gili, was set up alongside the track by Corporal John

O'Brien. Captain Schmedje was seated right beside him. 'He and I were on a little rise on the top side of the road and the tank was quite visible to us,' he said. 'Then he fired. We reckoned that he put a shot straight up the tank's barrel.'

Schmedje's assessment was optimistic. O'Brien managed to get away three shots from the Boys before the Japanese riding on the tank – no doubt startled by the enormous noise made by the weapon – returned fire by way of several hurled hand grenades. In fact, O'Brien had never fired a Boys rifle in his life, having only had a quick verbal instruction on its use that afternoon, which may account for his shots being inconclusive, although one of the tank's commanders was killed. Shrapnel from one of the grenades wounded O'Brien in the arm and a skirmish ensued. For his efforts, Corporal O'Brien was awarded the Distinguished Conduct Medal.

Schmedje dashed over to Brocksopp, who was also taking cover. 'John, we're not going to hold here,' he said. 'I can see them going around us in the bush. Come on, we're not going to sacrifice troops for a stupid little fight like this.'

Captain Brocksopp agreed and pulled his men back into the bush. The rout of the 2/10th Battalion continued.

•

Exhausted and broken, the 2/10th would play no further major part in the Battle of Milne Bay. Now it would be the turn of another of the 18th Brigade's untried militia battalions: the 25th, drawn from the farming areas of Toowoomba and Queensland's Darling Downs.

The 25th Battalion was under the command of another veteran of the First World War, Lieutenant Colonel Edward 'Ted' Miles, who had served in it for over a decade. Miles was said to hold a great affection for his men, knowing a good deal of them by name. It is to be hoped that he had also instilled them with courage: they were about to meet an invigorated Japanese force, and they would need it.

In anticipation of exactly the sort of breakthrough the Japanese had now spectacularly accomplished, Miles had earlier spread his men out along a 3-mile stretch of the Government Track leading east from No. 3 Strip. Closest to the Japanese was A Company, under Captain Basil Ryan, who stood with his raw men to meet the advancing enemy at the village of Rabi. Filing past him in the dark, however, were the retreating remnants of the 2/10th. In vain, Ryan implored the men to stand and fight with him, but these hard men of the AIF had had enough.

After the war, Ryan remembered:

As the 2/10th men straggled through, I made repeated requests for them to stay but the only answers I could get were, 'Not on your bloody life,' or words to that effect . . . the effect that the flight of the battle-trained veteran AIF battalion had on our unbaptised troops can well be imagined.

Ryan was about to learn that the reluctance of the men to continue the fight was not unfounded. Following hard on the heels of the 2/10th were the Japanese, moving up from the Gama River ford. They were now laughing and chatting as they swaggered up the Government Track, and no longer making any attempt to conceal themselves. While still uncertain of the location of the Australian airstrip, they nevertheless sensed that both it and complete victory were near.

Ryan spread his company through the bush on the inland side of the track, intending to ambush the enemy as they moved past, and push them across the track and into the sea. Such was the speed of the Japanese advance, however, that the Australians were still huddled and receiving their instructions when the Japanese arrived. Everyone could see instantly that their small and inexperienced force would be no match for what seemed an endless line of passing enemy troops, particularly as they would be attempting a difficult attack manoeuvre they had never rehearsed, and in the dark.

In an interview with author Peter Brune, Private Jim Hilton recalled that, as the Japanese passed by, 'I could have touched them, they were from me to you . . . they seemed to be going past us for bloody hours . . . they were making that much of a bloody racket they felt they owned the place!'

It only took a brief skirmish to scatter Ryan's force, which had no choice but to head north into the hills of the Stirling Range, where they joined men from the 2/10th who were making their way west to No. 3 Strip and Gili Gili.

Earlier that evening, the 25th's Regimental Sergeant Major, Warrant Officer Ken Barnett, had driven a three-ton truck laden with ammunition forward to KB Mission, but soon became hopelessly bogged in the mud on an impassable section of the track between Rabi and Kilarbo. Making a virtue out of a necessity, he decided instead to disable the vehicle entirely and use it as a roadblock against the advancing tanks.

At around 3 a.m. the Japanese arrived, but once again made short work of the scene. A Company's 9 Platoon put up a fight, but the Japanese quickly surrounded the position, and in the short but intense firefight the Australians were forced still further back along the track. Inspecting the abandoned truck, the Japanese were grateful for the stores of rations and ammunition they found inside, including a case of sticky bombs, which they would later return to the Australians in the heat of battle.

It was another intensely confusing situation, with the soldiers barely able to distinguish friend from foe. Lance Corporal Errol Jorgensen remembered: 'It was that bloody well confused … there were Japanese coming back, and 2/10th fellas behind them, and Japanese behind them. And we didn't know who we were shooting at. Didn't have a clue …'

The 25th Battalion was not the only unit to be rushed in to plug the gap punched by the Japanese at KB Mission. A short time after midnight on 29 August, Lieutenant Keith Acreman of the 101st Anti-Tank Regiment was at his post guarding a section of No. 3 Strip, listening to the increasing sounds of battle from the east. Suddenly, an urgent message – 'The tanks are coming' – was received, and Acreman was ordered to move some of his guns forward to the nearby village of Kilarbo, a little over a mile along the track. He set off quickly with two 2-pounder anti-tank pieces, one loaded onto a flatbed vehicle, the other towed by an American truck. For his protection, a section from the 25th Battalion were sent along with him, although exactly what protection a force of just ten men or so could offer was unclear.

Acreman had surveyed the area in the days before, and decided to situate his weapons on a part of the track which passed close to the beach and also crossed a bridge over a small creek. Before reaching the bridge, however, he was told by an alarmed infantry officer that the Japanese were perilously close. Without time even to dismount his weapons, he reversed the trucks a small way into the scrub and swung the barrels around towards the track.

Hardly were he and his bombardiers in position than soldiers began to appear from the jungle, heading west. Luckily for Acreman, they were Australians. Among them was Sergeant Winen, who informed Acreman that the track east was chaotic, with the advancing Japanese virtually running into the backs of the retreating Australians – and in the dark, nobody knew who was who. He warned that Japanese forward scouts were virtually on his tail and would soon arrive, and suggested the best thing Acreman could do was throw away the breech blocks of the guns and make a run for it. Acreman declined the suggestion.

Soon after Winen's departure, the night sky crackled overhead and a brilliant white phosphorous flare illuminated his position like daylight. Gunfire erupted as Japanese infantry poured around a bend and opened up with rifle fire, which pinged noisily off the anti-tank guns' protective shields.

The escorting section opened up in response as Acreman kept his eye on his gunsight for any sign of the tanks, occasionally joining in himself with his rifle. Years later, Acreman recalled: 'The Japs hit us . . . we heard them but didn't see them except their gunfire.' Returning it to them with small arms, he noticed the sound of the .303s of his escorting soldiers gradually fading. Then, during a brief lull, a gunner remarked in the dark: 'That's funny, not much firing going on.' Looking around, Acreman realised that his escort had withdrawn and they were alone.

At the next gun, a ricocheting bullet killed Bombardier Raymond Vize as he sat in the loader's seat, and Acreman began to run out of ammunition. Suddenly, in the dark, he heard Japanese voices ahead of him – and, even more alarmingly, behind. With the tanks having failed to materialise, Acreman decided to pull out his remaining men, and they slipped away into the dark. As Acreman attempted to retrieve the guns, one truck became hopelessly bogged, forcing him to abandon it. Then, still under fire, he reconsidered Sergeant Winen's earlier idea, and raced around to remove both weapons' firing mechanisms, rendering them useless to the Japanese.

In the terrible confusion of the withdrawal, Acreman was aware that appearing unexpectedly in front of his men could draw a quick response in gunfire from his own side, so he ordered a 25th Battalion signaller to tap into the telephone line to warn of their approach. As to why the expected Japanese tanks had failed to appear, he had no idea.

•

In fact, Acreman had not been abandoned. One of the senior NCOs in the section protecting him was Sergeant Stan Steele, a 24-year-old labourer from Stanthorpe, Queensland. Over the previous few days he had organised the construction of a small clearing on the bottom edge of No. 3 Strip, a few hundred yards from the runway itself, to be used as a dispersal area for the aircraft when they arrived. It was to this stronger position that Steele had withdrawn. In the chaos of battle, however, the message he'd sent to Acreman had failed to reach him.

It would be here, in a small area near the Government Track, the beach and the airstrip, that the defenders of Milne Bay would make another stand. With sixteen men from his own 25th Battalion, bolstered by a few stragglers from others, Steele set up an ambush with Bren guns and rifles. As the terrible night began to finally wane in the eastern sky, they sat under cover and waited.

The first men to appear were more of his own, whom Steele gladly co-opted to his force. To discourage them from continuing to the safety of the airstrip, the imposing figure of the 25th's Regimental Sergeant Major, Warrant Officer Ken Barnett, stood in their path, brandishing not one but two service revolvers he had somehow acquired. 'I'll shoot the next fella that bloody well takes another step,' he growled menacingly. The encouragement proved sufficient, and Steele's small band was further bolstered. Instructing them to lie in lines before the guns, one behind the other, Barnett's instructions were simple: 'When one fella gets killed, the next moves up.'

At 5 a.m., as Steele's men waited, the Japanese emerged along the track and, as one soldier later put it, 'swung right into us'. The trap was sprung. Thompson submachine guns, the heavier Brens and hand grenades cut the Japanese to pieces as they attempted to storm the clearing. Japanese snipers attempted to climb the trees and fire on the Australians but were blown down with hand grenades hurled into the treetops, their fuses set to four- and five-second delays.

At one stage, an artillery barrage from the 25-pounders of the 2/5th Field Regiment – sighted to come down on the clearing in the face of the advancing Japanese – was called off when the gunfire was heard and an urgent message of 'Hold fire!' was relayed to the gunners by field telephone just as they were poised to open up. A 'friendly fire' catastrophe was avoided by seconds.

Around 7.30 a.m. the small battle of what became known as Steele's Clearing petered out, and the Japanese, following their established pattern, retreated to the shelter of the jungle for the daylight hours. Some would even be withdrawn to the rear. Not one had succeeded in breaking through to the far side, and for the loss of not a single Australian life, an estimated 40 to 50 of the enemy had been killed. For his quick thinking and leadership, Sergeant Steele was awarded the Military Medal.

The enemy had been stopped, but no Australian was under the delusion that the halt was anything but temporary. The Japanese would soon regroup and resume their advance, and now, for the first time in the campaign, they were within sight of their goal of the airstrip. Even better for the Japanese, that afternoon a cruiser and eight destroyers were spotted heading south to Normanby Island. Reinforcements were on the way.

CHAPTER 26
THE KITTYHAWKS DEPART

In four days of battle, the Kittyhawks of 75 and 76 Squadrons had expended nearly 200,000 rounds of half-inch ammunition, every one of which was powerful enough to punch a hole through a brick wall. At sunrise each morning, the pilots climbed into the air and sprayed it into the jungles and along the beaches of Milne Bay, seeking out anything that may have arrived during the night. The wrecked barges were fired on again and again, in case repairs had been carried out overnight. So much ammunition was being expended, in fact, that a fully laden B-17 was flown in from Port Moresby to replenish the garrison's dwindling stocks.

The fighters were now working in tandem with the three Hudsons of 6 Squadron, which likewise used every minute of daylight to patrol, reconnoitre and bomb. Not a moment's rest was to be afforded the Japanese. Try as they might to seek shelter and rest in the daylight, the Kittyhawk pilots would do their best to find them and blast them.

Visible Japanese soldiers were always targeted, and the results were brutal, as 76 Squadron pilot Sergeant Ian Loudon stated in one of his combat reports after he had caught a party of Japanese on the beach: 'personnel reeling – staggering – groping – crawling and generally left in a chaotic condition'. Flight Lieutenant Nat Gould of 75 Squadron one morning spotted 30 or 40 newly embarked Japanese soldiers waving at his aircraft, believing it to be one of their own. 'They were initially told the only aircraft they would see would be those of the Japanese Navy,' he later recounted. 'We quickly corrected their assumption by turning around and strafing them. I think we killed the lot of them.'

Later in the battle, he came across a platoon-sized group of Japanese soldiers crossing a stream in the open. Approaching from behind, he opened fire at low level without the slightest hesitation, unleashing a decapitating storm of lead. The massacre left Nat completely untroubled. 'It was terribly brutal, but then so were the Japanese. I felt nothing, not then and not since,' he told the author.

Usually, however, the Japanese were highly adept at concealing themselves under the foliage of the jungle, and the pilots often had to pass several times along the same stretch of coast or track before they could locate anything to shoot at. Sometimes it was pure instinct that told them what might be lurking under a particular clump or canopy, but the flare system the army employed worked well. Another method of marking targets – which was unofficial but more accurate – also evolved: the soldiers would fire smoke rounds on either side of a target. These were spotted easily by the pilot, who would strafe between the two rising columns.

Both 75 and 76 Squadrons worked with an attached army liaison officer, who sat on one end of a field telephone and relayed the daily targets the men in the jungle had requested. Another officer in the operations tent at Gurney Field pencilled down the information and conveyed it to the pilots. In the absence of detailed maps, coordinates were of little use, so the pilots' familiarity with the features and landmarks was of utmost importance. The possibility of firing on their own men was constant, and one or two instances of this did occur in the battle, although no casualties were recorded.

The gratitude the soldiers felt for their aerial weaponry was immeasurable. Gone were the prejudices against the air force, the sulking resentment of the men on the ground having to slog the hard yards while the 'Brylcreem boys' – as the soldiers once dubbed the pilots – returned each day to clean sheets and a drink in their comfortable mess. There was not much Brylcreem to be found at Milne Bay, and certainly no clean sheets.

Indeed, with the niceties and regulations of Melbourne – even of Port Moresby – now seeming another world away, all vestiges of RAAF uniform protocol were discarded. Beards were grown, hair was left uncut, footwear and helmets apparently became optional. One soldier marching back towards Gili Gili on the Government Track one morning was waved at by a passing pilot from his open canopy as he flew towards the Japanese line. The soldier waved back, noting the pilot's distinctive red beard, bare head and apparent lack of anything resembling a shirt.

Flying Officer John Piper resorted to flying his trips in bare feet and pyjama shorts, reasoning that as he had to be up out of bed at dawn, and would grab a nap when he could during the day, he may as well stay in them.

'But what about your boots?' asked a concerned ground staffer, as Piper strapped himself into his cockpit one day. 'If you come down you'll need your bloody boots!'

'I don't care,' was the weary and fatalistic reply.

Disease, particularly malaria, continued to exact a terrible toll from all at Gurney Field. Bill Deane-Butcher would treat a full third of 75 Squadron's personnel, and the levels of infection in 76 Squadron were roughly the same. Many men, though sick, would continue to work, and even fly. Flight Lieutenant Nat Gould simultaneously suffered both malaria and dysentery, but kept to his flying roster nonetheless. 'I suffered diarrhea and vomiting at the same time,' he recalled. 'I would be airborne, and pull my oxygen mask away from my face to vomit while filling my trousers and my boots. Horrible, just horrible . . .'

As the battle wore on, the airstrip's metal mesh was continuously pounded into the slush underneath, until it resembled 'a horrid ribbon of mud'. Ground staff, exhausted and filthy, did their best to scrape the slime off the aircraft, often using their bare hands. They cleared it from ailerons, gunports and undercarriage legs, and took particular care with the ammunition ejection slots, which, if fouled, could cause the spent shells to jam up behind the guns and stop them dead. On wing surfaces, rippling layers of caked mud could alter the flying characteristics of the aircraft. Some pilots reported decreased manoeuvrability and drops in speed of up to 20 miles per hour. Keeping them clean was a continuing nightmare.

The two squadrons took turns – one would be up and fighting while the other was on the runway refuelling and rearming – but the aircraft themselves were being hammered. Gun barrels were wearing out, with pilots reporting that the tracer rounds placed at the end of each belt to warn that ammunition was nearly expended were observed to be firing off in wide spirals rather than directly ahead.

Nat Gould remembers his armourer giving him a quick demonstration between sorties. Removing a well-used barrel from its position in the Kittyhawk's wing, he held it up in front of Nat and dropped a new half-inch shell into one end. Both watched as it slid clean out the other end onto the ground, the rifling having been worn to a smooth bore.

The CO of 75 Squadron, Les Jackson, came up with a novel way of protecting the gun barrels and breech blocks from the mud: condoms stretched over them before each flight. The idea caught on quickly. Prophylactics were standard issue but the men had no use for them at Milne Bay, so they were pooled into general service. But with so many flights a day, hundreds were needed and even these began to run out. A most unusual request was therefore sent to RAAF HQ, and soon a tea chest full of rubber prophylactics was flown in from Townsville, after every civilian outlet in the town was hurriedly relieved of them.

Servicing the aircraft was a virtually impossible task in the primitive conditions at Gurney. The chief engineering officer of 75 Squadron, Bill Matson, performed the same miracles he had achieved at Port Moresby, running his hands over the wings and other surfaces – he was 'like a horse-whisperer', one pilot said – before deciding on the most time-effective way to keep it airborne. Despite the terrible conditions, the two squadrons maintained an average of 28 airworthy aircraft between them on a daily basis. As each Kittyhawk was armed with 1500 rounds of half-inch bullets, it was little wonder the army dubbed them the 'airborne artillery'.

•

By 28 August, with the Japanese closing to within 5 miles of Gurney Field, the decision was made to relocate the camp and move the aircraft out of harm's way – albeit temporarily – to Port Moresby. Squadron Leader Keith Truscott, who had only taken command of 76 Squadron the day before, following the death of Peter Turnbull, was disgusted by the decision, regarding it as a betrayal of the men on the ground. Even worse, only the pilots were to be evacuated, leaving the ground crews to their fate. But the order had come directly from Clowes, who had consulted with the new overall RAAF commander, Group Captain William 'Bull' Garing, who had arrived by Hudson from Port Moresby just that day,

The first thing Garing had done on arrival was tour Gurney Field. He sensed the panic and vowed to put a stop to it. 'If anyone has an escape plan, tear it up now,' he said to the men. 'If anyone has a kit packed to get away into the jungle, throw it out. We're staying and there's to be no talk whatever of escape.'

The Japanese were expected to make an attack on No. 3 Strip later that night, and the prospect of the aircraft falling into their hands was unthinkable. After the day's usual sorties against ground targets, therefore, at 4.45 p.m. the pilots set off one by one for Seven Mile Strip at Port Moresby – just an hour's flying time away – with orders to return at first light the next day. Lifting off the sodden runway, twenty aircraft from 75 Squadron and ten from 76 Squadron – the entire complement of Milne Bay's airworthy fighters – flew away, leaving a strange and unfamiliar silence in their wake.

The pilots left behind without planes were valued even more highly than the aircraft themselves, and so were likewise ordered to evacuate. Once again, 6 Squadron's redoubtable Flight Lieutenant Henry Robertson was called upon, not this time to conduct a reconnaissance flight but to pack his Hudson full of as many young airmen as he could and ferry them to safety.

In the gathering, drizzly dusk, seventeen nervous pilots climbed aboard the Hudson and squeezed into any space they could find. Flight Lieutenant Jeff Wilkinson remembered the atmosphere:

There was a lot of comment because some people thought we were abandoning the ground staff and the army . . . we were so crowded we couldn't sit down. We all had to stand and we were worried that the Hudson wouldn't get off the strip.

It was one of the most potentially disastrous take-offs in the history of the RAAF, as Robertson's overladen Hudson required the entire length of the runway to become airborne: even with his engines at full pelt, the plane seemed destined to career headlong into the trees. Some men jammed into the Perspex nose reported that a branch or two was indeed collected, but in Robertson's capable hands they cleared the jungle, swung to the left and landed at Moresby without further incident.

As Seven Mile's mechanics descended on the aircraft to spend the night carrying out drastically needed maintenance and servicing, the pilots headed for the RAAF Officers' Club in the town. Filthy, bearded and dishevelled, they drank into the evening. When the proprietor threatened to close the bar, the men simply placed their .38 Webley revolvers on the counter. The establishment was suddenly more than happy to extend its hours.

One pilot, however, had remained at Gurney Field. Squadron Leader Truscott had meticulously overseen the departure of all the Kittyhawks, then supervised the loading of the Hudson, offering a joke and seeking an assurance from the men that they would not proceed directly to the Officers' Club on arrival, an assurance that was rowdily given in a chorus of smiles. For himself, however, orders or no, here was where he would remain.

Just before he closed the Hudson's door on its uncomfortable passengers, it pushed open against him, and out stepped another pilot, Truscott's flying companion from their Spitfire days in England: Flight Lieutenant Clive 'Bardie' Wawn, who was likewise going nowhere. Truscott remonstrated with him but Wawn was unmoved. Truscott even threatened to pull rank, but Wawn simply stated that as long as Truscott was staying, so would he. Truscott relented, and as the two watched the Hudson climb away to the west, Truscott patted his old friend's back and quietly thanked him.

The soldiers had been surprised to hear the Kittyhawks taking off again in the late afternoon, then surprise turned to despair as they watched them form up and disappear, their engines fading away to the west. Group Captain Garing did his best to assure the men that their departure was strictly temporary, and that, come the morning, they would return. The soldiers, as cynical as soldiers anywhere, but having come to rely on their airborne artillery, decided to believe that one when they saw it.

The departure of the Kittyhawks may not have been permanent, but the relocation of the RAAF's camp was. In his remarkable memoir *Fighter Squadron Doctor*, 75 Squadron's medical officer, Bill Deane-Butcher, recalled the chaos of the move, and the sense of desolation after the aircraft and pilots had departed: 'About three hundred men were left on the strip including Bill Matson, the engineering officer, and me. We were an Air Force Squadron with no aircraft and no pilots and no-one seemed to be in charge.'

Believing they were about to be overrun in a Japanese break-through, many of the 'orphaned' ground staff huddled in groups to discuss their prospects. None had been trained or equipped for ground fighting, yet many were prepared to defend the airstrip as best they could. Some, wrote Deane-Butcher, checked the meagre stocks of ammunition and reacquainted themselves with their rifles. 'One man had a piece of sandpaper busily sharpening the tip of his bayonet. Some took their guns and set off to join the Army in the fighting.'

Others, meanwhile, were compelled to relocate to the new camp, in the middle of one of the larger coconut plantations, a mile or so to the south towards Clowes' Milne Force HQ at Hagita. This, if anything, was an even more blighted place than the one they had left, even lacking running water.

The journey was particularly torturous for the worst of Deane-Butcher's malaria patients. There being no transport available, the doctor led them himself – a procession of wretched men who could barely place one foot in front of the other – across miles of knee-deep mud. He reported that he himself was 'weary, parched and confused'.

Rounding a bend, he was struck by a surreal scene. In the muck, a trestle table was neatly set up, and beside it stood a smiling man who was wearing an unfamiliar and impossibly neat uniform. 'Would you like a cup of tea, sir?' the man asked, indicating a tidy row of cups and a steaming urn.

From that moment, and for the rest of his days, Bill Deane-Butcher was never reluctant to utter the phrase: 'Thank God for the Salvos.'

•

To the relief and surprise of the Australians, the Japanese did not launch their attack on No. 3 Strip that night. The Kittyhawks, as promised, returned the next morning, their engines re-tuned and replenished with clean oil and new filters. Overnight, the Port Moresby mechanics had also removed the mud with high-pressure hoses, and the US Army Air Corps stores had been plundered for brand-new half-inch Browning machine-gun barrels, which had been earmarked for their own Airacobra squadrons.

The night of Saturday, 29 August was also quiet. Like the Australians, the marines of 5th Kure SNLF, having fought nonstop for three days and nights in the most unforgiving conditions, with barely a scrap to eat, were exhausted. At Steele's Clearing, their advance had been checked, their first real setback of the campaign. For the moment, they were content to rest and regroup, but their immediate objective remained unconquered.

CHAPTER 27
REINFORCEMENTS

The most iconic image of the Milne Bay campaign was captured by the official war photographer's lens somewhere along the Government Track near the village of Kilarbo on 2 or 3 September. It shows a small number of Australian soldiers, their backs to the camera, making their way east, away from the viewer. The men are in shorts and tin hats, their rifles slung over their shoulders. Although their identities are unknown, there is no doubting the historical significance of the moment as, beside them, on either side of the track, like a pair of primordial beasts, lie the two Japanese Type 95 Ha-Go tanks, abandoned.

Exactly what happened will never be known, but the picture tells at least part of the story. Having rampaged their way up the track after being offloaded from one of the larger Japanese barges on the night of the invasion, having crashed their way through KB Mission, and then striking their way up the track and scattering the best efforts of the Australian defenders, having lit up the inky night with their powerful headlights and machine-gun fire, they had finally come to grief a mile or two from their objective of No. 3 Strip – yet more victims of the Milne Bay mud.

Lieutenant Acreman's brave stance at Kilarbo had been prompted by the panicked cry that 'the tanks are coming', but as he and his men of the 101st Anti-Tank Regiment were forced by the Japanese infantry to retreat from their position, he could only wonder what had prompted the enemy to abandon their invincible battering ram. The answer was simpler than he might have guessed: they'd got themselves bogged.

In the photograph the tanks face west, somewhere short of Kilarbo; both are halfway off the path, their outer track sunk into the morass, and one of them is tilted at a crazy angle.

No record exists of the frantic attempts that were surely made to extricate them, but it seems that their 120-horsepower engines proved insufficient for the unforgiving terrain of Milne Bay. In an extraordinary stroke of ill-fortune for the Japanese, both tanks had foundered simultaneously, preventing one from coming to the aid of the other, and no other vehicle had been landed that could pull them out. For the Japanese, it was a disaster. Their armour, which had so far swung the battle in their favour and confounded their enemy, was now dead by the side of the road. From now on, the Japanese marines would have to continue the battle on their own.

•

At first light on the morning of Friday, 28 August, at the Japanese rear HQ in the little village of Hilna, just to the east of KB Mission, Paymaster Captain Chikanori Moji stood in a small clearing beside the grass hut he was occupying and once again turned his ear to the west. In the gathering daylight he remained motionless, listening intently to sounds of the dawn, his hopes gradually rising, until one far-off note caught his ear, followed by another. Above the sound of the birds and the incessant rain, he could now clearly make out the distant throb of aircraft engines.

Moji's shoulders sagged, and once again he cursed this wretched place. For yet another night, the marines had failed in their objective of taking the Allied airfield, and the Kittyhawks would soon be in the air once again. Another hellish day lay ahead.

By this third morning of the battle, Moji could not remember when he had last slept. Communications with the front areas had been sporadic at best. Wounded men had made their way back in small parties, telling of the successes at KB Mission and how the Australians had melted before the Japanese combination of tanks and infantry. For a while, hopes for victory had been high.

Moji knew, however, that the men were hungry. Each night the navy had ferried more supplies ashore and removed many of the wounded, but, come the daytime, the prowling aircraft would attack, forcing the dumps to be established further and further back from the beach, deeper in the jungle. But the Australian pilots seemed possessed with an uncanny second sight, scenting out their targets even here, and attacking them through the cloak of jungle green.

As the morning wore on, news trickled in of a fight at a clearing following the victory at KB Mission which had not gone well. The Australians had lured the marines into a trap, raking them with machine-gun fire and grenades, killing a score of men, before the remainder, for the first time, were forced to pull back into the jungle. This unsettling news however, was upended around midday when Lieutenant Fujikawa, commanding the small detachment of 200 or so men of the 5th Sasebo, rushed into Moji's hut brandishing a small sheet of paper. 'Reinforcements being sent. Secure coastline,' read the message from Rabaul. That very night, the cruiser *Tenryu* would deliver 568 fresh troops of the 3rd Kure SNLF, as well as a further 201 from the 5th Yokosuka. It was the best news possible – and had arrived just in time, as a major attack on the airstrip was then being planned.

Moji, however, tempered the enthusiasm with a question: 'Where will they be landing?' There would be little point, he believed, in the men arriving at the same lonely piece of shore they had mistakenly claimed on the night of the invasion, and the torturous trek towards the airfield would soon exhaust the freshness of even the new soldiers. Further, with the element of surprise gone, they would be advancing on the well-prepared Australians from an expected direction. As Moji said after the war: 'The failure would be repeated unless the reinforcements landed on the other side of Rabi or immediately in the vicinity of Rabi.'

Fujikawa agreed, and arranged for a signaller to communicate with the *Tenryu* and advise the captain to proceed further to the west.

•

At 8.15 that evening, the *Tenryu* led a convoy of six ships into Milne Bay. They were earlier than expected. During the afternoon, despite the low cloud and bad weather, the ships had been discovered and attacked by a 6 Squadron Hudson piloted by Squadron Leader David Colquhoun. In a daring low-level pass through intense anti-aircraft fire, he dropped his four 250-pound bombs on a ship at the rear of the convoy – but for little result, beyond shaking the confidence of the raw Japanese soldiers onboard.

It was pitch dark when the ships dropped anchor in the still, ink-black water, not far from the shore. The signaller frantically relayed messages to the ships, but by the time they were noted the barges had been dispatched, and Fujikawa and Moji heard the familiar sounds of their motors in the darkness. The captain of the *Tenryu*, edgy from the afternoon's air attack, had ignored their advice and landed his men at exactly the same spot as three nights earlier.

Moji decided that the CO of the expedition, currently with his men near the airstrip, Commander Masajiro Hayashi, must be consulted, and headed off along the muddy Government Track to find him. Not far along, however, he encountered a large column of men heading back towards him. Hayashi had made a decision to withdraw the bulk of his forces for a few hours' rest. At the head of the column were the walking wounded. They were in terrible shape, thought Moji, although even the fit men hardly looked in better condition. He recalled:

[T]hey were truly a column of troops exhausted by combat, staggering noiselessly along the pitch-dark muddy road in two columns; hobbling along leaning on tree branches, some supporting wounded around the shoulders, others being carried on backs, some on stretchers. Others had arms in slings, limping and bowed.

These men had endured three days of fighting and with hardly a mouthful of food nor a moment of sleep, their white bandages grubby and smelling of blood.

'Is the CO here?' Moji asked, but no-one answered.

He searched the length of the column but Hayashi could not be found. Returning to Wahahuba, he found that Hayashi had beaten him back to the beach, and was in a deep and tense conversation with the CO of the newly arrived 3rd Kure SNLF, Commander Minoru Yano.

Having just stepped off the boat, Yano looked resplendent, though faintly ridiculous, in stiff white webbing, trimmed moustache and a perfectly pressed uniform. He was keen to get his men into battle. 'Let's go into the attack straight away!' he urged Hayashi as his troops filed off the barges and formed up on the beach.

Moji stood off, but listened intently to the conversation between the two officers, who knew, but did not like, one another from their officer training class. The somewhat imperious Yano was the same rank as Hayashi, but was expressing his fury at his colleague's decision to withdraw his men.

'They're all exhausted,' Hayashi responded slowly, with lifeless eyes. He explained firmly that the men were in need of rest, food and medical attention. It would be unreasonable to expect them to attack immediately.

There was an ominous silence; Yano was not the only one astonished by Hayashi's apparently timorous attitude. Moji later confessed that 'this was not an attitude I had previously heard from a Japanese commander'.

After further argument about which of them was in charge, they found a compromise. With the capture of the airstrip being of paramount importance, the marines – both the fresh and exhausted – would immediately make their way up the track to establish a foothold as far west as possible. Then they would rest, dispersing into the jungle during the day to await the order to attack the airstrip the following night.

Getting as close as possible to the Australians, it was argued, might lessen the chance of air attack, with the Kittyhawk pilots being wary of hitting their own. Hayashi reluctantly agreed to the plan, knowing that his weary men would now have to turn around and slog some of the eight miles back up the track to the airstrip before they could grab some rest.

Captain Moji regarded the young and eager Yano with disdain. 'You'll soon get yours,' he thought darkly to himself. Behind him, the wounded lined up to be transported back to the ships and evacuated. Some had collapsed into the mud; Moji had no idea if they were dead or alive.

The fresh troops of the 3rd Kure were shocked at the condition of their colleagues returning from the airstrip. One soldier recorded: 'From within the darkness, the soldiers of the Hayashi unit came out and scared us . . . according to what some of the wounded said, they had not eaten one mouthful because the food had been bombed by the enemy.'

At 11.30 p.m., with the troops unloaded and the wounded withdrawn to the ships via the barges, the combined force of marines turned towards the track and, each placing one weary foot in front of the other, headed back towards No. 3 Strip.

CHAPTER 28
NO. 3 STRIP

By 30 August, a strange, expectant lull had fallen over the Allied camp at Milne Bay. For two nights following the battle of KB Mission and its aftermath, the Japanese had remained relatively inactive, and signallers from Gili Gili to No. 3 Strip were becoming used to reporting 'All quiet' on the half-hour. For two nights soldiers had sat in lonely vigils, manning soaked machine-gun pits, eyes focused on the black wall of jungle in front of them. Nerves were frayed to breaking point. To exhausted eyes that were not permitted to rest, the stumps of coconut trees appeared to get up and move. Guns were drawn and cocked at the sound of bats; men jumped at the thud of a falling coconut. And still came the rain, soaking and incessant. One man remembered beginning the night in a slit trench with water around his knees. By the time he was relieved in the morning, it was up around his chest.

Now the tide of battle would shift towards the incomplete No. 3 Strip, on the eastern edge of the Allied base. It was here that the decisive action of the Milne Bay campaign would be fought.

As they had done at Gurney Field, the Americans of the 43rd and 46th Engineer Battalions had constructed a considerable piece of infrastructure in extremely trying conditions and in a very short space of time. Using bulldozers and ingenuity, by the beginning of the battle they had carved into the jungle a strip runway roughly 5000 feet long and 100 feet wide, running almost down to the beach in a west-north-westerly direction.

On the eastern side, a long knoll – named after the colonial administration house situated at one end as Stephen's Ridge – met the runway a third of the way down from its northern end, before running back several miles into the jungle. This natural barrier to any approach from the southern beach was augmented on both sides of the strip by parapets of bulldozed earth and tree trunks piled up by the engineers during construction. Beyond the western or Gili Gili side lay the large defensive area where some of the Milne Force units had been dispersed in camps. Behind them was jungle, and more of the ubiquitous coconut plantations.

No. 3 Strip was not yet complete, with the Marston matting still to be laid down. This was not a reflection on the efficiency of the engineers, but due to the proximity of the enemy. For the moment, the engineers had exchanged their tools for .50-calibre and .30-calibre machine guns, although most felt inadequately trained in their use.

Running down the entire length of the recently graded runway was a barbed-wire fence, with a small gap every 100 yards or so, built not to keep out the enemy but to prevent Australian soldiers and other personnel from taking short cuts across the construction site.

The Australians knew that the crucible of the battle would be the point where the Government Track met the centre of the runway before continuing west towards Gili Gili. Approaching from the village of Kilarbo a mile or so to the east, the track hugged the coast for several hundred yards before making a sharp right-hand turn and continuing virtually parallel with the runway before the crossing point. This was the direction in which the Japanese would travel to reach the eastern edge of the runway, while the Australian and American defenders would be on the other side.

The western side of the airstrip, therefore, would form the lynchpin of a comprehensive system of defences. Once again – as Clowes had envisaged all along – the men of the militia would bear the brunt of it.

Having barely rested after their initial defence of KB Mission, Lieutenant Colonel Meldrum's 61st Battalion dug in along Stephen's Ridge at the northern end of the strip, with the men of D Company rushed into the position after their eventful trek back from Ahioma. Ordered to stay quiet and not reveal their position, their task was to block any attempt to outflank the ridge via its eastern side. Shots were not to be fired under any circumstances before the battle, and tins were cleverly strung up on wire at ankle height across the track to warn of the enemy's approach.

At the lower end of the runway, which reached almost to the small beach, were the men of Miles' 25th Battalion. Unlike in previous engagements, here they were properly prepared, dug in, and in possession of a devastating array of firepower that was suited to the conditions – particularly their venerable Vickers machine guns.

Although a weapon of the previous war – it even seemed like something of a museum piece compared to more modern weapons – the Vickers was reliable and deadly. Its drawback for mobile infantry, particularly in the jungle, was its considerable weight, and the fact that it had to be transported in two sections. Here, though, with time to set it up in a static position, the machine-gun companies of the 25th and 61st would come into their own. Lighter Bren guns were also set up, with their fields of fire overlapping with those of the Vickers guns, covering every foot of the eastern side of the airstrip.

Machine guns were trained on the junction of the track and the airstrip, where mines had also been laid; to the rear, several 3-inch mortar teams had been set up. Further back still were the 25-pounders of the 2/5th Field Regiment's 9th Battery. More machine-gun pits were dug by the men of the American 709th Airborne Anti-Aircraft Battery, who placed their 0.5-calibre Browning guns at either end of the strip, and the 43rd US Engineers brought up two of their big half-track vehicles, backing them up to the edge of the strip to provide elevated gun platforms for their .30s and .50s.

In all, several hundred men were dug in along the western edge of No. 3 Strip, waiting for the Japanese to appear, determined they would go no further. For the past two nights, however, they had waited, their weapons at the ready, watching the darkness for movement, but the jungle in front of them had remained empty. Such inactivity was an enemy in itself. With the men constantly wet and unable to get dry or change their boots, their feet were beginning to swell agonisingly, the first sign of 'trench foot', the awful condition that had plagued the men of the trenches in the 1914–18 war. At night the temperature dropped, and men in static positions were denied even the opportunity to move about and warm up.

Two long nights spent waiting, in the dark and the discomfort, for the Japanese. When, they asked themselves, were they coming?

•

At Gili Gili, the past two days had been anything but uneventful, even witnessing the only incident of the campaign that could be vaguely described as comical. On the afternoon of 29 August, the entire garrison stood still, struck by the reverberations of explosions coming from the direction of No. 3 Strip. Instantly the rumour flashed around that the Japanese had broken through and were on their way to the centre of the camp. Panic descended, particularly at the rear. Radios were destroyed, files burned and those who had harboured plans to evacuate – despite the dire warnings of Bull Garing – grabbed their pre-packed survival kits and prepared to disappear west along jungle tracks to Mullins Harbour, or even Port Moresby, 220 miles away.

Others went forward to meet the Japanese, taking up positions behind coconut trees, ready to fire on the first figure that moved in the pouring rain. A panicked signal even reached Brigadier George Wootten, who was told the Japanese were about to descend on positions to his west. 'Well, why doesn't anyone shoot the bastards?' was his characteristic response. In fact, Wootten was sceptical, believing that any Japanese advance in his direction would have been noticed, and he had seen nothing.

The panic even spread to the main store, the quartermaster being told by a group of men passing on a truck that the Japanese were close by, prompting him to lay explosive charges in the canteen and blow up a good proportion of it – creating another large bang, which fomented even more panic.

Soon, however, the decided absence of any Japanese deflated the panic, and Major General Clowes issued a general order to stand firm: no breakthrough had occurred, and everyone should calm down. The culprit turned out to be not Japanese marines but an unfortunate herd of resident Zebu cattle, which the plantation owners kept around to eat the grass between the rows of coconut trees. One of their number had apparently wandered into a minefield and blown itself up, setting off a panic among the remaining animals, which in turn detonated more mines. American machine gunners then opened up on the beasts to prevent them from setting off even more ordnance, before finally, their numbers significantly reduced, they scattered into the jungle.

The panic subsided, but from the men's point of view, the most tragic aspect of the whole incident was the destruction of a great proportion of the store's beer, the remnants of which many did their best to secure.

•

There was no levity whatsoever in the following day's proceedings, which saw a number of small patrols push forward into the Japanese-held area east of the airstrip, and which for the first time revealed to the Australians the depravity of the enemy they were fighting.

Still concerned about the two Ha-Go light infantry tanks, which seemed to have vanished, patrols were sent forward to locate and, if possible, disable them. Lieutenant Aubrey Schindler was selected from the 25th Battalion, and he set off eastwards along the Government Track with a handful of men on the gloomy morning of 29 August. A more stressful expedition can hardly be imagined, as Schindler probed carefully forward along the muddy road. Communication with his men was by hand signals only. Each soldier's eyes scanned the road ahead, as well as the jungle verges, for signs of an ambush, taking note of fresh fronds and branches that had fallen to the base of palm trees, which might indicate the presence of a sniper above.

Having covered nearly 2 miles without incident, Schindler's men rounded a bend a little short of Gama River, where they found the abandoned Japanese tanks. One seemed to have swerved off the road: its belly was jammed up on the verge, its left track unable to gain traction, marooned like a turtle. Surprisingly, they seemed to have been simply left by the Japanese, with not even a sentry to guard them. Schindler later recalled:

> [The tanks] seemed to have run out of juice and were aban-
> doned on the side of the track. [One] was facing in the
> direction of the Strip and all we had to do was blow off
> the tracks (with two blobs of gelignite and a couple of well
> directed shots from a rifle) and destroy the engine. It was
> undefended and seemingly with no Kittyhawk damage and
> no blood stains.

Author Nicholas Anderson makes the valid point that the tanks' demise was in no small way attributable to the shooting of Corporal John O'Brien, who, several nights earlier at Gama River, had levelled his Boys rifle at one of the Japanese drivers and delivered a fatal shot. Though the tank was undamaged, its new driver was apparently less skilled than the man who had manoeuvred it into KB Mission, and on this narrow part of the track had evidently lost control and driven it into a bog. The following tank, trying to avoid it, had also come unstuck. O'Brien's Distinguished Conduct Medal was well deserved.

His feet raw and burning from their many days in mud and water, Schindler was happy to return to No. 3 Strip, his job of neutralising the most significant threat to the Australian infantry at Milne Bay complete.

Another patrol was ordered that day, led by the officer who had already so distinguished himself at KB Mission, Captain Charles Bicks. With just four men, including the redoubtable Lieutenant Herbert Robinson, Bicks set off at dawn to glean as much information as he could about the current Japanese dispositions. After reaching the knocked-out tanks, they cautiously pushed further, past Rabi and towards Gama River, where they began to find Australian and Japanese bodies strewn along the track, dead where they had fallen in the skirmishes of several days before.

Crossing the Gama itself, they made their second gruesome discovery of the day, a former Japanese field hospital. Lying in a row were several Japanese dead, naked except for the bandages covering their leg and head wounds. Then the men noticed that each had a neat bullet wound above the heart. In silence, they contemplated what this meant: their enemy was prepared to kill their own wounded rather than let them become prisoners. There was far worse to come.

Treading down the very same track along which the Japanese had pushed them in panic on the night of the KB Mission attack, the men carefully contemplated every corner, ready to scatter or return fire at the slightest indication of an ambush. In all likelihood, the Japanese were watching them from their jungle hideouts but, loath to reveal their positions to the terrible ground-attacking Kittyhawks, they kept silent.

As they approached the recent battleground of KB Mission, even greater horror was revealed. The Japanese, it seemed, did not confine their cruelty to captured combatants. The first Papuan Bicks' patrol encountered was a young man who had been bayoneted and shot, his hands tied behind his back with signal wire. Then they found another, and still more. Some were tied to trees, having apparently been used for bayonet practice, their heads slumped down over their broken and dismembered bodies. Others had been disembowelled.

Carefully entering the now quiet compound at KB Mission, the four men saw bodies scattered everywhere, already putrefying in the heat and humidity. Some were alone, some in bunches, resembling piles of used rags. Occasionally Japanese and Australian dead were mingled together.

The bodies of the two 2/5th Field Regiment forward observation officers, Lieutenants Gilhooley and Baird, were found beside a hut – and then came the most chilling discovery of all. Tied to a number of trees was a group of Australian soldiers in shorts, indicating them to be from Bicks' own 61st Battalion. Multiple puncture wounds attested that they too had been used in bayonet charges. Their limbs were smashed by multiple gunshot wounds, no doubt inflicted before they died, and their faces had been mutilated beyond recognition. Bicks and his patrol were sickened, and enraged, by the discovery.

In stunned silence, they progressed to where 11 Platoon had made its stand. As they moved between a series of huts a little further on, they heard a trio of chattering Japanese soldiers, oblivious to the Australians' presence. Probably they were bringing rations to their forward positions. Wasting no time, Bicks and Robinson – a renowned crack shot – raised their rifles and killed two of them on the spot. The third, much to their consternation, escaped. The killing did little to assuage their rage.

Turning back along the Government Track, they began the slog back towards No. 3 Strip, trying in vain to process what they had just seen – the cruelty, the barbarity, the utter pointlessness of it all. It was the first they had seen of the depths to which Japan's soldiers were capable of sinking, a level that was utterly alien to them. To kill in battle was one thing, but to inflict such agonies on surrendered soldiers, let alone on civilians, was, to these young Australians from ordinary backgrounds in a peaceful country, something much worse than war. This was a darkness – perverted, sadistic, and far beyond human.

CHAPTER 29
THE GREATEST BATTLE

As the sun began to go down on Sunday, 30 August, the Japanese emerged from their hiding places in the jungle. Despite the day's rest, many were already weary. Days of hunger, acute discomfort and the permanent danger of air attack were wearing them down, even before battle commenced. Like the Australians, they were permanently wet, grossly underslept and suffering the effects of sodden, swollen feet.

There was some room, however, for optimism. The reinforcing convoy had at last enabled some decent rations to be brought up, and the new men of the 3rd Kure and 5th Yokosuka – still fresh for the fight – imbued their weary comrades with a revitalised spirit. Despite the difficulties, the Australians had, for the most part, been swept aside, and just one more effort was now needed to dislodge them completely. The Japanese sensed success, as one marine's diary, captured afterwards, attested: 'The concerted attack has been ordered ... All of us are in good spirits ...

Nothing but serving the Emperor . . . We make our sortie, all hopeful of success.'

It was a simple enough plan: the 5th Kure would arrive at the airstrip first and begin the attack, providing the battering ram to charge the airstrip and seize it. They would then be backed up by the newer units of the 3rd Kure and 5th Yokosuka, as they arrived along the track and were funnelled forward into the battle, before pushing on to the main Allied camp beyond. None of these units, however, possessed the single devastating weapon for which the Australians had found no answer: the tanks.

The Japanese marines were confronted with their once mighty metal monsters as they moved up the track. The implications of their demise dawned slowly on the soldiers as, quiet with dread, they passed them by. Their most potent weapon now would be a handful of anti-tank guns, which could also be used for infantry support. But these were heavy – over 660 pounds – and had spoked wooden wheels which stuck constantly in the mud, and had to pulled out by the cursing, exhausted men.

It had been a difficult night's march westward, with the 5th Kure's Commander Hayashi once again leading the way. The newer units found the track particularly hard going. Their light split-toe boots were sucked off in the mud, and in the rain and the dark, men tripped and stumbled. Soon, large gaps opened in the line of advance between the units. The progress began to slow, then backed up and stalled around Wahahuba Beach where they had started.

It was past 2 a.m. when the first elements of the 5th Kure reached Kilarbo. Some men were surprised at the lack of resistance they met, at each bend expecting to be fired upon, but the jungle on this night was silent. What were the Australians up to? Where were the ambushes and roadblocks that they'd met along this road during the previous night attacks? Had the enemy already retreated? Had the road to the airstrip and the base beyond been abandoned?

The sky was thick with cloud and drizzle and offered no light. The soldiers placed white paper discs on the backs of their helmets for those behind to see, and officers donned white armbands so they could be recognised, but even these were virtually invisible in the gloomy tropical night.

Just before 3 a.m., the first elements of the 5th Kure reached the point where the track met the airstrip, and they began to fan out along its western edge, taking up positions behind the line of logs and earth which the American engineers had thought-fully provided, making as little noise as possible. Occasionally, brief patches of moonlight would allow them to catch a shadowy glimpse of the almost mystical prize that had so far eluded them: the Allied airstrip. The entire battle thus far had led to this, and now all they had to do was take it.

The Japanese had no idea that there was more than one airstrip at Milne Bay, or that the one before them was not the home of the harassing Kittyhawks, nor even was it yet operational. Nevertheless, they believed that this airstrip – and, by implication, the entire Allied base at 'Rabi' – was now within their grasp.

Each man made a short, silent prayer to his parents, and some to the Emperor, and awaited the signal. The decisive engagement of the fight for Milne Bay was about to begin.

•

On the other side of No. 3 Strip, the Australians and a handful of Americans had settled in for another long, wet and uncomfortable night. Whether it would bring a Japanese attack was still unknown. Men huddled under groundsheets, some smoking cigarettes, with the light carefully concealed. Some chatted quietly, in short bursts, but their eyes and ears remained cocked towards the blackness ahead.

Suddenly, 150 yards from the eastern side of the strip, a loud metallic *clang* was heard. From an observation post near the parked US half-tracks, the Australians sent up a flare. Some men remembered it as red, others white. In any case, in its ghostly illumination – like a great, seething carpet of olive-grey – a huddled mass of uniformed men was revealed. Every man on the western side saw it, and a collective gasp went up. How had the Japanese managed to get so close without being noticed? Now everyone waited for the word to attack.

There was a brief lull, during which both sides could throw away their cloaks of concealment and prepare for battle. Unlike at KB Mission, no chanting came from the Japanese side, but there was plenty of shouting. One voice was heard over the top of the cacophony, stating in excellent English: 'It's no use, we're coming over!' To which the indomitable Regimental Sergeant Major of the 25th Battalion, Warrant Officer Ken Barnett, was heard to reply, in his booming sergeant major's voice, 'Pig's arse you are! Hit 'em with everything you've got!' The words immediately inscribed themselves into Australian military folklore. No more encouragement was needed, and the silent black sky was split open by a storm of gunfire.

At first the Japanese were protected from the bullets by the earth and log barrier. A few mortar rounds landed but they were sporadic and wide.

In a command post near the half-tracks, Lieutenant Keith Acreman, who had ranged his anti-tank guns on the Japanese at Kilarbo a few nights earlier, assessed the situation in front of him:

> [A] flare went up from our lines and an Australian machine-gunner opened up. More flares went up and more Australian firing took place but I think the enemy had not been identified until they opened fire. Then it became obvious that they were forming up on the eastern side of the Strip near its junction with the road . . . It turned out later that this was not an isolated pocket of Japanese but the main body which had dragged up some of their mountain guns and machine guns on wheels. All this had been done so quietly that none of us in the Troop saw or heard anything. When the Japanese started firing, we all took up positions.

As at Kilarbo, however, the quick-thinking Acreman executed a piece of action which would have a profound bearing on the battle. Earlier that afternoon, in the waning hours of daylight, he had arranged for a signals officer to run a telephone line to his position, connected to the rear. Observing that both mortar crews were firing off target, he picked up the receiver of the field telephone, gave the dynamo handle a few cranks and asked to be connected to the mortar officer, Lieutenant Schindler, whose patrol had recently discovered the stranded Japanese tanks.

'You're dropping short,' said Acreman. 'Quick, give me a ranging shot on the road and the strip.' Almost instantaneously, a whistling projectile dropped from the charcoal-black sky, landing a few feet away from Acreman's position. It happened to be a dud, but it told Acreman what he needed to know. The mortars were targeting the junction of the airstrip and the Government Track, but on its western, not eastern side.

Instantly, Acreman gave the vital correction: 'Up 400, go!' Then, over his shoulder, he shouted a one-word order to all who could hear it: 'Gunfire!'

Simultaneously, the Japanese emerged from behind their protective earth barrier to make their first attack on the airstrip, and every machine gun, rifle and mortar let loose.

Lurid colours lit up the night. Tracers made darting lines back and forth as the Vickers and Brens opened up, and the Japanese returned fire with their Type 92 'woodpecker' machine guns, with their distinct punctuating, 'peck' sound. It was a powerful weapon, but crippled by its slow rate of fire.

Then the mortars arrived. Like an artillery barrage, Schindler's men poured round after round on the Japanese side of the runway. The infantrymen were amazed by their rate of fire, and convinced that it could not possibly be coming from only two crews. It was carnage. Shrapnel from mortar blasts tore off limbs and heads, and hurled body parts up into the trees, obliterating the first line of the Japanese attack. Hardly any managed to lay so much as a foot on the runway before being cut to pieces.

From their position up on Stephen's Ridge, a few hundred yards away, the men of the 61st Battalion looked down the length of the runway and were awestruck by what they saw. 'It was a pretty sight,' one of them said, 'the tracers just kept going and going and going . . .' One of the American engineers likened it to the Fourth of July, and recalled that with all the tracer flying about, he had enough light to read a map or even a newspaper.

Flares of various colours tore the cover of darkness from the attacking Japanese, exposing their ranks, which were then targeted by the overlapping belts of Vickers and Bren machine-gun fire. Now verbal orders shouted back corrections to Schindler's mortars. 'Up 50, 2 degrees right! Now up 10!'

The Japanese, in desperation, chose their best English speakers to shout countermanding corrections. Some Australians were taken aback at their powers of mimicry, but the men on the mortars were not easily fooled. If a specific target could not be found, Schindler directed his men to aim for the trees just behind the Japanese, causing devastating tree bursts that would blast wood into the Japanese soldiers, causing horrendous wounds.

Hayashi dared not peer over the earth parapet, but he could see that this first attack was failing. Men were falling everywhere. He quickly ordered a company commander to make a secondary attack on the Australian line down towards the sea end of the strip, but only ten fit men could be found to carry it out. The leading elements of the 3rd Kure had begun to arrive, but they became jammed up behind those of the 5th Kure, and could not fire for fear of hitting their countrymen in the back. Attempts were made to set up their 37-millimetre anti-tank guns, but the Australian mortars discovered them under the flares and ranged in mercilessly.

Not that the mortar crews were immune from danger themselves. Being a mere 250 yards from their targets, their muzzle flashes attracted fierce retaliation from the Japanese machine gunners. What amounted to a duel ensued, as each position attempted to knock out the other.

•

The battle of No. 3 Strip was particularly vivid for the handful of young Americans of the US 43rd Engineering Regiment, who would distinguish themselves as being the very first Americans to go into combat against the Japanese in the south-west Pacific – a task for which they were wholly untrained. Having been instructed in the skills of engineering and construction, these men were far better acquainted with bulldozers than machine guns; even their basic military training had been minimal. This, however, in no way dampened their enthusiasm for fighting alongside the Australians, for whose benefit they had been toiling these past weeks building the airstrips of Milne Bay.

Staff Sergeant Sidney Sleeth, of Rochester, Minnesota, was not supposed to even be at No. 3 Strip. As ordered by the 43rd's CO, Major Ludlow Adams, his job had been to deliver supplies to the Australians and then to proceed back to Gili Gili, out of harm's way. Deciding he wanted a story to tell his grandchildren, however, he adopted the Australian vernacular and declared, 'Bugger the Major! I'm staying to see what's going to happen here tonight.' Sleeth joined a group of fellow engineers assigned to the guns atop the two US half-tracks. In the quiet hours before the fight, he had surprised his pal (and fellow Minnesotan) Corporal Lionel Jierre by climbing onto one of the vehicle's decks and declaring himself ready for action.

The Australians were more than grateful for the presence of the Americans and their half-tracks, not just for their firepower but for the added height their armoured steel plating afforded them as they observed the enemy positions across the strip. Mostly the Australians had to be content with assessing the enemy from ground level, behind their low barrier of earth and logs.

After several wet and miserable hours in the dark, just before 3 a.m. Jierre heard noise from the other side of the strip and watched an Australian flare sail into the sky. 'This looks like the big thing,' he said to his crew, rousing them from under groundsheets. Suddenly the peaceful, rainy tropical night became a bedlam of noise.

There being room enough in the half-tracks for only a handful of men, the other Americans were dispersed among the Australians on the ground. One corporal hit upon the idea of filling the magazine of his Thompson entirely with tracer bullets, so he could light a path to a Japanese machine-gun position he had spotted in the gloom on the other side. Above him in the half-track, the American gunners opened up with their larger half-inch and .3-calibre weapons. Sergeant Paul Marquis and Private Henry Coffman recalled expending no less than 900 rounds between them. 'The barrels of our machine-guns were so hot they shone like Neon lights,' Coffman later recalled. Having forgotten to put on his shoes, he was forced to dance a jig to avoid the hot spent shells that clattered onto the metal floor at his feet.

At one point an Australian officer, Lieutenant Pat Livingstone, climbed up to direct some of the American fire. Suddenly, he yelled, 'Duck!' and grabbed two Americans by the collar, pulling them below the protective metal shield as a streak of

Japanese machine-gun fire whined through the space occupied the moment before by their foreheads.

Sergeant Sleeth was not so lucky, receiving a bullet in his arm as he tried to clear a jam in his .50-calibre gun. Previously, he estimated, he'd expended upwards of 1700 rounds in three hours.

Other Americans also fought with Australians for the first time beside No. 3 Strip. Anti-aircraft gunners and men trained to man coastal batteries added their weight to the firepower that utterly overwhelmed the Japanese. One awestruck US serviceman later commented that it was impossible to walk more than two feet along the western side of the strip that night without encountering a man with a machine gun or a rifle.

•

With his ranks thinning around him, Hayashi ordered his men to regroup a few hundred yards away in the jungle, and attempt a second attack. The lull in the fighting allowed the Australians to reload, and further deliveries of mortar bombs replenished the dwindling piles of ammunition. Meals, too, were delivered by the tireless army cooks, who risked their lives to bring simple but hot meals in dixie tins to the men manning the guns defending No. 3 Strip.

Just after 4 a.m. the second Japanese attack began. This time, blood-curdling shouts and screams accompanied their attempts to cross the runway, but their efforts to intimidate the defenders were unsuccessful. Again, the word went up – 'Fire!' – and Australian bullets shattered this second wave of Japanese marines as it had the first, their falling shadows illuminated eerily by the pale light of crackling flares. This second attack likewise petered out in the face of overwhelming Australian and American fire-power. One Japanese sailor recalled that 'there didn't seem to be any place we could put ourselves . . . we advanced but we were like rats in a bag and men were falling all around. I thought we were going to be wiped out . . .'

Still Hayashi refused to consider a withdrawal, convinced that Commander Yano would soon appear with the balance of his men of the 3rd Kure to save the day. It was not to be. When Yano did finally arrive, his men found the situation chaotic, and all but irredeemable.

A well-aimed hand grenade then burst beside Commander Hayashi, wounding him mortally in the face and leg. His men urged him to withdraw, but even as he refused, more of his staff of the 5th Kure fell around him.

Commander Yano, seeing that further frontal assaults on the junction of the runway and the track would be fruitless, ordered Lieutenant Yoshioka Fumiharu to take his 200 fresh marines of the 5th Yokosuka up a track that seemed to wind away to the north, and from there attempt an outflanking manoeuvre around the top of the airstrip. But the men of the 61st Battalion, dug in on Stephen's Ridge, were waiting for just this moment.

The Japanese made no attempt to disguise themselves as they charged up the slopes of the ridge. As in a terrible infantry battle on the previous war's Western Front, they were scythed down by the Australian Bren guns. Some Australians even remembered hearing the rattle of the tins set up along the path as the Japanese stumbled into them. The warning was soon redundant, as the enemy attempted in vain to storm the ridge.

Three attempts were made by the Japanese to storm across No. 3 Strip and push beyond, and each failed. Finally, in the grey pre-dawn, the Australians and Americans heard the unfamiliar sound of three short bugle blasts, the rarely used signal to withdraw.

In the carnage and confusion, the Japanese units had become scattered and their leadership collapsed. With Hayashi and several of his senior officers dead, no-one knew who was in charge, and as the dawn came up, the defeated marines made their way towards the cover of the jungle and the Government Track. As they did so, a terrible but familiar sound reached their ears: the deep-throated roar of aircraft engines.

•

Several miles to the east, emerging from a hut near Wahahuba, Captain Moji heard the aircraft as well – as he had done every morning since his arrival in this blasted place. This night, however, he had also been listening to the sounds of the battle drifting across from the airstrip. The question that burned in his mind – how had his men fared? – was emphatically answered by the sound of the Kittyhawks preparing, once again, to wreak destruction on the Japanese at Milne Bay.

CHAPTER 30
THE COUNTERPUNCH

As the dawn appeared, the Australians and Americans adjusted their eyes to the growing light, barely believing what the day was revealing. The Japanese had fallen silent. Their cries, and the distinctive staccato of their heavy machine guns, had gradually fallen away, so that now only a few ill-directed shots could be heard. The men were ordered to be ready for the enemy to make a dawn charge, but as the minutes ticked by the silence continued.

Then, slowly at first, the notion dawned that the Japanese – who had conquered everything before them, who had slashed their way through Asia, and whose soldiers were almost revered as a race of supermen – had, in this wet patch of tropical mud, been finally stopped. The men looked at each other, not wanting to jinx the moment by articulating the thought.

By 8 a.m. the Kittyhawks were in the air, searching for quarry, jauntily waggling their wings to the men on the side of the strip as they bolted overhead to begin their 'morning rounds'.

The day began to reveal the carnage of the night. Along the eastern side of the runway, a green mass appeared to have been dumped, lying in odd configurations: this was the Japanese dead. Then, more and more, a chorus of moans could be heard from the wounded who had been left behind in the jungle. It was, for most of those listening, an intolerable sound, but after a while the sounds of single pistol shots were also heard. As the cries gradually diminished, it became clear that the Japanese were killing their wounded.

Private Don McFarlan remembered of the morning: 'The sight across the Strip was a mess. We were gazing on what had been dense jungle and it looked like a field of tomato stakes. It was unbelievable what the firepower had done.'

Major General Clowes, having for a week been uncertain as to the Japanese strength and intentions, and also blinded by the weather, a lack of maps and a paucity of intelligence, now knew that the enemy's primary tactic had been to attack the airstrips and the Allied camp directly along the track, an attack which had now been shattered along the eastern edge of No. 3 Strip. Finally, the fog of war was lifting. No subsequent follow-up forces had been deployed, and the plan Clowes had nurtured since the start of the conflict could now begin.

It was not a moment too soon. For the last week, Clowes had endured rising criticism from generals MacArthur and Blamey and, less directly, the Deputy Chief of the General Staff, George Vasey, over his management of the battle.

Vasey's letters and directives of the time are illustrative, revealing a man unsuccessfully trying to steer a path between conflicting egos and vastly different approaches to the conduct of the war. 'I'm afraid the last week was a trying time for many of us,' he confided in a note to Sydney Rowell in Port Moresby. 'GHQ [i.e. MacArthur's HQ] is like a bloody barometer in a cyclone. Up and down every two minutes!' Vasey explained that, in the eyes of the man he obliquely referred to as 'the Great', meaning MacArthur, Clowes had committed the unforgivable sin of not carrying out their hastily issued directive of 'Clearing the Northern shore of Milne Bay' by moving against the Japanese immediately, and with everything he had, following their landing.

Clowes had then exacerbated GHQ's petulant frustration by denying their demands, issued several times daily, for blow-by-blow descriptions of his progress. In this, Vasey conceded his own annoyance: 'I am more convinced than ever that our reports need to be written in Americanese. They don't understand our restrained English . . .'

Rather than waste time explaining to the higher powers in faraway Brisbane the impossibility of quickly moving large numbers of men across country that was little better than a quagmire, to attack an enemy whose strength and ultimate aims were still unclear, Clowes chose simply to get on with the job of soldiering.

On the morning of 1 September, he could at last report that a large Japanese attack had been repelled at No. 3 Strip, and they appeared to be in retreat. So on edge had HQ been throughout the campaign that the news was received with euphoria, which led an unimpressed Vasey to comment: '[O]ne would have thought they had just won the Battle of Waterloo.' Nonetheless, despite what they regarded as his opaque tactics and sullen refusal to communicate them, the powers that be at the pinnacle of Australia's war effort finally had reason to be pleased with Cyril Clowes. Whether it would redeem him in their eyes in the long run, however, remained to be seen.

In any case, the successful defence of the airfield meant Clowes could now launch his long-awaited counterpunch. In preparation, he had ordered one of his unused AIF units to prepare for battle, the 2/12th Battalion under the command of Lieutenant Colonel Arthur Arnold. The youngest of a large farming family and a professional soldier, Arnold hailed from a strong military background – both his father and brother had fought at Gallipoli – and was renowned among his men for being a strict but fair disciplinarian.

The 2/12th had been raised in 1939 in Tasmania from farming communities in and around Brighton, on the Derwent River a little north of Hobart. Coincidentally, the 7th Brigade's CO, John Field had been the unit's first commander. There not being enough Tasmanians to fill the ranks of the 2/12th, however, it had been topped up with Queenslanders from the Brisbane area, making it one of the most geographically diverse units in the Second Australian Imperial Force. Arnold had served with his men in the Middle East and Tobruk with distinction, but their real test would come here, in the tropics of New Guinea.

For a week now, the 2/12th could only listen to the sounds of battle from a distance, but now, as the fight for No. 3 Strip began, they were ordered from their camp to the appalling Government Track, where they would begin their long war with the Japanese. Road transport had initially been arranged, but the track had now become virtually impassable to all but foot traffic. Sometimes pushing through the knee-high porridge-like mud, and having to carry all their equipment, the men groped their way several miles from their bivouacs around Gurney Field towards No. 3 Strip, ready to take over from the exhausted men who had stopped the Japanese along the runway.

By 6.30 a.m. they had arrived, but they were ordered not to attempt a crossing of the strip before 8 a.m. As the men peered through the early light, they wondered what awaited them on the other side of the runway. Soon they would be the first men of Milne Force to pursue the Japanese back along the Government Track, all the way to where they had landed, in the dead of night, six days earlier.

•

Pouring east, the battered Japanese could barely comprehend what had occurred during the night. The 3rd Kure staggered back along the right-hand side of the track, while what was left of the 5th Kure took the left. Some had terrible wounds, others carried comrades on their backs, while yet others could do little more than crawl through the mud.

For each man, the sensation of defeat and retreat was new and bitter. No provision had been made for the inconceivable prospect of a withdrawal, so the marines had been given no position to which they could fall back. In any case, the officers of both regiments had been all but wiped out, with the 5th Kure virtually ceasing to function as an effective unit.

Men hurried along as best they could, one eye towards the sky in anticipation of another air attack. Their great fear now was that a quick advance by the Australians through the jungle might cut off their escape route. For the Japanese soldier, retreat was shameful enough, but the prospect of capture was unthinkable.

•

At 9 a.m., the 2/12th Battalion's D Company, commanded by Captain Geoff Swan of Richmond, Tasmania, spread out in a line along the eastern side of the runway of No. 3 Strip and, rifles in hand, began walking. Their ambitious objective: to harass the Japanese retreat and push them back all the way to KB Mission by 4 p.m. that afternoon. Shortly before their departure, Swan had encountered 61st Battalion's commander, Lieutenant Colonel Meldrum, who had warned of the rearguard the Japanese were bound to have left, and to expect heavy casualties.

Treading cautiously, D Company reached the other side, where the scale of the previous night's horror revealed itself. The men stared at the scene from hell before them. A giant brush cutter appeared to have vented its anger on the jungle, which was now a shredded mess of bare branches and shattered trunks. Japanese bodies lay everywhere. Another soldier who would cross the strip that day, Lieutenant David Radford of the 9th Battalion, recalled:

> [T]here was only one thing you can call it, a butcher shop. It was just littered with bodies and parts of bodies of these Jap marines. Because, you see, small arms fire at fifty yards range doesn't just kill you, it cuts you to bits . . . it was just a charnel house. I've never seen anything like it before or since.

Corporal Errol Jorgensen of the 25th Battalion likewise journeyed across with some of the Americans, who were so sickened that they turned around and went back. 'There were legs up trees, arms, heads, everything,' he recalled. 'It was repulsive, really.'

Private Jim Hilton described a tangle of Japanese bodies around a machine-gun post:

> [A]t least twenty blokes were killed in a row behind [it]. One bloke must have strapped on and then he'd get killed, and then another bloke [would] take over and he'd get killed. There were even blokes, all with legs crossed over each other . . .

It soon became apparent that not all Japanese were dead or had surrendered. Although it was quiet on the edge of the runway, as soon as the Australians pushed back to the clearing which had been the Japanese assembly point for the night's attack, sniper fire began to ring out, no doubt from those marines who had decided to embed themselves in the trees and fight it out to the bitter end. In this, the Australians were happy to oblige, and a message was sent back to request that the Kittyhawk pilots be guided by the coloured flares and strafe the crowns of the trees. Several Japanese fell out and dangled in midair, restrained by ropes tied around their waists or ankles, twisting macabrely like hideous ragdolls.

Still the sniping continued. A favoured tactic was to fire on the Australians – particularly the officers – after they had passed by, as a warning that the Japanese were not yet beaten. To disguise their rank, officers discarded their service revolvers and carried rifles along with their men. Badges of rank were removed, and saluting – rare in the field in any case – was now avoided completely.

Nor were the men safe on the ground among the myriad enemy corpses – some of which, it transpired, were far from dead. The tactic, which would continue to haunt the Allies wherever they fought the Japanese in the Pacific, involved men lying 'doggo' among their own dead, concealing a hand grenade or rifle, then flinging it or firing into the enemy when their backs were turned.

One of the first casualties of this alarming trick was D Company's Captain Swan, who was said to have responded to the cry of a wounded Japanese soldier, and approached him to give aid. As he drew near, the man sprang up, and although he was quickly shot down by Swan's men, he managed to let go a hidden grenade, shrapnel from which caught Swan in the neck, severing an artery. Only the quick action of Private Joe Eager, who kept pressure on the officer's wound with finger and thumb, stemmed the bleeding and saved the officer's life.

More men would bear witness to the same tactic. As the Australians proceeded along the track, dubbed this day the 'Avenue of Death', a 2/12th platoon commander was passing a group of about twenty 'dead' Japanese when one was seen to move and was quickly shot. Suddenly the remainder sprang to life. One began firing a light machine gun and a firefight quickly ensued, but the Australians had the advantage and wiped them out on the spot, the Japanese quickly resuming their former poses, only now in reality. It was unofficially decreed that no enemy would be considered dead unless he had been 'killed' several times over by passing Australians, usually by means of the bayonet.

It was a grim turning point in the way the two sides fought out the remainder of the war. These and other Japanese tactics appeared to the Allied forces as abhorrent, beneath any rules of war, and played into the contemporary idea that the Asian races were inferior in general.

Sergeant Arthur Traill, who had witnessed Captain Swan's attack, later said:

> From then on the only good Jap was a dead one . . . our policy
> was to watch any apparent dead, shoot at the slightest sign
> of life and stab with bayonet even the ones who appeared to
> be rotten. It was all-out from then on, neither side showing
> any quarter and no prisoners were taken.

Even clearly dead and dangling Japanese snipers would be fired upon as the Australians passed underneath; one was later cut down and found to be riddled with hundreds of bullets. Men would also walk backwards after passing groups of enemy dead, to make sure they were not taken by surprise.

•

As the morning of 1 September progressed, the 2/12th moved along the Government Track. One company would move forward while another remained to mop up, then they'd alternate. This yielded a huge store of Japanese equipment, including two anti-tank guns, machine guns of various calibres, pistols and rifles. Of even more importance, vital intelligence documents were also recovered. On Commander Hayashi's body was found a complete set of plans for the Japanese attack on Milne Bay.

Progress, however, was slow. In a reversal of the situation of several days earlier, it was now pockets of Japanese who lay in wait to ambush the advancing Australians. At right angles to the track, narrow corridors in the thick scrub and jungle had been cut, in which groups of marines would hide, emerging to fire upon the Australians as they passed. Each cutting therefore had to be reconnoitred and neutralised, slowing the Australian advance to a crawl. Through the tireless work of the signallers, who rolled out and connected literally miles of telephone cable, contact with the rear was maintained.

It was now that the last of Brigadier Field's militia units were brought up, the 9th Infantry Battalion, who were ordered to send two companies along the track, divide into platoons and secure various points from No. 3 Strip to KB Mission. The men of A Company were to camp closest to the airstrip, at Kilarbo, while C Company pushed on towards the mission itself.

Late in the day on 1 September, Arnold had decided to split his 2/12th Battalion into two: Companies A and D would continue on to retake KB Mission, while Companies B and C would dig in for the night along Gama River, a mile or so to their rear, to protect against a Japanese counterattack from the jungle. As the sun began to go down on this monumental day, the scene was set for the last major battle of the Milne Bay campaign.

Forming a 100-yard box around the natural boundary of the Government Track, the short but steep bank of the Gama River and the shingle beach into which it flowed, the men of the 2/12th's B and C Companies were relaxed enough to risk a dip in the Gama before preparing their defences for the night. After their slog up to No. 3 Strip the previous night, they hoped it would be a quiet one. Everyone desperately needed some sleep.

While preparing their main defensive line along the west side of the track, the expected direction of a Japanese attack, a platoon from the 9th Battalion's C Company passed by, heading to their designated camp further east; they were led by Captain Colin Kirk, a 27-year-old bank clerk from Toowoomba. The two units greeted each other, and the militiamen disappeared down the track into the fading light.

Meanwhile, the men of the 2/12th busied themselves constructing shelters and gun positions for the night with whatever they could find around them. Across the mountain side of the track, four listening posts had been dug, shallow pits manned by two men, and spaced twenty or so yards apart, to give early warning of a Japanese incursion from the jungle.

Up a coconut tree on the defence perimeter, Private Merv McGilvery hacked with his bayonet at some palm fronds he planned to use as bedding. From below, a loud whistle caught his attention. His mate Private Vince 'Pug' Geason, a burly Tasmanian, crouching in one of the listening posts on the far side of the track, was pointing hard towards the west. Looking ahead, McGilvery watched a group of figures making their way towards him along the track.

'Natives?' called Vince.

McGilvery, with the advantage of height, did not have to look twice. 'Natives be damned,' he replied, 'they're Japs!'

Descending the tree as quickly as he could, McGilvery sounded the warning to his unit. In a show of remarkable discipline, the 2/12th assumed their firing positions, brought their weapons to bear and prepared to meet the oncoming Japanese in total silence, luring them into the trap.

The approaching Japanese formation was from Lieutenant Fumiharu's 5th Yokosuka detachment, and the previous night had been beaten back as they attempted to storm Stephen's Ridge at the mountain range end of No. 3 Strip. Instead of rejoining their doomed comrades at the junction of the track and the runway, they had dispersed into the jungle, where they had rested during the day. Now they were attempting to reach their rear areas around Wahahuba to the east. They had no forward scout to warn them of the Australians lying in wait, and, incredibly, nor were they making any attempt to conceal themselves, chatting away loudly and, as some of the Australians recalled, even laughing.

With the men of the 2/12th crouched in their positions, waiting to spring the ambush, soon there would be very little for them to laugh about.

If this situation was not extraordinary enough, from the opposite direction more approaching voices could be heard – but they were of a quite different tone. Not knowing what to make of this, the soldiers waiting to spring the ambush could do little more than shrug their shoulders and concentrate on the job in front of them.

The second group of voices belonged to the men who had passed by an hour or so previously, 15 Platoon of the 9th Battalion's C Company. Captain Kirk had been ordered to camp near Rabi, but had overshot the mark; when his men were some way past Gama River, he'd realised his mistake and turned around to come back. It was just as Kirk's men prepared to pass the 2/12th's position for a second time that the shooting broke out.

The Japanese were caught by surprise, their first line being mowed down by the Australian gunfire from point-blank range. This forced them back into the jungle, right onto the four listening posts, where hand-to-hand fighting erupted. Several Japanese landed directly on top of Private 'Pug' Gleason's position. The next morning, the man who had first spotted the approaching enemy was found dead, with a large number of Japanese bodies around him. His companion, Private Henry Franklin, was badly wounded but managed to crawl out of his position towards the track; despite his cries for help, he died before his mates could reach him.

The surprised men of C Company, having stumbled into the battle, wisely sought the safety of the 2/12th's perimeter, inside which they were ordered to repel any Japanese incursions, but only with the use of their bayonets, as the risk of hitting their own men was too great in this night-time melee.

The Japanese made several ferocious attempts to breach the 2/12th defensive perimeter, at one stage even using the sticky bombs they had captured from the abandoned ammunition lorry a week earlier. Now, however, they seemed to work far better than they had in the hands of the Australians at KB Mission. The irony was not lost on the 2/12th defenders at Gama River.

Finally, a group of Japanese decided to attempt an outflanking manoeuvre by wading into the sea and working their way around – but they were spotted and a series of carefully lobbed hand grenades put an end to their efforts.

By 1 a.m. it was all over, and once again the Japanese limped back into the jungle. In the morning light, round the 2/12th perimeter, the Australians counted nearly 100 enemy dead, including the unit's commander, Lieutenant Fumiharu. Not a single one had succeeded in breaching the Australian defensive line.

More horror was to await the Japanese that night, as the 2/12th's remaining companies, A and D, successfully retook KB Mission, primarily with a determined bayonet charge that resulted in a further 60 dead. Another skirmish at Motieau Creek brought the total for this single night to somewhere around 200 Japanese fatalities. The Australians, by comparison, lost barely a handful of men.

•

As the sun came up on the second day of September, it became obvious that the Japanese at Milne Bay were finished. There would be more skirmishes over the ensuing days, some flashes of fierce resistance, and even some acts of astonishing bravery, but the fight at Gama River marked the last major confrontation between the Australian defenders and the Imperial Japanese Navy's Special Naval Landing Force marines, who had believed victory would be theirs in a matter of days, if not hours.

It was, instead, the first defeat of Japanese land forces in the entire Second World War.

CHAPTER 31
THE END FOR THE JAPANESE

On the evening of Sunday, 6 September, the remnants of Japan's Milne Bay invasion force waited anxiously in the dark behind a small beach six miles east of Rabi, every man's ears straining for the sound of the barges which would emerge out of the pitch-black sea and take them away from this nightmarish place at the end of the world. The marines were exhausted and hungry, and many were wounded or had feet which had swelled so much that their boots would have to be cut off them. Some were virtually naked, their uniforms lost, shredded or caked with blood. Nonetheless, they were grateful, as until midday of this day, none of them had expected to leave Milne Bay at all.

'We have reached the worst possible situation,' was the fatalistic signal sent to Rabaul by Commander Yano the previous day. 'We will together calmly defend our position to the death. We pray for absolute victory for the Empire and long-lasting fortune in battle for you all.'

Many of the wounded had already been evacuated. The first few nights had been orderly enough, but as the situation became more desperate, and as more and more men appeared on the beach requiring evacuation, it had degenerated into chaos. Now men with minor wounds would push others aside to secure a place, some threatening the medical officers with hand grenades. Others, pushed all the way back along the track to the beach where they had landed, and who could not bear the shame of defeat, took their own lives.

At midday, Captain Moji had intercepted an excited signals runner carrying a piece of paper, which bore a message from Rabaul: 'Decided to evacuate all personnel tonight. Advise evac point.' Disbelieving, Moji ran to as many of the positions where the defeated clusters of men had gathered as he could. He told them to assemble on the beach that night, but was careful not to evoke their shame by using the word 'evacuation'. Every man answered quickly and affirmatively, in tacit understanding of the true purpose of tonight's exercise.

Including the wounded, a total of around 600 men would be taken off the beach. Many more, however, were being left – both dead and alive – in the ghastly jungles of Rabi.

Moji himself was one of the last to be taken away. As the barge made its way from the beach, its full contingent of defeated soldiers sat in silence until, eventually, the hull of the destroyer *Tenryu* loomed over them. A hand pulled Moji over a ladder and a rail, and he was on the deck, surrounded by others of this vanquished force. Not a word was spoken to them, nor did they utter a sound. All they were now capable of doing was to lie prostrate on the deck of the ship and allow the exhaustion they had managed to hold off for so long to finally crash over them.

•

In reality, the Japanese expedition to seize the airstrips and garrison at Milne Bay was doomed even before the invasion convoy set sail from Rabaul on 24 August. The Allies had performed brilliantly in keeping the existence and size of their base a secret, and the Japanese were convinced that whatever it was they were heading to attack would only be defended by a battalion or so. How confident they would have been knowing they were in fact sailing towards a stronghold defended by nearly 10,000 men can never be known.

The fact that the Imperial Japanese Navy sent their men to Milne Bay without proper intelligence, in the form of maps and reconnaissance, speaks to their military folly. The SNLF marines were dropped miles from their intended landing beach, and had no idea where their objective, the Australian airstrip, even was. This, as much as anything, suggests that the Rabi operation was put together with guesswork. At no time did the Japanese at Milne Bay know exactly where they were, a situation amplified the further west they advanced.

Aerial photographs were non-existent, and the Japanese command expected reconnaissance to be carried out by the marines after they had landed. Added to this madness, they were extraordinary lax in their own security. Arrogantly believing a quick victory would be theirs, the Japanese brought ashore reams of important documents indicating their intentions and displacements. The Milne Bay battle plan found on Commander

Hayashi's body at No. 3 Strip was quickly translated by the Allies. Many of the most important documents were placed in the trust of the Paymaster, Captain Moji, and he left them on the beach when he boarded the barge to the *Tenryu*. The notion that an Australian officer would carry into battle such sensitive documents was unthinkable.

The vaunted Japanese marines – both the men and their officers – were, after all, not up to the job. To be fair, the SNLF were sailors rather than soldiers, trained to storm ashore and quickly seize a location of strategic importance, but not to withstand the rigours of even a short infantry campaign – and particularly not one so traumatic as Milne Bay. They carried inferior weapons, their grenades generally far less potent than those of the Australians, and lacking short-barrel submachine guns such as the Thompson, which the Allies considered essential tools of jungle warfare.

Both AIF and militia soldiers later reported that their adversaries were surprisingly slow to react, both in an ambush situation and on the trigger. Even with their rifles, the Japanese marksmanship was poor, with many committing the classic mistake of firing high, a characteristic of under-trained troops, particularly at night. At KB Mission, many diggers felt the air above their heads continually moved by Japanese bullets, even when the shooting was at close quarters.

The Japanese officers, too, were poor. As seen with their military enterprises all over the Pacific, the Japanese very often had no Plan B once their initial effort had been repulsed. At No. 3 Strip, for instance, the doomed attempt to storm the runway was followed by another, and still another, until the force was completely defeated. Commander Hayashi made no attempt to regroup, rethink or reconsider his options in the face of military reality. Admittedly, Yano ordered Lieutenant Fumiharu up the runway towards Stephen's Ridge, but it was a sloppy and poorly thought out assault that was doomed to fail.

Japanese air power played almost no role in the battle, and their troops on the ground were left wondering why their famed Zeros had vanished, allowing the dreaded Kittyhawks to roam the skies at will. The answer lies, in part, with another air force, one which has gained scant recognition in the Milne Bay story: that of the United States.

Far from the Milne Bay area, the American pilots of the 80th and 41st Fighter Squadrons flying their Bell P-39 Airacobras waged a relentless, behind-the-scenes war against the Japanese airstrips in the leadup to the battle. Despite being vastly inferior to the Zero as a fighter, in ground attack the Airacobra was effective enough, providing it had the element of surprise. Time and again, the American pilots would take off from their base at Port Moresby's Seven Mile Strip and tackle the hump of the Owen Stanley Range to hit the Japanese at their new base at Buna, on Papua's north coast. Their daring was notable.

On one occasion in late August, three pairs of Airacobras dived through the cloudy dawn sky to rake six Zeros as they were taking off to attack Milne Bay. Three were destroyed, two of them caught just as they were retracting their wheels. Two more Zeros were shot down in similar circumstances the next day.

Lieutenant Bill Turner was so determined on 27 August to hit a Zero as it sat on the ground that he flew straight through a clump of trees. Remarkably, his aircraft kept flying, but both wings would need replacing. Twin-engine Japanese bombers and transports were also hit, the American pilots leaving the Buna airstrip a blazing wreck.

The American bomber crews flying their Marauders of the 22nd Bomb Group also carried out raids on Buna, on one occasion being lucky enough to arrive when the defending Zeros were away from the base: they left the runway cratered and severely damaged.

On 29 August, the Buna commander declared his airstrip untenable and withdrew his few remaining aircraft back to Rabaul. Although it was much closer than Rabaul to Milne Bay, Buna played no subsequent part in the battle. This suppression of Japanese air power by the US Army Air Forces was vital in allowing the Kittyhawks to patrol the skies over the Milne Bay battlefield unchallenged.

The role in the victory of the RAAF itself, however, cannot be overstated. Even from before the main battle began, the Kittyhawk pilots smashed the ambitious Japanese plan to outflank the Milne Bay garrison from the north by destroying their barges on Goodenough Island. Nor were the barges in Milne Bay able to be used to outflank the Australians along the shore, as these had likewise been holed or reduced to splinters by the guns of 75 and 76 Squadrons. On each day of the battle, without exception, the Australian aircraft took off and prowled overhead, hungry for targets, wearing out their guns by shooting at anything Japanese that moved, or which might be lurking under trees. Their relentless presence wore the Japanese down and drove them to despair. As one Australian witness on the ground put it, after the Kittyhawks had passed over, 'Palm fronds, bullets and dead Japanese snipers came pouring down with the rain.'

The Australian soldiers were immensely grateful for their 'airborne artillery', but it must not be forgotten that, unlike the Japanese marines, they themselves fought above the level expected of them – particularly Brigadier John Field's poorly rated 7th Brigade, militiamen whose experience of fighting before the battle was precisely nil. Although they were pushed back initially, the 61st Battalion never considered that they were defeated, and were able to recover from setbacks such as that at KB Mission. Milne Bay proved conclusively and forever that militia soldiers could fight with courage and aggression alongside the best of the AIF.

Outstanding individual efforts from untried officers and men abounded, such as the 61st Battalion B Company's cool-headed Captain Charles Bicks, who, despite having been promoted only recently, after being told he was too old to join the army, for two nights held off the Japanese in a bitter running battle. He was later awarded the Distinguished Service Order. Sergeant Stan Steele of the 25th Battalion demonstrated a quick-thinking ability to improvise: first stemming the Japanese with his ambush on the edge of No. 3 Strip. Steele too was decorated, with the Military Medal. Not bad for 'choccos' in their first battle.

The higher powers, however, did not hold so sanguine a view of the Australian fighting man at Milne Bay, nor of their leader, Major General Cyril Clowes. General Douglas MacArthur never forgave Clowes for disregarding his direction to throw everything he had against the Japanese on the first night of the invasion, and then no doubt felt he was being kept out of the loop after Clowes' refusal to issue gleefully written hour-by-hour updates on the progress of the battle. Despite others – such as his friend, and the CO of New Guinea Force, Lieutenant General Sydney Rowell – coming to Clowes' defence, General Thomas Blamey was likewise dismissive of Clowes, and begrudged him his victory. In a letter to Rowell (who Blamey was soon to sack) on 1 September, just as the Japanese had been routed at No. 3 Strip, the Australian general wrote:

> I would like to congratulate you on the complete success of the operations at Milne Bay. It, of course, is extremely difficult to get the picture of the whole of the happenings, but it appeared to us here [at GHQ] as though by not acting with great speed Clowes was liable to have missed the opportunity of dealing completely with the enemy and thus laying himself open to destruction if after securing a footing, the enemy was able to reinforce their first landing party very strongly.

Had Clowes complied, and the Japanese then landed elsewhere, the Australians could well have lost the battle. This is not to say he was blameless in every aspect of his direction of the conflict. His wearing out of the 2/10th Battalion, whom he shuffled about like chess pieces on the eve of their defence of KB Mission, was ill-thought, as was his lack of oversight concerning some of the unfortunate decisions of his subordinate, Lieutenant Colonel Dobbs, not least his refusal to carry anti-tank weapons in the face of the threat of Japanese tanks.

But Clowes did emphatically win the Battle of Milne Bay, and with relatively low casualties. His instructions from the beginning were to protect the vital airstrips, and in this he succeeded, without once having to substantially alter his initial plan of using the 7th Brigade to defend, and the 18th Brigade to attack. Out of a force of over 9000 men, 161 were killed and 212 wounded. The Japanese figures are vaguer, but have been estimated at 750 killed from a force of 2800 men, with 1318 evacuated and the remainder left to perish over the following weeks.

The garrison of Milne Bay was saved, and became a substantial military base for most of the remainder of the war. On 14 September, No. 3 Strip was up and running, and officially renamed as Turnbull Field, in honour of 76 Squadron's gallant commander, who had lost his life protecting his mates on the ground from one of the Japanese tanks.

Gurney Field also became the unmarked burial ground for more than 80 Japanese marines. After only a few days, the eastern side of the strip became putrid with the stench of decomposing bodies, exacerbated by the heat and humidity. The dangers of disease were particularly great, given that No. 3 Strip still needed substantial work by the engineers.

Some men gave in to their curiosity and inspected the awful scene. Blackening bodies, often dismembered, lay bloating in their green uniforms in hideous clumps. Flight Lieutenant Jeff Wilkinson of 75 Squadron was inspecting the dead one day when his blood froze. Ahead of him, against a tree, was an upright Japanese soldier. Upon closer inspection, Wilkinson realised he too was dead, caught by a bullet or shrapnel blast while relieving himself against a tree. 'Here were these people lying dead,' remembered the young pilot, 'but they were going to come and take our country off us.'

Burial parties came to clear the corpses. The operation took four days to complete, and affected the men of the clean-up team profoundly. Sergeant Noel Despard-Worton, of the 61st Battalion, remembered: 'We were all beginning to experience the strange, revolting, horrible, nauseating and sickening smell that got down into your lungs and into the sweaty wet clothes. It is very hard to describe . . .'

The task became so great that one of the American bulldozers was utilised to dig a single long pit, into which the bodies were interred. The traumatised bulldozer driver regularly had to stop his work to vomit. 'It was a most gruesome sight to see human bodies rolled into a mass grave by a bulldozer as though they were logs of timber,' recalled one man.

A few weeks after the battle, a small monument was erected on the eastern side of the runway above the mass grave. It was a simple wooden plank, attached to which was a white painted board that read: 'This marks the western-most point of the Japanese advance, Aug-Sep. 42. 85 unknown marines lie buried here.'

It remained a modest monument to a great achievement, summed up in the words of Brigadier John Field:

Small in comparison to some of the sustained and desperate fighting which took place in the Pacific . . . yet it was the first Australian victory against the Japanese invader, and brought to a halt the long series of territorial gains which the enemy had seemed to achieve with relative ease. Henceforth the tide was destined to turn.

None of this, however, washed with General MacArthur. On 6 September, even after the Japanese had evacuated the remnants of their shattered force, MacArthur wrote to his superior, General George Marshall, in Washington:

> The Australians have proven themselves unable to match the enemy in jungle fighting. Aggressive leadership is lacking. The enemy's defeat at Milne Bay must not be accepted as a measure of relative fighting capacity of the troops involved.

MacArthur was never convinced of the Australians' fighting ability, becoming renowned thereafter for issuing press releases describing their setbacks and defeats as Australian, but their victories as Allied.

Cyril Clowes was never appointed to another field command. Soon after the battle, malaria swept through the Milne Bay garrison in an epidemic even more virulent than that which had pervaded since the Allied arrival. Clowes, who was later partially blamed for the prevalence of the disease, was himself invalided out. He spent the rest of the war in virtual obscurity, now without friends in high places, posted in 1943 to run the purely administrative Victoria Line of Communication Area.

He never complained. Clowes placed himself on the army retired list in 1949, his chest bare of decorations save for one – awarded him by at least one grateful government, that of Greece. For his efforts defending their country in 1941, he was awarded the Greek Military Cross.

•

As the last Japanese marines were loaded onto the barges, a bugle rang out to signal their impending departure. Scattered through the jungle, singly or in groups, wounded or simply lost, many Japanese soldiers heard it and made a final, desperate dash to the water. An unknown number – but somewhere in the hundreds – heard it in despair, realising they were now stranded.

Over the next days and weeks, they would be sought out and dealt with by the victorious Australians. Some would die in brief skirmishes or hopeless suicidal charges, many would kill themselves quietly, and a handful would be taken prisoner. Others would simply be swallowed up in the vast tropical jungle, attempting a hopeless overland march back to their people, succumbing eventually to starvation or disease.

Others still would fall into the hands of the Papuan people. One account describes a group of disarmed Japanese who were followed at a set distance for weeks by groups of villagers who simply stared and said nothing, hurling stones and other objects, refusing to allow the Japanese a moment's rest, day or night. Eventually, in despair and exhaustion, they hung themselves from branches of trees.

Theirs was, in fact, a merciful end, as the Papuan people had no reason whatsoever to show the Japanese invaders the slightest shred of mercy.

CHAPTER 32
THE WEBB REPORT

In the halls of the High Court of Australia, in Canberra, the gilt-framed portrait of Sir William Flood Webb looks down on the busy comings and goings of the most venerable legal institution in the Australian Commonwealth, on whose hallowed full bench he for many years occupied a seat. Not that there was anything in William Webb's upbringing to suggest he would attain so lofty a position. Born in Brisbane to an English shopkeeper and a young Irishwoman whose other three sons had died in infancy, William was only four when his mother passed away herself. Thereafter he was brought up on a small Queensland sheep property near Warwick, where the nuns at his convent school (Webb remained a devout Catholic all his life) noted his searing intelligence. After a scholarship education, he rose quickly up the legal ranks, and by 1940, aged 53, Judge William Webb had become the eighth Chief Justice of Queensland.

A legend of Australian law, Webb, with his large brown eyes, Roman nose and impassive smile, was noted for being 'the model of polite, courteous behaviour'. According to the Australian Dictionary of Biography, 'he was patient and understanding; he did not easily ruffle'. Nothing, however, could have prepared him – nor anyone else – for the findings of the commission he accepted in June 1943 from Prime Minister John Curtin 'to conduct an enquiry into whether there had been any atrocities or breaches of the rules of warfare by the Japanese in the Australian territory of New Guinea and Papua'.

It was not to be a trial of any individual, but a report of the testimony of those witnesses he found reliable. Many of the soldiers who had served throughout the battle were called, such as Sergeant Albert Ramsden, who had been aboard the *Elevala* on the first night. Evidence was also heard from the now Major Charles Bicks, DSO, of the 61st Battalion. Many Papuans from tiny Milne Bay villages such as Lilihoa and Wandala West were also asked to travel to the court and tell Justice Webb what they remembered of the Japanese during the battle.

The findings would shock not just His Honour, but the entire civilised world, which for the first time would come face to face with the true depravity of Japan's military machine.

Many months were spent, both in Australian courts and in visits to Milne Bay itself, interviewing hundreds of Papuan and Australian witnesses, before Justice Webb's report was released in July 1944. Even today it makes for difficult reading; various historical sources state that its details of Japanese atrocities were considered so revolting that, despite its obvious use as a propaganda tool to inspire even greater loathing for an already hated enemy, the public was shielded from them for years.

Webb began his long summary: 'I find that the Japanese Armed Forces, between August 26 and September 6, 1942, at Milne Bay, without justification or excuse, killed the following natives under the circumstances stated . . .'

From the moment the marines of the Special Naval Landing Force stepped ashore at Milne Bay on 26 August 1942, a storm of unspeakable suffering was unleashed on the Papuan people. Having little or no idea where they actually were when they landed at Wahahuba Beach, the SNLF marines stormed into the surrounding coastal hamlets, demanding intelligence. Nonsensical maps were thrust into the faces of bewildered villagers, with officers demanding, 'Where is Rabi?' Any hesitation was met with immediate and savage violence. Men were roused from their beds and, at bayonet point, ordered to lead the way down the tracks towards the Australians. 'Take us to the airstrip!' they shouted in garbled English. When the going was not fast enough, or the Japanese felt they were being led in circles, they turned on their guides with brutality.

Justice Webb began his long catalogue of Japanese crimes with a list of fifteen Papuan names:

(1) PAKALASI, who was tied to a tree and bayoneted.

(2) ODA TOM, who was bayoneted.

(3) TIMOTEO, who was bayoneted through the chest as he sat up after waking . . .

Some are described in more detail, such as number twelve:

(12) KININURI, was one of the crew of the BRONZEWING and was caught by the Japanese at Moteo village, they tied

his hands behind his back and bayoneted him through the stomach.

The next section of Justice Webb's report begins:

I ALSO FIND that the Japanese armed forces at Milne Bay between the dates aforesaid without justification or excuse killed the following natives whose names are unknown and under the circumstances stated . . .

It then outlines a true catalogue of horrors. As the battle wore on, and the expected victory eluded them, the Japanese seemed determined to vent their fury on the local population with escalating barbarity, even sadism. Women, in particular, were brutalised. Webb describes:

(17) A native female near Moteo whom they tied to the ground and mutilated. Each wrist and leg was tied to a stake with signal wire. She was naked and lying on her back. She had been ripped from the stomach upwards and there was a knife slash across her stomach . . . (20-21-22) Two native females and a native male whom they tied to trees with their hands tied behind, and killed with a bayonet or sword . . . (26) A native girl whose breasts they cut off . . . (27) At Rabi, a native male whose hands they tied behind his back and tied [to] a native house-pole and whom they slit across the stomach X-wise . . . (33) Near Wagu Wagu, a native, sex unknown, whose arms they stretched out and whom they cut up the crutch . . . (34) Between Rabi and KB and about five hundred yards from KB a native whose hands they tied behind his back with signal wire and bayoneted in the anus . . . (47) A thousand

yards east of KB a native woman in her early teens whom they stripped and staked out and whose breasts they cut off . . . (6-9) The Japanese came upon four men whilst they were seated. The Japanese spoke to them, but they did not understand what was said. The Japanese then bayoneted HINANULI in the right side, and, when he fell, they bayoneted him again. The Japanese then bayoneted IAOKI in the chest. DIABEOEO and SAKARAISI were shot.

Thus Webb's list continues, relentlessly detailing no less than 59 innocent Papuan men, women and children whose fate it was to be tortured by these *bushido* knights of the South Seas, who supposedly followed a noble warrior creed steeped in honour. The sensibilities of the times initially prevented Webb from including the fact that the Papuan women and children were almost always raped, repeatedly and brutally, before their murder.

Then the report listed the 36 Australian soldiers captured at Milne Bay by the Japanese, not one of whom survived.

(1-6) At KB, six soldiers whom they tied up with signal wire and bayoneted in the stomach and whose identity discs and other means of identification they removed . . . (13) Half a mile inland from Rabi Mission, a soldier whom they tied to a coconut palm with his arms around it, the wire cutting deeply into his wrists, and then shot in several places . . . (14) Between KB and Wagu Wagu, a soldier whose hands they tied in front and whom they badly bayoneted in the stomach, ripping it out . . . (27-28) At Wagu Wagu, at the Japanese headquarters, two militiamen (Names expunged) whose hands they tied behind their backs with fish cord made by the natives and one of whom was tied six feet away from the other to a tree . . . both men were badly bayoneted. The man on the ground had his hands tied in front of his chest below his throat, and was so marked as to indicate that he had been trying to protect himself against bayonet thrusts after being tied. His buttocks and genitals were cut to ribbons. The tops of his ears were cut off. His eye sockets were missing. He had about twenty knife or bayonet wounds in his body . . .

At the bottom of the last listing, Webb states blandly:

I find that each of these killings constituted a breach by the Japanese armed forces of the rules of warfare to the effect of Article 4 of the Hague Rules and Article 2 of the Prisoners of War Convention of 1929. I also find that each of these killings constitutes an atrocity, as having been savagely brutal.

Only at virtually the last line of the summary does Webb allow his revulsion to seep through the legal language, adding: 'Only fiends could use men for bayonet practice.'

Herbert Vere 'Doc' Evatt, Australia's attorney-general and a future president of the United Nations, said of the report:

[I]ts contents are such as to shock and dismay the feelings of every decent human being . . . If those responsible of these outrages are allowed to escape punishment, it will be the grossest defeat of justice and a travesty of principles for which the war has been fought.

Evatt's fears sadly came to pass. The atrocities committed at Milne Bay eventually blended into the great dark ocean of Japan's crimes, committed in almost every part of Asia in which her soldiers fought and occupied. At war's end, after presiding over three war crime commissions, Webb began a long series of trials lasting until the early 1950s. In all, 924 enemy nationals were tried for war crimes in 196 trials conducted by Australian military courts in eight separate locations. Of those found guilty, 148 were sentenced to death and executed, with an additional 496 given prison sentences.

Few of these, however, pertained directly to the crimes committed at Milne Bay. The final report was rushed and incomplete, signed off hurriedly by Webb the very day he departed in 1946 for Japan after being appointed, at MacArthur's instigation, as president of the far larger International Military Tribunal for the Far East, whose work became known as the 'Tokyo Trials'.

On this vast stage, Webb found himself completely out of his depth, and he was unable to manoeuvre through the minefield of global Cold War politics. His fervent desire to see Emperor Hirohito himself indicted as a war criminal was shunted aside in the name of post-war expediency and came to nothing.

The names of the AIF servicemen and the militiamen in Webb's report are – mercifully for their families – withheld, but the details, overwhelming and heartbreaking, eventually blur into images of young men suffering ghastly, lonely deaths at the hands of fiends.

EPILOGUE
TOKYO, 2018

In Jeffrey Grey's popular 1990 volume, *A Military History of Australia*, dozens of battles and engagements in which Australia's armed forces took part are thoroughly and thoughtfully analysed, from the colonial period to the Vietnam War. The information is authoritative and well written, and Grey's book continues to be reviewed favourably by readers today, with one of the most repeated accolades being 'comprehensive'.

Yet when it comes to discussing Australia's fight on its own doorstep against the Japanese in the Pacific, not a single reference – even in passing – concerns Milne Bay. The name does not appear in the index. Needless to say, there is no mention of Major General Cyril Clowes.

In this omission, however, the author is far from alone. Several other revered works on Australia's wars, particularly those published prior to 1980, likewise lack any reference to the first land defeat of the Japanese in the Second World War.

The reasons for this are mysterious, but perhaps stem from the thankfully waning era of the 'cultural cringe', in which our national inferiority complex downplayed and even expunged the virtue of any achievement won by us alone. Even the Kokoda campaign – more extensive and more bloody by far than Milne Bay – took years to come to the awareness of the public, who were finally overcoming their national reluctance to stare honestly into the face of our own accomplishments.

Seventy-seven years on, and with all the participants now passed, it may serve a generation with scant regard for history of any kind to understand just what it was we achieved, virtually alone, in our darkest hours, in the steaming jungles to our north.

Spare a thought, however, for the young people of today's Japan. A visit to the extremely modern Yushukan War Memorial Museum, near the Imperial Palace in central Tokyo, will take the interested visitor past myriad groups of young Japanese schoolchildren admiring the magnificently restored Zero fighter that sits in the foyer. These same children will then be led past superb displays of swords and armour – purportedly the best collection of both in the world – from feudal times and the Sakoku years, when Japan was closed to the world for more than three centuries, until 1853, when Commodore Matthew Perry forced his way into Tokyo Bay on the USS *Mississippi*.

Throughout the museum, information is set out on touch-screens and interactive digital displays, with brilliantly reproduced images and realistic displays of heraldry and ancient weapons. The excited children love every bit of it.

Watching the youngsters as they absorb Japan's early twentieth-century history, however, is far less satisfying. Alongside the illuminated screens filled with Japanese writing explaining the war in China and beyond until 1945, are other screens, identical, but written in English. What one reads on these is deeply disturbing.

Here, the dark crimes of Japan's mid-century nadir are utterly washed away. No prisoners or locals were mistreated; the gallant soldiers of the Emperor were welcomed lovingly wherever they set foot throughout Asia; and the only crimes committed were by the vengeful Allies. Needless to say, there is no mention of the ghastly fates of 59 Papuans and 36 Australian prisoners of war at Milne Bay.

The children read everything quietly and, as young Japanese do, listen studiously to their teacher-guide, leaving eventually, once more past the old green aeroplane, and emerging again into the sunlight having learned not an iota of truth about their country's recent past.

It is a shame indeed that the children and grandchildren of the soldiers of the Battle of Milne Bay, on both sides, remain so unaware of the deeds of their forebears, both the good and the bad.

SOURCES AND ACKNOWLEDGEMENTS

In telling the story of the Battle of Milne Bay, I have freely drawn on a number of excellent primary and secondary sources, the most interesting of the latter being Clive Baker and Greg Knight's *Milne Bay 1942*, published in the early 1990s, when many of the Milne Bay veterans were still living. While no longer easy to get hold of, this large – at times even rambling – work provides a unique and comprehensive day-by-day account of the build-up, the battle and its aftermath, with a great deal of first-person quotes, biographies and narratives.

Peter Brune's magnificent canvass of Australia's involvement in the entire Pacific War, *A Bastard of a Place*, includes a large section on Milne Bay and was also utilised throughout, as was his earlier *The Spell Broken: Exploding the myth of Japanese invincibility*. Brune, as always, provides a compelling picture of the politics behind the campaign, as well as the view from MacArthur's and Blamey's headquarters in Melbourne and Brisbane. His breakdown of individual engagements, such as that of Gama River, are invaluable.

Two excellent published personal accounts were used, both written by men who served at Milne Bay during the battle. James Henderson's *Onward, Boy Soldiers: The Battle for Milne Bay, 1942* not only takes us through the author's journey as a Western Australian signaller, but provides a close look at the battle from the Japanese perspective, gained from his unique research and interviews in Japan after the war, particularly with the paymaster of the 5th Kure, Captain Chikanori Moji.

Brian Boettcher's *Eleven Bloody Days* is another personal memoir from an eyewitness to the battle. The infantryman's descriptions of the conditions in which the engagement was fought were invaluable.

Bill Deane-Butcher, 75 Squadron's redoubtable chief medical officer, self-published his own vivid account of the battle in *Fighter Squadron Doctor*, which once again proved an invaluable source.

A more recent account is that of Nicholas Anderson, published in 2018 as part of the Australian Army Campaign Series. Being from a military background, Anderson provides a skilful breakdown of the military aspect of the campaign.

The Australian government official histories were naturally used, and, despite being penned in the mid- to late 1950s, possess a surprising freshness and vitality. Particularly useful were: *Volume V: South-West Pacific Area – First Year: Kokoda to Wau* by Dudley McCarthy, and *Volume IV: The Japanese Thrust* by Lionel Wigmore. The RAAF official histories proved likewise useful, namely *Volume I: Royal Australian Air Force, 1939–1942* by Douglas Gillison.

In regards to the RAAF's vital role at Milne Bay, Mark Johnston's *Whispering Death* and Anthony James Cooper's *Kokoda Air Strikes: Allied Air Forces in New Guinea, 1942* were highly informative. Historian David Wilson was also used, particularly his history of 75 Squadron, *Seek and Strike* and *The Decisive Factor*, the first book to thoroughly examine the RAAF's role in the early part of the New Guinea campaign both at Port Moresby and Milne Bay.

An unexpectedly vivid and detailed article on the battle appears in the otherwise somewhat general *The History of World War II* by Lieutenant Colonel E. Bauer published by Paul Hamlyn in 1979.

Ivan Southall, himself a former Second World War pilot, brings to life the characters of Peter Turnbull and his successor as 75 Squadron's commanding officer, Squadron Leader Keith Truscott in his 1958 classic, *Bluey Truscott*.

Many primary sources were also used. Although all the participants of the battle have now passed, I am once again grateful to the foresight of the archivists at the Australian War Memorial and the National Library of Australia for their efforts to record so many of the voices of the men and women who fought in our wars before their stories were lost. A good number of participants of the Milne Bay battle – particularly RAAF pilots and ground crew – have given long and detailed interviews as part of the Keith Murdoch Sound Archive and the NLA's Fred Morton collection. An excellent resource, now available to all. I myself was also fortunate in being able to interview some of the veterans before they passed, including Milne Bay pilots Nat Gould and Roy Riddell. Listening once again to the cassette tapes on which I had recorded their voices in their own homes a decade or so ago was a most moving experience.

I have also been greatly assisted by excellent material provided by several family members of veterans, particularly – once again – Peter Tucker, son of 75 Squadron Kittyhawk pilot Flying Officer Arthur Tucker, Richard Deane-Butcher, son of 75 Squadron doctor, Bill Deane-Butcher, and Clive Wawn, whose father, Flight Lieutenant Bardie Wawn flew alongside Turnbull and Truscott in Milne Bay as well as many other engagements, cementing his reputation as a true hero of the RAAF.

Although the sound quality is not the best, Tim Gellel of the Australian Army History Unit provides an excellent lecture on Milne Bay on Youtube: https://www.youtube.com/watch?v=dJotmqHe57M.

I am likewise most grateful for material provided by Wing Commander Bill Evans, former CO 75 Squadron, and Bruce Whealey and his wife, Margaret, whose father Len Scaysbrook served with No. 10 RAAF Repair and Salvage Unit.

BIBLIOGRAPHY

Allchin, F., *Purple and Blue: The History of the 2/10th Battalion AIF (The Adelaide Rifles) 1939–1945*, 2/10th Battalion Association, Adelaide, 1958.

Anderson, N., *The Battle for Milne Bay, 1942*, Army History Unit, Canberra, 2018.

Baker, C. and Knight, G., *Milne Bay 1942*, Baker-Knight Publications, Sydney, 1991.

Barrett, J., *We Were There: Australian Soldiers of World War II Tell Their Stories*, Viking, Sydney, 1987.

Bateson, C., *The War with Japan: A Concise History*, Ure Smith, London, 1968.

Bauer, E., *The History of World War II*, Paul Hamlyn, London, 1979.

Boettcher, B., *Eleven Bloody Days: True Story of the Battle for Milne Bay*, published by the author, 2009.

Brune, P., *A Bastard of a Place: The Australians in Papua*, Allen & Unwin, Sydney, 2004.

Brune, P., *The Spell Broken: Exploding the Myth of Japanese Invincibility*, Allen & Unwin, Sydney, 1997.

Brune, P., *Those Ragged Bloody Heroes: From the Kokoda Train to Gona Beach 1942*, Allen & Unwin, Sydney, 1991.

Buggy, H., *Pacific Victory: A Short History of Australia's Part in the War Against Japan*, Department of Information, 1946.

Cooper, A., *Kokoda Air Strikes: Allied Air Forces in New Guinea, 1942*, New South Books, Sydney, 2011.

Daily Mirror, 'Japs took first drubbing from Australians in Jungle Battles', *Daily Mirror*, 21 August 1953.

Day, D., *Reluctant Nation: Australia and the Allied Defeat of Japan 1942–45*, Oxford University Press, Melbourne, 1988.

Deane-Butcher, W., *Fighter Squadron Doctor*, published by the author, 1989.

Ewer, P., *Storm Over Kokoda*, Murdoch Books, Sydney, 2011.

Gillison, D., *Volume I: Royal Australian Air Force: 1939–1942*, Australian War Memorial, Canberra, 1962.

Graeme-Evans, A.L., *Of Storms and Rainbows: The Story of the Men of the 2/12 Battalion*, 2/12 Battalion Association, Hobart, 1991.

Grey, J., *A Military History of Australia*, Cambridge University Press, Melbourne, 1990.

Ham, P., *Kokoda*, Harper Collins, Sydney, 2004.

Henderson, J., *Onward, Boy Soldiers: The Battle for Milne Bay, 1942*, University of Western Australia Press, Perth, 1992.

Horner, D., *Crisis of Command: Australian Generalship and the Japanese Threat, 1941–1943*, Australian War Memorial, Canberra, 1978.

James, K., 'General Clowes of Milne Bay', *Wartime Magazine*, issue 59, Australian War Memorial, 2012.

Johnston, M., *Whispering Death: Australian Airmen in the Pacific War*, Allen & Unwin, Sydney, 2011.

Lucas, W., 'Battle of Milne Bay', *Central Queensland Herald*, 3 September 1942, p. 14.

Mannix, P., *We Served, No. 10 Repair and Salvage Unit, RAAF Unit history. Papua New Guinea, Milne Bay, Queensland, 1942–1946*, published by author, 2004.

McCarthy, D., *Volume V: South–West Pacific Area – First Year: Kokoda to Wau*, Australian War Memorial, Canberra, 1959.

Pfeffer, R., Milne Bay Diary of Roy Frederick Pfeffer, 61st Australian Infantry Battalion.

Piper, R., 'Gurney and his Airfield', *Wings Magazine*, Winter, 1983.

Piper, R., 'Number One Strip Milne Bay', *Paradise: Air Nuigini inflight magazine*, November 1983, p. 68.

Rowell, S.F., *Full Circle*, Melbourne University Press, Melbourne, 1974.

Ryan, P., *Fear Drive My Feet*, Melbourne University Press, Melbourne, 1959.

Southall, I., *Bluey Truscott: Squadron Leader Keith William Truscott, RAAF*, Angus and Robertson, Sydney, 1958.

Thompson, P., *Pacific Fury, How Australia and Her Allies Defeated the Japanese Scourge*, William Heinemann, Sydney, 2008.

Wigmore, L., *Volume IV: The Japanese Thrust*, Australian War Memorial, Canberra, 1957.

Wilson, D., *The Decisive Factor*, Banner Books, Melbourne, 1991.

Wilson, D., *Seek and Strike: 75 Squadron RAAF, 1942–2002*, Banner Books, Melbourne, 2002.

Yank: The Army Weekly, 'Battle of Milne Bay', 27 August 1943.

INDEX